RETHINKING THE CHICANO MOVEMENT

In the 1960s and 1970s, an energetic new social movement emerged among Mexican Americans. Fighting for civil rights and celebrating a distinct ethnic identity, the Chicano Movement had a lasting impact on the United States, from desegregation to bilingual education.

Rethinking the Chicano Movement provides an astute and accessible introduction to this vital grassroots movement. Bringing together different fields of research, this comprehensive yet concise narrative considers the Chicano Movement as a national, not just regional, phenomenon, and places it alongside the other important social movements of the era. Rodriguez details the many different facets of the Chicano movement, including college campuses, third-party politics, media, and art, and traces the development and impact of one of the most important post-WWII social movements in the United States.

Marc Simon Rodriguez is Associate Professor of History at Portland State University and the managing editor of the *Pacific Historical Review.*

American Social and Political Movements of the Twentieth Century

Series Editor: Heather Ann Thompson, University of Michigan

Rethinking the American Anti-War Movement
By Simon Hall

Rethinking the Asian American Movement
By Daryl J. Maeda

Rethinking the Welfare Rights Movement
By Premilla Nadasen

Rethinking the Gay and Lesbian Movement
By Marc Stein

Rethinking American Women's Activism
By Annelise Orleck

Rethinking the Chicano Movement
By Marc Simon Rodriguez

RETHINKING THE CHICANO MOVEMENT

Marc Simon Rodriguez

 Routledge
Taylor & Francis Group

NEW YORK AND LONDON

First published 2015
by Routledge
711 Third Avenue, New York, NY 10017

And by Routledge
2 Park Square, Milton Park, Abingdon, Oxon OX14 4RN

Routledge is an imprint of the Taylor & Francis Group, an informa business

Library of Congress Cataloging-in-Publication Data

Rodriguez, Marc S., 1968–
Rethinking the Chicano movement / Marc Simon Rodriguez.
    pages cm.—(American social and political movements of the
twentieth century)
   Includes bibliographical references and index.
  1. Chicano movement—History.   2. Mexican Americans—Politics and
government.   3. Mexican Americans—Social conditions.   I. Title.
E184.M5R5875   2014
973'.046872—dc23   2014022362

ISBN: 978-0-415-87741-1 (hbk)
ISBN: 978-0-415-87742-8 (pbk)
ISBN: 978-0-203-08172-3 (ebk)

Typeset in Bembo
by Apex CoVantage, LLC

Printed and bound in the United States of America by Publishers Graphics,
LLC on sustainably sourced paper.

CONTENTS

Editor's Series Introduction   *vii*

Introduction: Mexican Americanism and the Long
Chicano Movement   1

1 A Growing Militancy: The Farm Workers in California
and Political Activism in Texas   23

2 The New Urban Politics: Chicanos and the War on Poverty   53

3 Youth and the Campus: Chicano Students and Chicano
Education   93

4 News and the Movement: Newspapers and Ideas in the
Chicano Movement   117

5 Art and the Movement: Chicano Murals and
Community Space   139

Conclusion: Rethinking to Move Forward   165

Bibliography   *175*
Index   *197*

EDITOR'S SERIES INTRODUCTION

Welcome to the *American Social and Political Movements of the 20th Century* series at Routledge. This collection of works by top historians from around the nation and world introduces students to the myriad movements that came together in the United States during the 20th century to expand democracy, to reshape the political economy, and to increase social justice.

Each book in this series explores a particular movement's origins, its central goals, its leading as well as grassroots figures, its actions as well as ideas, and its most important accomplishments as well as serious missteps.

With this series of concise yet synthetic overviews and reassessments, students not only will gain a richer understanding of the many human rights and civil liberties that they take for granted today, but they will also newly appreciate how recent, how deeply contested, and thus how inherently fragile, are these same elements of American citizenship.

Heather Ann Thompson
Temple University

INTRODUCTION

Mexican Americanism and the Long Chicano Movement

From the dusty border towns of Texas to the busy streets of Chicago and Los Angeles, the impact of the Chicano Movement is still felt in the daily lives of all Americans.[1] The Mexican American civil rights movement, which flourished in the 1960s and 1970s, pushed the boundaries of US citizenship, provided the impetus for modern bilingual education, and continues to expand the historical understanding of what it means to be a long-standing racial minority in the United States. This social movement, with aims comparable to those of the African American civil rights movement, sought to end generations of formal and informal discrimination against Americans of Mexican ancestry and to remedy past discrimination by creating support for educational, social, and employment opportunities for Mexican Americans. Comprised of many regionally based movements, the Chicano Movement had several important loci of activism, rather than a central leadership. In some ways parallel to the Black Power Movement, it built upon an established tradition of Mexican American civil rights activism, even as it saw itself as a radical and youth-driven movement dedicated to the creation and celebration of a distinctly Chicano culture and politics.

The Mexican American, or Chicano, community has not always been generally recognized as a historically significant presence in the United States, and the Chicano civil rights movement, in particular, is comparatively little known. Informed people are aware that Mexican Americans (or 'Spanish Americans' or 'Latins') have populated the US Southwest as a distinct regional minority group for generations, and some would also locate Chicanos alongside Native Americans and Asian Americans as one of the smaller minority groups with a long history in the United States. However, these 'lesser' minority groups often remain outside the US historical imaginary. The typical worldview among both everyday people and scholars has created a black/white binary of understanding when it comes to race and history in the United States. For example, most Americans have heard of the landmark 1954 *Brown* v. *Board of Education* case, but how many know about *Hernandez* v. *Texas* decided that same year?[2] This view has led to historical interpretations of race, ethnicity, and immigration that neglect the long and diverse history of minority groups nationwide. As the second-largest minority community in the United States at the time, Mexican Americans in the 1960s and 1970s, via the Chicano Movement, challenged this black/white binary of racial understanding.[3] The Chicano Movement altered common understandings of the history of racial and ethnic discrimination and introduced language rights into the national civil rights debate.

The American Social and Political Movements of the Twentieth Century series is itself an effort to expand common understandings of the variety of twentieth-century social movements; in this spirit, the current book is an effort to rethink the Chicano Movement and place it alongside the important social movements of the era.

Who are the Chicanos?

Terminology

Perhaps the confusing terminology employed by the government, the media, and community groups to label the 'Hispanic' community is one of the reasons that many Americans know so little about the Chicano Movement. Today one might refer to members of Spanish-speaking or Latin American-origin communities as 'Hispanics' or 'Latinos,' yet these terms are too broad to convey any meaningful content. 'Hispanic' refers both to an expansive group including long-term domestic minorities, such as Mexican Americans and Puerto Ricans, with long histories of domestic discrimination, and to immigrants from Spain, refugees from Cuba, and the growing number of immigrants from the Caribbean and Latin America.[4] This definition may also include high-status Latin American graduate students who stay in the United States after graduation and become citizens. Each of these Latino peoples, as far as the government and many employers are concerned, qualify as 'Hispanics'—a definition labeling them as disadvantaged minorities in regard to hiring, educational, and governmental diversity policies, regardless of prior discrimination within the United States.[5] Interior to this confusing definitional terrain, many Latinos and recent immigrants themselves know very little about the Chicano Movement.

Chicano has had wide application in the scholarship on Mexican Americans in the United States. In some early texts written during the movement Chicano was used to encompass all Mexican-ancestry people in the United States regardless of citizenship. In most cases, however, Chicano was used to identify those who participated in the social movements of the 1960s and 1970s and also as a term to replace the hyphenated 'Mexican-American' identity. For many activists, Chicano was applied to those people of Mexican ancestry born in the United States (Mexican Americans) even if individuals rejected the term. Others embraced Chicano as a way to demand a 'brown' racial status and to reject historical claims to a 'white' identity. In this sense, Chicanos were neither Mexicans nor white Americans, but rather represented a self-fashioned US minority group with its own history and culture. In this book Chicano and Mexican American will be used interchangeably in some cases, but in the main Chicano will be used to differentiate the activist viewpoint and community from the broader Mexican American community.

Demographics

Mexican Americans have long been the second-largest domestic minority group after African Americans in the United States. Within the increasingly diverse modern Latino community, Mexican Americans represented the dominant group, comprising nearly 60 percent of the population. While an estimated 500,000 or more Mexican Americans lived in the Great Lakes states, and in smaller settlements in the Pacific Northwest and Southern states, the vast majority of the population remained concentrated in the states of the Southwest (Texas, New Mexico, Colorado, Arizona, and California). By 1960, the Mexican American population had reached 3.5 million people in the five Southwestern states (certainly an undercount), with 85 percent US-born. Nearly half were the children of at least one Mexican-born parent. For much of the period between World War I and the 1960s various programs had brought legally sanctioned guest workers from Mexico known as 'Braceros' to the United States, where they mixed with domestic residents and the large number of unsanctioned Mexican workers. This rich mix of ancestry and citizenship groups meant that Mexican Americans born in the United States were part of often transnational and translocal interstate labor communities.[6] By 1960 nearly four million people could be counted as Mexican American and their population was rising. By 1970 there were over 4.5 million Mexican Americans in the Southwest with the vast majority still comprised of US-born residents. If one considers undercounts and the population of Mexican Americans outside the Southwestern states, a population of nearly five million Mexican Americans in 1970s seems reasonable.[7]

Language and Class

While it is true that many twenty-first century Mexican immigrants speak Spanish, it is also true that a majority of Chicanos in the 1960s had some Spanish-language proficiency while a significant number spoke mainly English. Among the Mexican American population, *Tejanos* (Texas Mexicans) and *Hispanos* (colonial-descendant New Mexicans) spoke distinct heritage dialects of Spanish. In these communities, while English was spoken, Spanish was often the dominant language of the home. In Los Angeles and other places long-term residents spoke a form of either Chicano Spanish or Chicano English which blended aspects of both languages, whereas newcomers often spoke predominantly Spanish and increasingly took advantage of expanding Spanish-language media outlets. Significant numbers of urbanized Mexican American youth in the 1960s were primarily English speakers and knew little or no Spanish even if they were from families that included Spanish speakers. This great linguistic diversity meant that while there were Spanish-language newspapers, bilingual newspapers, and even Spanish-language television, many Chicano youth were most comfortable speaking English in the 1960s. Even with this linguistic variation, many Chicanos, even those who did not speak Spanish, considered bilingualism a goal of the Chicano Movement. Thus, English-speaking Chicanos and Spanish-speaking Chicanos often engaged in activism that sought bilingual and bicultural education. The Chicano Movement itself was mainly organized using English, but it was English heavily laden with Spanish, and language use varied based upon region.[8]

The Mexican American community was predominantly a working-class urbanized population in the 1960s and 1970s. Early in the twentieth century a majority of Mexican Americans were farm laborers, and a significant number continued as agricultural laborers and migratory workers after 1960, yet the vast majority (one in six) had moved out of agricultural work as a result of increasing urbanization. As of 1960 over half of Mexican American male workers still held predominantly unskilled work in the 'factories, mines, and construction' category with 17 percent in the 'professional and clerical' category, a number comparable to that for African Americans. While Mexican American men were laborers, Mexican American women predominated in the clerical and sales category. As educational rates for Mexican Americans trailed those of African Americans, Mexican American workers earned wages that were slightly higher than those for African Americans yet did not rival those for Anglo Americans. While half of Mexican American children failed to complete high school, they also trailed African Americans and Anglo Americans when it came to college attendance with only 6 percent completing one year of college as opposed to 12 and 22 percent respectively. However, the trend toward high school graduation and college attainment was on the upswing and growing by 1970 as many more Mexican Americans completed high school and attended college. Still, the ranks of the middle class increased over time, and Mexican Americans were mainly a working-class population in the 1960s (a fact that was also true at the start of the twenty-first century).[9]

Rethinking the Chicano Movement: The Chicano Nation Imagines Itself

The world rapidly changed in the 1960s as the terrain of civil rights opened for minorities and women and as the nation confronted the war in Vietnam and the rise of a militant youth culture. Mexican Americans built upon a long tradition of civil rights activism, taking to the streets in a protest movement they soon referred to as the Chicano Movement. The movement, like many social movements of this era, was an amalgam of groups sharing the same general goals—civil rights, social and educational equality, economic opportunity, and cultural independence for the Mexican American people. The Chicano Movement expressed the desire of many Mexican Americans for equality in the United States.[10] Highlights of the movement included efforts to bring electoral democracy to segregated Texas, labor rights to the grape harvesters of California, and educational equality to children in Los Angeles and the Midwest. Influenced by developments in other social movements, including the Black Power Movement, the antiwar movement, and the American Indian Movement, as well as changes in women's understanding of gender and men's understanding of masculinity, the Chicano Movement was markedly militant compared to other historical civil rights movements led by Mexican Americans.[11] This book takes a broad view of the Chicano Movement, as it considers its main threads of activism and its many accomplishments, at both the local and national levels.

Rethinking the Chicano Movement is an effort to locate the movement within the dynamic times that created it. The Chicano Movement took shape in the late 1960s and grew through the 1970s, during a decade of national and global social movement awakenings. Many young people embraced change as what they perceived to be part of a struggle to remake society and end the racial, ethnic, and economic oppression of minorities, women, and poor people within the United States. The fact that minorities, counterculture, antiwar, and New Left radicals felt that they could dream and make these dreams a reality, as they created a new world free from oppression, racism, colonialism, and eventually sexism and homophobia, is itself a breathtaking statement of the optimism of the era. The goal of this book is not an exhaustive study of the Chicano Movement but rather its representation as the important national project it was. With this in mind, I have chosen to highlight specific activist moments, or individuals, exemplifying the movement's ethos in each chapter, so that the reader may understand the nature of the undertaking's *gestalt*.[12]

To step back and see the Chicano Movement for what it was, what it thought it was, and what the many young people who made it hoped it would become is a central objective of this book. I make a serious effort to acknowledge the differences and tensions within the movement; however, I do not allow an account of these organizational issues to overwhelm the accomplishments of the movement. Too often radical movements for change are cast as fairly simple rise-and-fall narratives, and while the most utopian (or dystopian) goals of movements are seldom achieved, many of the central goals of social action become realities with lasting impact for future generations. After decades of research and a stimulating wave of new scholarship, there is both an opportunity and an obligation to reassess the movement. The Chicano Movement, as reflected in the youthful experimentation of its participants, focused in equal measure on revolutionary and reform efforts, as activists consciously sought to carve out a place within the economic and social fabric of the United States for the Mexican American people.

Rethinking the Chicano Movement aims to understand the ways in which the movement sought both radical reform and practical changes within the framework of American society. While the rhetoric of the movement often had overtones of revolution and irredentism (efforts to claim the land on behalf of Chicanos through violence if necessary), its goal was frequently more concretely reformist in nature. Mexican Americans, in claiming the mantle of Chicanos (much as African Americans proclaimed pride in Black Power), wanted to be themselves, to create and refashion themselves in a way that made sense outside the realm of conformity and assimilation. In addition to the identity construction and cultural nationalist tendencies within the movement, Chicanos, like the reformist Mexican American activists who came before them, sought to remedy the poor living, working, and educational conditions within their communities by altering their relationship to the state. These practical reforms were at the heart of the Chicano Movement in every place it took root, as activists demanded community control of the institutions providing them with services, safety, education, and opportunity—and they were willing to be militant in these demands, leading wave after wave of marches, sit-ins, walkouts, and demonstrations nationwide. The Chicano Movement dared to dream radical, even revolutionary, dreams, even as they took to the streets calling for practical change for future generations of everyday Mexican Americans.[13]

Rethinking the Chicano Movement considers the movement's many links to other radical movements to reveal an ethnic movement, driven mainly by an experimental group of young activists and a small group of movement elders. The youth activists shared a deep commitment to global and domestic freedom struggles. The Chicano Movement reflected and refracted the radical era that gave birth to it, yet it remained a domestic movement at its core, seeking racial, ethnic, and economic justice for Mexican Americans. Chicanos demanded that their people should no longer be allowed to fall between the cracks in social policy left by the overly simplistic black/white binary espoused by government officials, politicians, mainstream reformers, and academics. Chicanos sought access and opportunity, demanding that representative government, private industries, labor unions, public schools, colleges, and universities create opportunities and space for their community. If the institutions or industries faltered, Chicanos took direct action—engaging in boycotts, walkouts, and other forms of protest. Chicanos worked with and borrowed tactics from other people of color, and in urban centers such as Chicago they worked in a pan-Latino environment including Puerto Ricans and others. Action for diversity led to diversity in action for many Chicanos.[14]

War, Conquest, and the Birth of the Mexican American People

While its militancy and unapologetic tone were departures from past movements for civil rights among Mexican Americans, the Chicano Movement did not 'awaken' a docile community but, rather, expanded established traditions of domestic resistance. In fact, Mexican Americans had long fought for civil rights following the conquest of the American Southwest by the United States. Manifest Destiny, a doctrine according to which the United States should span 'from sea to shining sea,' had several problems as a policy, since such a destiny required the conquest of newly independent Mexico, which stood in the way of westward expansion. In the Mexican state of Coahuila y Tejas, recent arrivals from the United States, as well as some native Tejanos (Texas Mexicans), rebelled against Mexico in 1835 and, in 1836, opened the Republic of Texas to legal Anglo migration and settlement. In 1845 the United States annexed Texas and invaded Mexico, crossing what Mexico considered the international border at the Nueces River. The United States, which claimed the border was at the Rio Grande, soon conquered Mexico, occupied Mexico City, and took control of the northern half of Mexico by annexation and purchase.[15]

The Treaty of Guadalupe Hidalgo formally ended the war in 1848 and made those Mexicans remaining in the ceded territories US citizens. The treaty guaranteed the property and civil rights of these new American citizens; despite formal legal protection, however, these former Mexicans experienced massive land loss and social discrimination under the new regime. The US conquest resulted in Mexican Americans losing 'homeland' property rights. Moreover, as Anglos poured into the region, Mexican Americans faced a rapidly established system of racial oppression, economic exploitation, and a lynch-law culture of violence, which cost many of them their property and lives in often gruesome displays of legal chicanery and racial violence. Some Mexican Americans rebelled against this oppression, and the conquered territories were disturbed by armed uprisings for the next six decades. By the early decades of the twentieth century, however, as immigration from Mexico increased exponentially following the Mexican Revolution of 1910 and the last armed uprisings came to an end, Mexican American activists pursued a path of nonviolent civil rights politics and litigation in a process mirroring that of African American activist groups. Many Mexican immigrants maintained emotional attachments to Mexico and some remained foreign nationals; yet, the shift among the US born and naturalized population toward citizenship activism became central after 1930.[16]

Under the provisions of the Treaty of Guadalupe Hidalgo Mexicans were not defined as a racial minority by the federal government, even though local Anglo officials treated them as an inferior group and many Anglos discriminated against them.[17] The US government considered Mexican Americans 'Caucasians,' since the treaty included naturalization provisions. By making Mexicans eligible for citizenship, the United States made all Mexican-ancestry people 'white' by law. Thus, Mexican American civil rights politics ran parallel to but did not often overlap with the African American civil rights movement until the 1960s, as the states often deemed African Americans a separate racial group, allowing for their legal segregation from whites. Mexican Americans, without the backing of either the state or racially conscious philanthropists, existed in a racial 'in-between' status. Because of this ambiguity, civil rights organizations adopted a litigation approach to defend their meager rights as 'Caucasians' (whites) rather than seeking to embrace the as yet undefined legal space of race-conscious Equal Protection activism. It took the racial politics of the Chicano Movement and several landmark Supreme Court cases for Mexican Americans to embrace a 'brown' racial status under the law.[18]

From Moderate to Militant Mexican Americanism: The Chicano Movement

Early accounts of the Chicano Movement portrayed it as part of a *longue durée* of Chicano history. Many early Chicano scholars, influenced by colonial theory, portrayed Mexican Americans as a colonized nation within a nation.[19] By this reasoning, Mexican Americans, following the defeat of Mexico in 1848, comprised an 'internal colony' within the United States suffering under a system of colonial exploitation in the cities and rural areas of the Southwest. This perspective played a significant role in the early development of Chicano historical scholarship in general and Chicano Movement ideology in particular.[20] Chicanos had lived in what had recently become the American Southwest since the seventeenth century and had fought a nearly 400-year struggle to preserve their communities and culture.[21] These early efforts to recover Chicano history, much like the art and poetry of the movement itself, tied the civil rights activities of the 1960s and 1970s to a long-standing legacy of persistence and resistance on the frontiers of the Spanish Empire, Mexico, and the US–Mexico borderlands.[22]

In this new historical imaginary, young Chicanos and Chicanas regarded existing civil rights organizations, such as the League of United Latin American Citizens (LULAC) and the American GI Forum (AGIF), as overly moderate in the face of oppression. However, this view is too simplistic. While these groups appeared moderate by the standards of 1960s-era activism, and while some leaders who supported 'Caucasian rights' may have absorbed Southern-style racist attitudes and language when it came to African Americans, it is also the case that some members of these organizations saw themselves in racial terms. These members lent assistance and support to the Chicano Movement as it developed. As the young Black Power activists found the old-guard African American civil rights organizations, such as the National Association for the Advancement of Colored People (NAACP), too moderate and tentative for the political climate of the 1960s, Chicano activists likewise rejected the tactics and strategies of their most recent civil rights predecessors.[23]

LULAC embraced patriotic Americanism and rejected a 'racial' identity for Mexican Americans, although it originally emerged in response to the fight against discrimination in Texas—where Mexican Americans and African Americans faced segregation and racial violence. For much of the early twentieth century, LULAC supported litigation efforts to end the segregation of Mexican American students across the Southwest and California. In the 1950s, the newly formed AGIF, together with LULAC, supported a variety of cases, including *Hernandez* v. *Texas*, which ended discriminatory jury selection for Mexican-ancestry people and expanded the meaning of the Fourteenth Amendment of the Constitution to protect Mexican Americans as a distinct and identifiable 'other' white group rather than an identifiable minority group. In places where lynch law, social segregation, and employment discrimination were rampant, LULAC and the AGIF fought, often with limited resources, against discrimination and created a strong foundation for future activism and eventually for a nonwhite racial status for Mexican Americans.[24]

The postwar growth in Mexican American activism was due, in part, to the demands of returning veterans. After serving in World War II and the Korean War, Mexican American veterans, inspired by the wartime rhetoric of patriotism and American exceptionalism, demanded civil rights at home.[25] These veterans, returning to civilian life, became the backbone of the AGIF across the Southwest. Frequently employed in civil service occupations and as professionals, Mexican American veterans helped establish and reinvigorate local AGIF and LULAC chapters, often in the face of Anglo harassment. In fact, in Crystal City, Texas, one AGIF member asked the organization's founder, Hector Garcia, if the group was similar to the NAACP. While Garcia rejected this characterization of the AGIF as a race-based organization, the growth and development of these local chapters indicates an attitudinal shift from the politics of 'whiteness' to a more nuanced, racially informed approach to remedying discrimination. By the early 1960s, as citizenship-focused groups grew more militant, the stage was set for a more aggressive style of activism.

Mexican American activism prior to the Chicano Movement—while dedicated to civil rights—operated in the ambiguous space between those rights guaranteed Mexican Americans as nominal 'whites' and the policies used by Anglos to limit equality. These early efforts earned successes for Mexican Americans who won access to better education, jobs, and voting rights across the Southwest, even as they lagged behind Anglos economically, socially, and in most measures of upward mobility. The 1960s witnessed the abandonment of the 'in-between' ethnic status of 'other' whites among young activists who embraced a new identity, relying on the Mexican concept of *mestizaje*. *Mestizaje* describes the process of racial mixture in Mexico and the Southwest that made Mexican Americans a hybrid racial and ethnic group of mixed-ancestry people of indigenous, African, and European origins. The new Chicano identity, in embracing this unique racial patois, set itself apart from older Mexican American civil rights groups, as it no longer sought to maintain the myth of a Caucasian racial identity in the face of obvious difference.[26]

Identity formation and student activism drove movement growth as young people became participants in social movement activity. In the early 1960s, an increasing number of Mexican American teens graduated from high school during a period of Cold War patriotic indoctrination. These well-educated young people internalized notions of equality and rejected as 'un-American' the racial discrimination against Mexican-ancestry people in the Southwest, as they increasingly proclaimed pride in a racially defined Chicano identity. Moreover, unlike older Mexican American activists, young Chicanos and Chicanas viewed their struggle as part of a broader movement of social justice linked to the African American civil rights movement. These young activists tied their struggle for freedom to the revolutionary struggle in Cuba, as well as anti-colonial movements in Africa and Asia. While there were divisions and rivalries, there was much that bound the various social movement centers of the Chicano Movement together. The movement increasingly emerged as one driven by the shared goals of a national minority group seeking to define itself and claim social, educational, and political space. Much as scholars of the African American civil rights movement portray the complexity of the African American freedom movement, recent histories of the Chicano Movement now reveal it as a complex milieu of regionally situated yet nationally focused civil rights movements with their own leaderships, goals, and intermittent internal tensions.[27]

The Chicano Movement, as we explore here, continued a long tradition among Mexican American activists seeking both civil rights and space for ethnic pride in the United States. In this way, the movement that developed in the 1960s extended and amplified established demands for Mexican American inclusion, opportunity, and cultural freedom. Not only did it challenge the utility of old tactics, it also created a new Chicano culture that reflected community traditions and history. The new identity that became Chicano culture expressed the desire of young people to take ownership of their lives and the representations of Mexican American politics, art, and culture in the public sphere. In many critical ways, the Chicano Movement staked out a new radical political and cultural space for Mexican Americans, even as it preserved the reform-minded ethic of older civil rights movements within the community.

Chicano Nationalism: Chicanismo Considered

What bound the Chicano Movement together was commitment to the basic ideology of Chicano nationalism and the practice of Chicanismo. Chicano nationalism grew in tandem with and was influenced by the nationalist rhetoric of anti-colonialism in the 1960s. As former colonies in Africa and Asia threw off the yoke of European colonialism, African Americans and Mexican Americans—many attending university—drew analogies between colonial peoples' fight for self-determination and their own struggles within the United States. Argentine-born Cuban revolutionary Che Guevara, in particular, became an inspiration by proxy, despite Guevara's limited knowledge of the Mexican American people. Chicano nationalism, like anti-colonialism, made specific claims to nationhood and designated the Southwestern region won by the United States through annexation and war a 'homeland' named Aztlán, after the mythical homeland of the Aztec people. By mixing myth with reality, Chicano intellectuals and activists directed a community, seemingly marginal to the history of both Mexico and the United States, to place itself proudly at the center of history making. In art, popular culture, and politics, Chicano nationalists blended elements of European, Aztec, and Mexican history, culture, and myth to create a comprehensive history of the Chicano people—shifting their location from the periphery to the core of North American history.[28] Chicanismo as an ideology represented both a rejection of Mexican American identity and the effort to build a new consciousness among Chicanos. Chicanismo was an explicit rejection of assimilation in favor of a focus on 'self-respect and pride in one's ethnic and cultural background.'[29]

Perhaps the best 'snapshot' of the Chicano Movement's understanding of itself is 'Yo soy Joaquín' (I am Joaquín), a poem written by movement leader Rodolfo 'Corky' Gonzales. This poem is, perhaps, the preeminent expression of Chicano nationalism and Chicanismo. It ties the modern Chicano of the city *barrios* (ethnic neighborhoods) and the small farming communities of the Southwest to the native peoples of the Americas, Aztec kings, and Spanish conquistadors. Chicanos are hybrids. Chicanos are both conqueror and conquered: 'I am Cuauhtémoc, proud and noble' and 'I am the sword and flame of Cortes the despot.' According to Gonzales, Chicanos have absorbed the strengths of both Spain and the indigenous peoples of Mexico. Chicanos are workers who 'lost the economic battle and won the struggle of cultural survival.' Chicanos are attempting to preserve culture in the face of American capitalism. Chicanos are *men*.

It is unfortunate that the only reference to women in this epic expression of the dreams of Chicanos and the Chicano Movement seems an afterthought: women are 'black shawled' and 'faithful' actors who 'who die with me/or live depending on the time and place.' Regardless of its limitations as art and its lack of gender consciousness, however, the poem as a historical text gives one of the best-distilled views of the movement's view of history and culture available. 'Yo soy Joaquín' wrote the Chicano into history as it linked *barrio* residents and farm workers to the Aztecs, the conquest of Mexico, and the building of the American Southwest.[30]

If Chicano nationalism defined the broad historical and social contours of movement ideology, Chicanismo defined its praxis. Perhaps growing out of masculine practices of bonding and friendship known as *carnalismo* among young men and boys, Chicanismo set the terms of the social relationships by which Chicanos were to abide. With some long-standing regional variations, for example, the *pachucos* and *cholos* of Texas and California and the *manitos* of New Mexico, the links of unity drawing young men together in working-class Chicano communities served as the foundation for much of what became Chicanismo. Unlike locally constructed and limited ties among particular groups of young men in and outside of gang life, this new view of *carnalismo* tied all Mexican Americans (men and women alike) together in a family; they were now linked to an identity transcending the *barrios* of Texas, California, Illinois, or the smaller *colonias* of the rural Southwest.[31] Chicanismo, by expanding the bonds of friendship and obligation to the community as a whole, tied Chicanos together as a people—with obligations to one another and a shared history of struggle from which to draw.

With its strong links to a clearly gendered masculinity, Chicanismo, as practiced by some movement leaders and grassroots male activists, often embraced what some critics considered a primitive sexism. It was one area where Chicana women increasingly sought to define themselves as equals within *La Raza* (the race), as some increasingly began to refer to Chicanos. Chicana women who challenged sexism within the movement faced opposition and criticism from many activist men, as well as some women, yet also found allies in their effort to broaden the movement's challenge to the status quo. Women across other social movements likewise faced overt sexism and paternalism.[32] While the movement had many imbricated layers of differentiation and internal controversies, as did the other social movements of the era, the primary focus was the fight for the civil and cultural rights of Mexican Americans.

Chicano Social Movements for Community Control

One of the first episodes in what became the Chicano Movement for political participation took place in the small community of Crystal City, Texas. Electoral activism took on a militant ethnic tone in deeply segregated Crystal City in 1963, when that city's Mexican American migrant farm-worker majority erupted in protest and challenged a political system that had barred them from elected office. The national attention garnered by the effort to elect Mexican American representatives in Crystal City introduced the rest of the nation to the then second-largest minority group and its demand for civil rights. There had long been Mexican American democratic movements in Texas and California, but the tone of the rhetoric in the 1960s became more militant. The revolt in Crystal City bore radical fruit. Working-class Mexican Americans elected working-class men to office; they had mobilized the grassroots and won. Although these elected officials were ill prepared and easily coerced and subsequently left the stage for many reasons, youth activists had learned how to organize at the grassroots. After 1963 they joined students from San Antonio working with local politicians supportive of the Crystal City rebellion to found the Mexican American Youth Organization (MAYO) in 1967. Thus, events in Crystal City led directly to the establishment of MAYO, which became one of the leading Chicano Movement organizations of the era. In the late 1960s, some of MAYO's founding activists helped establish La Raza Unida Party (RUP) in Texas, which as it expanded became a viable third-party challenger in Southwestern politics, ran candidates in Texas and California, and supported candidates across the Midwest.[33]

The shift from accommodation to militancy in Mexican American civil rights activism took place fairly rapidly in the early 1960s. LULAC and the AGIF put a primary emphasis on their citizenship and patriotism, but, while the new militant voices heard in Texas, California, and across Mexican America still made claims as citizens, they also took explicit pride in their culture and embraced their status as minority people and workers. In making the case for an end to anti-democratic practices or poor working conditions, they no longer feared speaking openly about the present-day impacts of past discrimination and oppression. This language upset many Anglos, who accused leaders of reverse racism, and angered those Mexican American activists committed to the policy of accommodation; yet this new rhetoric of militancy spanned generations, as old and young alike increasingly asserted a sense of their own rights and place in history without apology.

To those familiar with 1960s-era Chicano Movement activism, Cesar Chavez and the United Farm Workers (UFW) immediately come to mind. Although the UFW kept its focus on labor organizing and never defined itself as a 'Chicano' organization, the farm workers' movement and the national grape boycott it led were a central training ground for many Chicano Movement activists. In 1966, California farm workers, after years of organizing under the Agricultural Workers Organizing Committee (AWOC), joined with the group that would eventually become the United Farm Workers Organizing Committee (UFWOC). Headed by charismatic leaders such as Cesar Chavez, Dolores Huerta, and Larry Itliong, the UFWOC took a local movement for unionization among grape harvesters and built a national boycott that brought the plight of California's farm workers to the American dining-room table through its consumer boycott of grapes. The UFWOC inspired many Mexican American youths to join the grape boycott effort in cities and on campuses nationwide, where they gained important activist training and experience. Known as 'La Causa,' the grape boycott stimulated militant activism nationwide, portrayed the poor worker with dignity, and became a key gathering point as it grew in tandem with, and shared activists with, the Chicano Movement everywhere.[34]

Its distinctly youthful character and its demands for community control and immediate change set the Chicano Movement apart from long-standing civil rights movements among Mexican Americans. Within Mexican American communities, young people played an important role in altering the landscape of politics and protest by infusing it with very clear public critique of the status quo. Demanding full and speedy enfranchisement as citizens of the United States, high school students and recent graduates in East Los Angeles organized a walkout movement to end discrimination against Mexican American pupils. This high school protest intertwined with the establishment of the Brown Berets, a Chicano paramilitary organization fashioned on the Black Panther Party in Los Angeles. When students walked out of their high schools in 1968 to protest discrimination, an event known as the 'Chicano Blowouts' began. The protests focused national attention on the inadequate college preparation, discriminatory tracking, and abuse of Mexican American students in the schools of East Los Angeles. The Blowouts exposed issues that Mexican American children nationwide had long been facing and challenged the basic structure of an educational system that limited upward mobility for minorities. By embracing direct action and the militant rhetoric of Chicano pride, these events had a major impact on Chicano Movement activism as they inspired student protests elsewhere in California, Texas, Illinois, and other states.[35]

This book is an effort to both explain and rethink the contours of the history of the Chicano Movement for civil rights among Mexican Americans in the United States. Growing in tandem with the national social movement and civil rights culture that developed in the United States in the 1960s and 1970s, the Chicano Movement for civil rights was driven by the militant and unapologetic demands of young Mexican American men and women pushing for citizenship rights in all areas of the public sphere.

Organization of the Book

The chapters that follow explore important epochs in the development of the Chicano Movement by tracing the main contours of development along with case studies detailing exemplary activist moments.

Chapter 1 lays a foundation by introducing the primary organizations and individuals that led, shaped, or created an important basis for further movement activity, even if they did not support or adopt the Chicano appellation. Central to this chapter is the political effort in Crystal City, Texas, which in 1963 demonstrated that working-class Mexican Americans could, in fact, organize themselves to press for democratic participation in deeply segregated South Texas. Though short lived, this spark kindled persistent political mobilization in nearby San Antonio and inspired activism in places as far away as California and the Midwest. Next, the chapter explores the rise of the United Farm Workers Organizing

Committee (UFWOC), which provided activist training and a national network, in many ways facilitating the spread of the Chicano Movement nationwide and making Cesar Chavez an iconographic movement leader for many Americans.

The next four chapters explore activism across a number of Chicano Movement centers with a focus on community, campus, print media, and art.

Chapter 2 explores the development of Chicano community activism and the formation of organizations focused on community control during the 'War on Poverty' era in urban *barrios* and rural *colonias* across the Southwest and the Mexican American diaspora.[36] A variety of organizations took shape, both radical and reformist, pressing for change in Chicano communities; many challenged the relationship of Chicanos to the state as they demanded control of community resources, including schools and poverty programs. Some organizations focused on securing federal and state funding for community services, while others saw community engagement and ethnic pride as their central mission. Some within this milieu, such as the Crusade for Justice based in Denver, Colorado, considered their goal to be local community control, yet they never rejected Chicano nationalism. Lastly, Chapter 2 considers La Raza Unida Party (RUP) as a national third party.

Chapter 3 shifts our focus to college campuses, where young Chicanos established key organizations that pushed for recruitment of Mexican American students, for hiring and retention of Chicano and Chicana faculty, and eventually for Chicano Studies programs and departments. These efforts followed the East LA walkouts and other Chicano student-led high school boycotts nationwide and took place within an environment influenced by the Youth Conferences held by the Crusade for Justice and other student conferences in California and elsewhere. In 1968 the conferences resulted in the founding of the Movimiento Estudiantil Chicano de Aztlán (MEChA), a group that would lead the push for Chicano student representation, affirmative action, and Chicano faculty recruitment and retention efforts at colleges and universities nationwide. Chapter 3 explores the creation and development of Chicano Studies as a campus-based discipline and concludes with a consideration of the state of Chicano Studies on campuses today.

Chapter 4 examines the role of print media in the movement. The Chicano journalism movement served to spread movement ideology and symbols across the nation. Chicanos established new, often bilingual, newspapers during this period of movement activism. From Michigan, to California, Colorado to Texas, Chicanos and supporters established newspapers linked together by the Chicano Press Association (CPA), creating an outlet for creativity as well as a conduit for transmitting news across the Chicano community. The Chicano newspapers of the 1960s and 1970s included a variety of weekly, quarterly, and other publications serving a variety of communities, large and small, from coast to coast. Some were neighborhood papers infused with Chicano politics, while others highlighted art, poetry, and prose, and still others focused on arcane issues of radical theory and the politics of the university. These newspapers served as the mouthpiece for the movement's politics and ideology.

The community mural movement that developed in the 1960s linked Chicanos to other minorities living in the urban environment and provided a platform for the public—and often epic—telling of Chicano history, life, culture, and the story of the movement itself. **Chapter 5** explores the way in which a number of urban locations, including Los Angeles, San Diego, and Chicago, nurtured community artistic movements, often including significant contributions by Chicano, Anglo, Puerto Rican, and African American artists. These Chicano and other muralists created museums of the streets, telling the movement's histories and shedding light on local protest efforts, as they worked in a style influenced by the mural movement of Mexico. The Chicano murals told the long history of the Chicano people in accessible visual styles. This public art became a subject of activism and preservation, as the murals themselves frequently confronted the trauma of political attacks, neglect, and urban renewal polices that often led to the destruction of communities and of their art: thus, the murals themselves were transformed into sites of protest in many minority communities and these struggles, in turn, became part of the movement.

* * * * *

As reconsidered here, the Chicano Movement encompassed a diverse, and sometimes contradictory, set of goals. Its members sought civil rights and inclusion as citizens and protection for the rights of noncitizens, while also aspiring to create and maintain a distinct 'Chicano' identity in the face of acculturation. The Chicano Movement as a whole represented a variety of movements with different leaderships and goals, yet all agreed, more or less, on the basic demands of civil rights and respect for the ethnic and cultural practices of Mexican-ancestry people in the United States. In some cities, the Chicano Movement often included sympathetic Anglos, African Americans, Puerto Ricans, and other Latinos, as it built alliances and coalitions across communities. As the 1970s progressed, however, the movement grew increasingly splintered and weakened; many social movements of the 1960s transformed and changed character in the late 1970s and 1980s, as community-based organizations grew increasingly reliant on government and philanthropic donations, which implied restrictions on protest. Yet, even as organizations moderated their positions in order to survive, the influence of the Chicano Movement is felt today in the efforts of more moderate heirs, as they work to create educational, economic, and other opportunities for Mexican-ancestry and other Latino populations in the United States. Moreover, and perhaps most importantly, the Chicano Movement trained and nurtured a generation of politicians, academics, artists, and community leaders who felt that upward mobility was more than mere self-serving economic climbing: it was also about full citizenship and respect for the less fortunate members of the Chicano community.

The legacy of the Chicano Movement and the application of its protest models are evident today. The dynamic and sustained protests of immigrant-rights organizations nationwide are often led by coalitions that include former Chicano Movement activists and their children. The Chicano Movement created opportunities for many Latino immigrants who know very little about this civil rights movement led by Mexican Americans. Speaking Spanish in public is now acceptable, as is having ballots, instructions, and other forms available in Spanish and several other languages, thanks to the efforts of Chicano activists. Affirmative action for 'Hispanics' regardless of nativity and the expansion of educational opportunities at colleges and universities nationwide are all a direct result of the Chicano Movement. The Chicano Movement, along with other social movements of the 1960s and 1970s, opened American society in significant ways that are still continuing to change American life.

Notes

1 The term 'Chicano' came into use in the early part of the twentieth century, and while it may have originally been a pejorative it became widely used among activists and college students during the civil rights movement of the 1960s as a specific rejection of the term 'Mexican American.' Never fully accepted outside the activist or student community, its use declined in the 1980s yet continued to resonate with those committed to Chicano studies on college campuses. It is used here as a historical term to refer to the broad-based civil rights movement of Mexican Americans between the mid 1960s and the 1980s. Chicano should also be understood as a term that differentiates those Mexican-ancestry people born in the United States from Mexican citizens born in Mexico.

2 Ian Haney-López, 'Hernandez v. Brown,' *New York Times*, May 22, 2004.

3 By 'black/white binary' I mean the practice of viewing social problems and solutions in terms of the historical tensions and relationships between Anglo Americans and African Americans and the resulting psychological and policy impacts this has had and continues to have on 'other' long-standing domestic minorities, such as Mexican Americans. For a discussion of some of the issues related to the problem of the black/white binary, see Juan F. Perea, 'Ethnicity and the Constitution: Beyond the Black and White Binary Constitution,' *William and Mary Law Review* 36, no. 2 (1995): 571–611.

4 For an example of a Latino history separating Cubans as a successful group when compared to other Hispanics, see Fernando Hernández, *The Cubans: Our Legacy in the United States: A Collective Biography* (Berkeley: Berkeley Press, 2012). For a discussion of affirmative action and the blurring of identity, see Hugh Davis Graham, *Collision Course: The Strange Convergence of Affirmative Action and Immigration Policy in America* (Oxford: Oxford University Press, 2002).

5 On the unintended consequences of affirmative action and other identity policies, see Steven M. Gillon, *That's Not What We Meant to Do: Reform and Its Unintended Consequences in Twentieth-Century America* (New York: W.W. Norton, 2000); Graham, *Collision Course*; Peter H. Schuck, *Diversity in America: Keeping Government at a Safe Distance* (Cambridge: Harvard University Press, 2003); Walter Benn Michaels, *The Trouble with Diversity: How We Learned to Love Identity and Ignore Inequality* (New York:

Metropolitan Books, 2006). On the possibilities and problems of pan-Latino unity, see José Calderón, "'Hispanic" and "Latino": The Viability of Categories for Panethnic Unity,' *Latin American Perspectives* 19, no. 4 (Autumn, 1992): 37–44; Suzanne Oboler, *Ethnic Labels, Latino Lives: Identity and the Politics of (Re)Presentation in the United States* (Minneapolis: University of Minnesota Press, 1995); Christina Beltrán, *The Trouble with Unity: Latino Politics and the Creation of Identity* (Oxford: Oxford University Press, 2010).

6 See United States Bureau of the Census, *We the Mexican Americans = Nosotros Los México Americanos* (Washington, DC: Department of Commerce, Bureau of the Census, 1970).

7 For information on the population in 1960 see Leo Grebler, Joan W. Moore, and Ralph C. Guzman, *The Mexican American People: The Nation's Second Largest Minority* (New York: Free Press, 1970), 30. For information on the population in 1970 see United States Bureau of the Census, *Census of Population, 1970: Subject Reports, Final Report PC(2)-1A, 'National Origin and Language'* (Washington, DC: Department of Commerce, The Bureau of the Census, 1973), table 10, p. 70.

8 On the complexity of language use among Latinos and Chicanos, see John M. Lipski, *Varieties of Spanish in the United States* (Washington, DC: Georgetown University Press, 2008); Ilan Stavans, *Spanglish: The Making of a New American Language* (New York: Rayo, 2003); Ed Morales, *Living in Spanglish: The Search for Latino Identity in America* (New York: St. Martin's Press, 2013); Sara M. Beaudrie and Marta Ana Fairclough, *Spanish as a Heritage Language in the United States: The State of the Field* (Washington, DC: Georgetown University Press, 2012).

9 United States Bureau of the Census, *We the Mexican Americans*, 6–14; Edward Eric Telles and Vilma Ortiz, *Generations of Exclusion: Mexican Americans, Assimilation, and Race* (New York: Russell Sage Foundation, 2008), 135–58.

10 For the purposes of this study 'Chicanos' are defined as those US citizens of Mexican ancestry who embraced the militant radicalism of the social movement culture of the 1960s and 1970s, sought to maintain their distinct ethnic culture, and fashioned a new cultural identity as they made demands for civil, educational, and labor rights at home. Chicanos were radicals committed to social change, cultural preservation, and upward mobility on their own terms. When Chicanos spoke of 'Chicanos,' they often included all Mexican Americans and sometimes meant to include all Mexican-ancestry peoples (immigrants, non-citizen residents, and US citizens alike) residing in the United States.

11 For a lively discussion of the Chicano Movement's potential and limitations, see Ramón Gutiérrez, 'Community, Patriarchy and Individualism: The Politics of Chicano History,' *American Quarterly* 45 (March 1993): 44–72.

12 For a discussion of the New Left, labor, and youth movements, see Peter B. Levy, *The New Left and Labor in the 1960s* (Urbana: University of Illinois Press, 1994); Van Gosse, *Rethinking the New Left: An Interpretative History* (New York: Palgrave Macmillan, 2005); Jeffrey J. Rangel, 'Art and Activism in the Chicano Movement: Judith F. Baca, Youth, and the Politics of Cultural Work,' in *Generations of Youth: Youth Cultures and History in Twentieth Century America*, ed. Joe Austin and Michael Nevin Willard (New York: New York University Press, 1998), 223–39.

13 For a study of authenticity and the New Left, relevant in several key ways to Chicano activism, see Doug Rossinow, *The Politics of Authenticity: Liberalism, Christianity, and the New Left in America* (New York: Columbia University Press, 1998). For a consideration of the Chicano view of place, see John R. Chávez, *The Lost Land: The Chicano Image of the Southwest* (Albuquerque: University of New Mexico Press, 1984).

14 See Laura Pulido, *Black, Brown, Yellow, and Left: Radical Activism in Los Angeles* (Berkeley: University of California Press, 2006); Felix M. Padilla, *Latino Ethnic Consciousness: The Case of Mexican Americans and Puerto Ricans in Chicago* (Notre Dame: University of Notre Dame Press, 1985); Lilia Fernandez, *Brown in the Windy City: Mexicans and Puerto Ricans in Postwar Chicago* (Chicago: University of Chicago Press, 2012).

15 For more on Manifest Destiny, the Texas Revolution, and the invasion of Mexico, see (in Spanish) Leopoldo Martínez Caraza, *La Intervención Norteamericana en México, 1846–1848: Historia Político-Militar de la Pérdida de Gran Parte del Territorio Mexicano* (Mexico: Panorama Editorial, 1981); and (in English) Robert Walter Johannsen, *To the Halls of the Montezumas: The Mexican War in the American Imagination* (New York: Oxford University Press, 1985); Timothy M. Matovina, *The Alamo Remembered: Tejano Accounts and Perspectives* (Austin: University of Texas Press, 1995); Timothy J. Henderson, *A Glorious Defeat: Mexico and Its War with the United States* (New York: Hill and Wang, 2007); Raúl A. Ramos, *Beyond the Alamo: Forging Mexican Ethnicity in San Antonio, 1821–1861* (Chapel Hill: University of North Carolina Press, 2008); Robert W. Merry, *A Country of Vast Designs: James K. Polk, the Mexican War, and the Conquest of the American Continent* (New York: Simon & Schuster, 2009); Reginald Horsman, *Race and Manifest Destiny: The Origins of American Racial Anglo-Saxonism* (Cambridge: Harvard University Press, 1981).

16 See David M. Montejano, *Anglos and Mexicans in the Making of Texas, 1836–1986* (Austin: University of Texas Press, 1987); Tomás Almaguer, *Racial Fault Lines: The Historical Origins of White Supremacy in California* (Berkeley: University of California Press, 1994); Armando C. Alonzo, *Tejano Legacy: Rancheros and Settlers in South Texas, 1734–1900* (Albuquerque: University of New Mexico Press, 1998); Emilio Zamora, *The World of the Mexican Worker in Texas* (College Station: Texas A&M University Press, 2000); Benjamin Heber Johnson, *Revolution in Texas: How a Forgotten Rebellion and Its Bloody Suppression Turned Mexicans into Americans* (New Haven: Yale University Press, 2003); María Montoya, *Translating Property: The Maxwell Land Grant and the Conflict over Land in the American West, 1840–1900* (Lawrence: University Press of Kansas, 2005).

17 Although an inelegant term, 'Anglo' is used in this book to describe the various white ethnics in the United States and the American Southwest.

18 See Montejano, *Anglos and Mexicans in the Making of Texas*; George A. Martínez, 'The Legal Construction of Race: Mexican-Americans and Whiteness,' 2 *Harvard Latino Law Review* 321 (1997); Montoya, *Translating Property*; Johnson, *Revolution in Texas*; Richard Griswold del Castillo, *The Treaty of Guadalupe Hidalgo: A Legacy of Conflict* (Norman: University of Oklahoma Press, 1990); William D. Carrigan, *The Making of a Lynching Culture: Violence and Vigilantism in Central Texas, 1836–1916* (Urbana: University of Illinois Press, 2004); Michael A. Olivas, ed., '*Colored Men*' and '*Hombres Aquí*': Hernandez v. Texas and the Emergence of Mexican-American Lawyering* (Houston: Arte Público Press, 2006); Ignacio M. García, *White But Not Equal: Mexican Americans, Jury Discrimination, and the Supreme Court* (Tucson: University of Arizona Press, 2009); Neil Foley, *Quest for Equality: The Failed Promise of Black-Brown Solidarity* (Cambridge: Harvard University Press, 2010).

19 The *longue durée* (literally, long duration) is a school of history that gives priority to long-term structural and social changes over short-term events. By 'internal colonialism' authors meant that Mexican Americans were a people conquered by the United States and treated after this period as an internal colony—a subset population without full citizenship rights, despite their location within the United States and their formal citizenship.

20 For the classic internal colonial model, see Rodolfo Acuña, *Occupied America: The Chicano's Struggle toward Liberation* (San Francisco: Canfield Press, 1972) and Mario Barrera, *Race and Class in the Southwest: A Theory of Racial Inequality* (Notre Dame: University of Notre Dame Press, 1979). For a more recent survey following a similar model and orientation, see Armando Navarro, *Mexicano Political Experience in Occupied Aztlán: Struggles and Change* (Walnut Creek: Altamira Press, 2005).

21 Eventually, historians distanced themselves from the internal colonialism model due to the difficulty of applying the concept practically because Mexican Americans settled the Southwest as Spanish or Mexican colonists on land which belonged to Native Americans and were US citizens. However, a commitment to a narrative of long-term persistence, resistance, and Chicano cultural preservation remained.

22 For excellent studies following this persistence narrative, see Albert Camarillo, *Chicanos in a Changing Society: From Mexican Pueblos to American Barrios in Santa Barbara and Southern California, 1848–1930* (Cambridge: Harvard University Press, 1979) and Stephen J. Pitti, *The Devil in Silicon Valley: Northern California, Race, and Mexican Americans* (Princeton: Princeton University Press, 2003).

23 See Mario T. García, *Mexican Americans: Leadership, Ideology & Identity, 1930–1960* (New Haven: Yale University Press, 1989); David Gutiérrez, *Walls and Mirrors: Mexican Americans, Mexican Immigrants, and the Politics of Ethnicity* (Berkeley: University of California Press, 1995); Henry Ramos, *The American GI Forum: In Pursuit of the Dream, 1948–1983* (Houston: Arte Público Press, 1998); Craig Allan Kaplowitz, *LULAC, Mexican Americans, and National Policy* (College Station: Texas A&M University Press, 2005); Brian D. Behnken, *Fighting Their Own Battles: Mexican Americans, African Americans, and the Struggle for Civil Rights in Texas* (Chapel Hill: University of North Carolina Press, 2011).

24 See Carlos M. Alcala and Jorge C. Rangel, 'Project Report: De Jure Segregation of Chicanos in Texas Schools,' 7 *Harvard Civil Rights-Civil Liberties Law Review* 307 (March 1972); Olivas, '*Colored Men*' and '*Hombres Aquí*'.

25 Thomas Hietala defines American exceptionalism as 'the belief that the nation's politics and diplomacy have been uniquely altruistic, open, and beyond reproach.' Quote taken from Thomas R. Hietala, *Manifest Design: American Exceptionalism and Empire* (Ithaca: Cornell University Press, 2003), xvii.

26 On Chicanismo and identity, see Armando B. Rendón, *Chicano Manifesto* (New York: Macmillan, 1971); José Antonio Burciaga, *Drink Cultura: Chicanismo* (Santa Barbara: Joshua Odell Editions, Capra Press, 1993); Ignacio M. García, *Chicanismo: The Forging of a Militant Ethos among Mexican Americans* (Tucson: University of Arizona Press, 1997); Arnoldo C. Vento, *Mestizo: The History, Culture, and Politics of the Mexican and the Chicano: The Emerging Mestizo-Americans* (Lanham: University Press of America, 1998); Rafael Pérez-Torres, *Mestizaje: Critical Uses of Race in Chicano Culture* (Minneapolis: University of Minnesota Press, 2006). José Vasconcelos's 'La Raza Cósmica' served as the foundation for much thinking regarding race and ethnicity during the Chicano Movement era. See José Vasconcelos and Didier Tisdel Jaén, *The Cosmic Race: A Bilingual Edition* (Baltimore: Johns Hopkins University Press, 1997).

27 See Patrick James Carroll, *Felix Longoria's Wake: Bereavement, Racism, and the Rise of Mexican American Activism* (Austin: University of Texas Press, 2003); Zaragosa Vargas, *Labor Rights Are Civil Rights: Mexican American Workers in Twentieth-Century America* (Princeton: Princeton University Press, 2005); Mark Brilliant, *The Color of America Has Changed: How Racial Diversity Shaped Civil Rights Reform in California, 1941–1978* (New York: Oxford University Press, 2010); Marc S. Rodriguez, *The Tejano Diaspora:*

Mexican Americanism and Ethnic Politics in Texas and Wisconsin (Chapel Hill: University of North Carolina Press, 2011); Shana Bernstein, *Bridges of Reform: Interracial Civil Rights Activism in Twentieth-Century Los Angeles* (New York: Oxford University Press, 2011).

28 See Luis Leal, 'Octavio Paz and the Chicano,' *Latin American Literary Review* 5, no. 10 (Spring, 1977): 115–23; Rudolfo Anaya and Francisco Lomelí, eds., *Aztlán: Essays on the Chicano Homeland* (Albuquerque: University of New Mexico Press, 1991); George Mariscal, *Brown-Eyed Children of the Sun: Lessons from the Chicano Movement, 1965–1975* (Albuquerque: University of New Mexico Press, 2005). Many Chicanos saw Aztlán as the homeland of not only the Mexican people, but as the homeland for the Chicano people. Organizations in *barrios* were often considered homeland focused.

29 Quoted in Carlos Muñoz, *Youth, Identity, Power: The Chicano Movement* (New York: Verso Press, 2007), 97.

30 All quotations from 'I Am Joaquín, an Epic Poem, 1967' in Rodolfo 'Corky' Gonzales, *Message to Aztlán: Selected Writings of Rodolfo 'Corky' Gonzales* (Houston: Arte Público Press, 2001), 16–31.

31 The terms *pachuco, cholo, manito*, are all terms that relate to male-centered collective organizing models based on neighborhood, kin, and sometimes gang networks. While some view these terms as extremely limited geographically or historically their use within Mexican American communities continues to this day. *Barrios* are urban Mexican American ethnic neighborhoods (which often included immigrants and other Latinos). *Colonias* are the rural equivalent of the *barrio*.

32 See García, *Chicanismo*, and Burciaga, *Drink Cultura*, as well as Joan W. Moore and Robert Garcia, *Homeboys: Gangs, Drugs, and Prison in the Barrios of Los Angeles* (Philadelphia: Temple University Press, 1978); Anaya and Lomelí, *Aztlán;* Ana Castillo, *Massacre of the Dreamers: Essays on Xicanisma* (Albuquerque: University of New Mexico, 1994); Gonzales, *Message to Aztlán;* Richard T. Rodríguez, *Next of Kin: The Family in Chicano/a Cultural Politics* (Durham, NC: Duke University Press, 2009).

33 For more on Crystal City and the rise of La Raza Unida Party, see John S. Shockley, *Chicano Revolt in a Texas Town* (Notre Dame: University of Notre Dame Press, 1974); Ignacio M. García, *United We Win: The Rise and Fall of La Raza Unida Party* (Tucson: University of Arizona Press, 1989); Armando Navarro, *Mexican American Youth Organization: Avant-Garde of the Chicano Movement in Texas* (Austin: University of Texas Press, 1995); Rodriguez, *The Tejano Diaspora*.

34 For more on the UFWOC and Cesar Chavez, see Susan Ferriss, Ricardo Sandoval, and Diana Hembree, *The Fight in the Fields: Cesar Chavez and the Farmworkers Movement* (New York: Harcourt Brace, 1997); Marshall Ganz, *Why David Sometimes Wins: Leadership, Organization, and Strategy in the California Farm Worker Movement* (New York: Oxford University Press, 2009); Miriam Pawel, *The Union of Their Dreams: Power, Faith, and Struggle in Cesar Chavez's Farm Worker Movement* (New York: Bloomsbury Press, 2009); Randy Shaw, *Beyond the Fields: Cesar Chavez, the UFW, and the Struggle for Justice in the 21st Century* (Berkeley: University of California Press, 2011); Matt Garcia, *From the Jaws of Victory: The Triumph and Tragedy of Cesar Chavez and the Farm Worker Movement* (Berkeley: University of California Press, 2012).

35 On walkouts and related activism, see National Latino Communications Center and Galan Productions, *Taking Back the Schools* (Los Angeles: distributed by NLCC Educational Media, 1996); Ian Haney-López, *Racism on Trial: The Chicano Fight for Justice* (Cambridge: Belknap Press of Harvard University Press, 2003); Margarita Berta-Ávila, Anita Tijerina Revilla, and Julie López Figueroa, *Marching Students: Chicana and*

Chicano Activism in Education, 1968 to the Present (Reno: University of Nevada Press, 2011); Mario T. García and Sal Castro, *Blowout! Sal Castro and the Chicano Struggle for Educational Justice* (Chapel Hill: University of North Carolina Press, 2011).

36 The 'War on Poverty' was a set of government programs to assist communities in resolving issues related to poverty in the United States. Often controversial, due to the mandate that the poor be included in the management of poverty programs, the War on Poverty trained many minority and low-income activists in both governmental reform and politics.

1

A GROWING MILITANCY

The Farm Workers in California and Political Activism in Texas

Introduction

To grasp the long history of the Chicano Movement this chapter will explore the Mexican American civil rights organizations of the twentieth century. First, the chapter introduces several influential groups established by Mexican-ancestry people in the United States. In the early decades of the twentieth century, and increasingly in the post-1945 period, Mexican Americans organized to protect their civil rights and meet community needs. The chapter also briefly explores Cold War hysteria, which limited the activist terrain for all civil rights organizations in the United States, in order to set the context for this important era. To detail the important legacy of practical activism prior to the emergence of the Chicano Movement of the 1960s, the chapter considers influential predecessor civil rights organizations in some detail, as well as some of the smaller groups that had an impact on the community.[1]

To demonstrate this evolution in political activism, this chapter examines two cases of 1960s militant activism to highlight the shift in political tone and praxis that eventually gave rise to the Chicano Movement. The first example took place in Crystal City, Texas, where Mexican Americans organized an electoral campaign with the assistance of political and labor activists from nearby San Antonio. Rejecting the moderate politics of the recent past, this militant working-class movement, which flowered in 1963, embraced ethnic politics and 'Latin' pride, as grassroots leaders spoke openly of past Anglo discrimination. This struggle for political rights served as a training ground for many youth activists who became key Chicano Movement leaders in Texas and challenged the color-blind 'Caucasian' political strategy (rejection of minority status and continued whiteness claims) and moderate politics of many organizations established during the Cold War. The second example emerged out of the formation of the United Farm Workers (UFW) after 1962, led by Cesar Chavez and Dolores Huerta from headquarters in Delano, California. In 1965 the UFW began the largest boycott in US history, introduced the plight of Mexican American farm workers to the nation, and trained a generation of Mexican American youth activists nation-wide. The grape boycott led by these California labor organizers in many ways became the foundation upon which participants built a national infrastructure for the Chicano Movement. In these two important episodes of Mexican American social movement activity in Texas and California, movements peopled by youth activists rejected Cold War moderation in favor of militancy, direct action, and ethnic pride.[2]

While the Chicano Movement often characterized itself as a radical break from the past, many of the claims were amplifications of long-standing civil rights claims. For much of the twentieth century, Mexican-ancestry people sought inclusion, equality, and human rights in the United States. Many of the immigrant-led organizations maintained a focus on Mexican pride, while calling for humane treatment in their new home. Likewise, Mexican American groups, though they limited their membership to US citizens, also proudly sought to maintain personal and public connections to their language and culture while demanding their rights as citizens within an increasingly hardening regime of borders and exclusionary rights for the immigrant and undocumented population. The long history of activism on the part of Mexican-ancestry people is an evolutionary tale.

Mutual Benefit Organizations and Mexican Consulate-Supported Groups

In the tradition of other immigrant and ethnic groups, Mexican workers and long-term residents established mutual benefit societies, or *mutualistas*. These organizations aided Mexican-ancestry people by sponsoring social events and festivals as well as providing small insurance programs and death benefits, and they sometimes rose to defend the collective labor, civil, and political rights of Mexican-ancestry people in the United States. Some *mutualistas* involved themselves in Mexican politics and tried to maintain a Mexicanist orientation by encouraging Mexican citizens to reject acculturation and naturalization in favor of the preservation of Mexican cultural practices, language, and citizenship.[3] Such a hard line toward acculturation and naturalization makes sense considering the often prominent role played by Mexican consular officials in these organizations before and after the Mexican Revolution of 1910. Other *mutualistas* were primarily workers' organizations, and these often became centers for labor organizing as they sporadically emerged to defend workers' rights before receding to focus again on the provision of services to local communities of Mexican-ancestry people.

Mutualistas reflected the class and national-origin complexities of the Mexican-ancestry communities that gave them life. While some *mutualistas* were clearly working class in origin and orientation, others were led by Mexican nationalist elites, and class divisions played a role in the life of community activities. Not surprisingly, many of the *mutualistas* closely affiliated with the Mexican consulate maintained a focus on defending the civil rights of Mexican nationals and the preservation of Mexican citizenship. Others were clearly working-class or indigenous in character and organization, for example, La Sociedad Mutualista Cuauhtémoc, which organized chapters in Texas and the Midwest. Some have separately considered the role of elites in both *mutualistas* and Mexican Americanist organizations and have placed these groups in class-based opposition to one another. A more nuanced examination reveals that mutual benefit organizations, like later developing Mexican Americanist organizations, were often middle class in orientation, goals, and programming. While Mexican Americanist organizations disliked any comparison to the often negatively portrayed Mexican immigrant, however, many mutual benefit organizations also explicitly challenged the Anglo-held stereotypes of 'Mexicans' as shiftless impoverished people by sponsoring events that featured Mexicans' positive middle-class values. Mexican Americanist organizations and *mutualistas* publicly highlighted the Christianity and pride (albeit American or Mexican national pride) of Mexican people and emphatically characterized the community as hard workers. Class divisions existed in the broader Mexican-ancestry community, and these divisions were often a part of organizational life no matter the citizenship orientation of the group. *Mutualistas* and the Mexican Americanist organizations that followed both sought to portray Mexican-ancestry people in a positive light to the larger society in the United States.[4]

In 1894 residents in Tucson, Arizona, established the Alianza Hispano-Americana, to protect the rights of Mexican residents and organize politically. While not formally a political group, the Alianza served as a cross-class community organizing center that focused on organizing Mexican American opposition to discriminatory policies and politicians at the local level. The organization focused on the legal rights of immigrants and long-term residents and expanded to serve the Mexican-ancestry communities throughout Arizona and in California. This organization was typical of the mutual benefit organizations established in Los Angeles, San Antonio, Chicago, and the many other places where Mexican migrants found themselves working. Divisions existed between US citizens and Mexican nationals, elites and workers, and *mutualistas* were either independent or relied to varying degrees on support from consular officials, but the organizational model tended to be similar across Mexicanist organizations.[5] Many of these organizations continue to exist in the twenty-first century, providing burial insurance programs and halls for weddings, funerals, and community events.

The League of United Latin American Citizens (LULAC)

The League of United Latin American Citizens (LULAC) established itself in the early twentieth century and became one of the most influential civil rights organizations in the Mexican American community. Mexican American community leaders established LULAC in 1929 by the merger of a number of Mexican

American organizations at Corpus Christi, Texas. At this meeting held at a *mutualista* hall, the Salón Obreros y Obreras, the organizers decided that LULAC should clearly represent the interests of, and limit its membership to, US citizens of Mexican ancestry. This decision, central to the group's founding, led some noncitizen members of predecessor organizations to walk out of the founding meeting in protest. Established just a little over a decade after the most recent violent border conflicts between Mexican-ancestry residents of the Texas–Mexico border and the Texas Rangers, there were clear reasons to press for the rights of citizens and to model the organization along the lines of other 'hyphenated' American organizations founded by immigrants.[6] To this end, LULAC selected English as the official language of the organization, even though it supported bilingualism and most of those important to the group's establishment were Spanish speakers. Though considered 'integrationist,' LULAC pressed for an end to discrimination against Mexican Americans in employment, education, housing, and voting rights. LULAC was far from a rich person's organization; at most local levels it represented a diverse mix of middle-class and working-class members, although national and statewide representatives for the group tended to be from the minority professional class, as was often true for ethnic organizations generally. While LULAC is often defined as a 'middle-class' organization and while professionals and academics often won leadership positions, it is noteworthy that the Mexican Americans who formed LULAC held meetings in a mutual benefit workers' hall, and it recruited members from all levels of Mexican American society. Less antagonistic in practice to the working class and immigrants than perhaps assumed, LULAC's racial- and immigration-focused rhetoric, offensive by twenty-first-century standards, fit the contours of political life in Texas, a former Confederate state, where a conservative Anglo community dominated social and political life and used violence to maintain social control over African Americans and Mexican Americans alike. In Texas, with its history of racial oppression and lynch law, the hyperbolic public whiteness and patriotism claims of LULAC essayists was a way to enmesh Mexican Americans within the civic fabric of the state and the nation during a time of limited possibilities for the sort of equal protection reforms that materialized following the *Brown* and *Hernandez* decisions.[7]

Mexican Americanism and 'Whiteness'

LULAC, even with its Americanist political ideology, struggled to expand beyond its base in San Antonio and Corpus Christi for much of its early life. The group often faced opposition from ranchers and the Texas Rangers when it sought to establish rural councils (local organizations), yet it expanded in the Southwestern and Midwestern states, becoming a national organization. Even with a commitment to assimilation and public use of English, LULAC struggled to organize across the Southwest, where Mexican-ancestry people, regardless of nativity, were often simply labeled 'Mexicans' by Anglos who saw them as inferior. Despite this pervasive racism, LULAC demanded that the rights of Mexican Americans be protected and went to court to defend these rights.[8]

In its official publications and in comments made by leaders in the 1940s and 1950s, LULAC embraced a white racial status for Mexican Americans. The issue of 'whiteness' has been a controversial topic in Mexican American identity and history. Under the Treaty of Guadalupe Hidalgo (1848), Mexicans were eligible for citizenship, a right reserved to 'Caucasians' (and African-ancestry people after 1870) and preserved in *In re Ricardo Rodríguez* (1897) against the efforts of Anglos to define Mexicans as nonwhite and therefore ineligible for citizenship.[9] Following *Rodríguez*, Mexican Americans had the legal protection of 'whiteness' (naturalization, and the right to vote) in a society defined by Jim Crow segregation for African Americans and immigration restriction for nonwhites; however, this *de jure* (legal) white status did little to end the widescale *de facto* (actual) segregation of Mexican Americans. Thus, statutory protection, in the guise of racial privilege in fact worked against Mexican Americans in a practical sense. In this perilous environment defined by racism against nonwhites, LULAC pushed for an end to the segregation of Mexican American children in so-called Mexican schools across the Southwest and called for the integration of these 'Caucasian' students at the 'Anglo' schools. From Texas to California, Mexican American families played a game of legal cat and mouse as they used their 'whiteness' to call for an end to the 'Mexican' schools and the integration of their children.[10]

By the late 1950s, LULAC had successfully supported civil rights activism through protest and court cases, as it pursued a politics of active engagement. LULAC, like the National Association for the Advancement of Colored People (NAACP), tended to press for change through accepted channels of protest and thus often engaged in moderate political activism and supported civil rights litigation. For example, prominent members wrote letters to elected officials requesting remedy in the area of public accommodation in response to complaints from residents regarding issues of discrimination in public schools, swimming pools, and the court system. At other times, the organization supported grassroots protests, marches, and pickets. When issues were not resolved via negotiation, LULAC often helped families to hire individual Mexican American attorneys or joined with other organizations to support civil rights litigation. By the early 1960s, however, this approach seemed far too moderate to militant members and young activists. A politics that appeared to pander to Anglo sensibilities struck many as weakness rather than wisdom and the result of decades of timid and compromised activism—under the watchful eye of the Texas Rangers. Challenged by the rise of the Chicano Movement, LULAC changed its positions on issues of racial identity, women, and immigrants in the early 1970s, as it came to embrace many of the policies initiated by Chicano militants. LULAC continues today as the longest-operating Latino civil rights organization in the United States.[11]

Understanding the Cold War's Influence on Mexican American Activism

One of the burning questions in Mexican American history has to do with the degree to which Mexican American organizations sought integration within American society versus the degree to which they sought to maintain their Mexican identity. As is true in the case of other ethnic groups in the United States after 1945, adaptations on the part of US ethnic groups need to be seen through the lens of Cold War Americanism. Mexican American politics across the Southwest became increasingly organized after World War II, when groups led by military veterans joined the struggle to defend the civil rights of Mexican Americans in the Cold War era. As veterans returned from military service and the Americanist training gained by participation in the armed forces, they sought to enjoy the freedoms and rights they had fought to defend and expand to other nations. Veteran organizations and their leadership reinvigorated older institutions within the community and created new ones as they made the case for the greater inclusion of Mexican Americans in the public sphere. The orientation was Americanist, focused on the needs and civil rights of citizens, yet there was concern and activism on behalf of Mexican-ancestry peoples regardless of nationality.

The climate of the Cold War played a significant role in shaping and limiting the postwar Mexican American political imaginary, as anti-Communist attacks threatened reformist civil rights and labor organizations. During the war and afterward the federal government itself underwent a series of purges that sought to bar Communists, radicals, and gays and lesbians from public service and civic participation, while the private sector and labor unions likewise purged leftists and Communists. In this harsh climate, minority and progressive organizations worked to expand the meaning of US citizenship, walking a fine line between patriotic protest and suspect behavior. Mexican American organizations struggled to maintain a focus on the formal Americanist nature of their demands for equality in a world dominated by the global conflict between the Soviet Union and the United States and domestic fear of fellow-traveler radicalism. Militant protest in the United States had clear limits in the climate of Cold War jingoistic patriotism, anemic public discourse, and purges of radicals from all segments of society.[12]

The Cold War Attack on Civil Liberties

Right-wing conservatives and anti-Communists used the Cold War climate of fear to attack the civil liberties of Americans. Congress in a fury of anti-radical zeal passed the Taft-Hartley Act of 1947 and the McCarran Internal Security Act in 1950. The first statute severely limited the freedom of US labor organizations by demanding anti-Communist loyalty oaths from all leaders, and the second required that Communist and Communist-front organizations register with the Attorney General and submit membership lists and financial records. The government also breathed life into the Alien Registration Act of 1940 curtailing First Amendment rights well into the 1950s as it used this law, also known as the Smith Act, to devastate the Communist Party. These laws made any form of protest suspect, limited free speech, barred those branded as Communists from jobs and international travel, and threatened naturalized citizens with deportation among other penalties. In 1952 Congress passed the McCarran-Walter Immigration and Nationality Act, which subjected naturalized citizens to deportation if they had participated in 'suspect' organizations prior to coming to the United States. States and local governments passed similar laws. In such a climate where the penalties for subversion were draconian and real, Mexican American organizations wrapped themselves in the US flag and the rhetoric of Cold War patriotism as a means of survival in an era defined by hysterical anti-Communism.[13]

The American GI Forum (AGIF)

Following World War II, as veterans became important members in many fraternal organizations and a key constituency for elected officials, Mexican Americans once again met in Corpus Christi, Texas, and established the American GI Forum (AGIF). Initially focused on the needs of veterans, the AGIF lobbied for equality in the provision of veterans' benefits and a variety of programs that fell under the Servicemen's Readjustment Act of 1944, commonly known as the 'GI Bill.' The legislation was intended to help transition veterans into civilian society by offering low-cost mortgages, business loans, college, vocational, and unemployment benefits, yet many Mexican Americans felt that their access to these benefits was limited. The AGIF lobbied for greater efforts to make sure that all veterans had access to their benefits regardless of race or ethnicity. Moreover, the AGIF pressed for an end to discrimination on draft boards, at Veterans' Administration hospitals, and in regard to other veterans' services.

In 1949 the Felix Longoria Affair placed the AGIF at the center of racial and ethnic civil rights politics in the United States. Felix Longoria Jr. had died in the Philippines during World War II, yet the Army did not recover his body until 1948. When the Army sent his remains home to Three Rivers, Texas, a local funeral home operator refused to let the family hold a service. Longoria's family requested assistance from the AGIF, led by Dr. Hector Garcia who was also unsuccessful in his efforts to negotiate with the funeral home operator. Garcia wrote a series of letters to elected officials in Texas requesting assistance. The Texas press covered the story of discrimination against a fallen combat soldier, and a local story became a national one, shedding light on the long-standing discrimination against Mexican Americans in the Lone Star State. Seeking to end the controversy,

Senator Lyndon Baines Johnson acted quickly to arrange Longoria's burial at Arlington National Cemetery with full military honors.[14]

The AGIF grew in the 1950s and increasingly took on civil rights causes. While clearly a veterans' group open to all former service members (75 percent had to be veterans) the AGIF supported court cases in a variety of areas of importance to Mexican Americans and conducted investigations into the impact of undocumented immigrants on the working-class and migrant Mexican Americans of South Texas. The AGIF grew but, much like LULAC, had a difficult time establishing itself in the ranching and farming communities of South Texas, where Anglo minorities with support from the Texas Rangers oversaw a system of economic and racial/ethnic oppression. Despite these issues, the AGIF expanded across the Southwest. It became a national organization in the late 1950s, though it continued to have its strongest organizational base in Texas.[15]

The Hernandez Case

Most prominently, in the mid 1950s the AGIF joined with LULAC to support the case of cotton-picker Pete Hernandez. An all-Anglo (white) grand jury in Jackson County, Texas, had indicted Pete Hernandez, an agricultural worker, for the murder of Joe Espinoza, and an all-Anglo trial jury found him guilty. Claiming that Mexican Americans were barred from the commission that selected juries and from trial juries, Hernandez's attorneys tried to quash the indictment. Moreover, they tried to quash the jury panel called for service, because authorities excluded persons of Mexican descent from this case. The facts indicated that bias was customary practice, as a Mexican American had not served on a jury in Jackson County in over 25 years, and thus *Hernandez* claimed that the court system discriminated against Mexican-ancestry citizens as a special class in Jackson County. The trial court denied the motions. At this point, the all-Anglo jury found Hernandez guilty of murder and sentenced him to life in prison. In affirming, the Texas Court of Criminal Appeals found that 'Mexicans are . . . members of and within the classification of the white race as distinguished from members of the Negro Race' and rejected the petitioners' argument that Mexican Americans were a 'special class' under the meaning of the Fourteenth Amendment. Further, the court pointed out that 'so far as we are advised, no member of the Mexican nationality' challenged this classification as white or Caucasian. The 'Caucasian' status of Mexican Americans and the strategy of claiming such a legal status backfired against the minority litigant in the *Hernandez* case.[16]

The AGIF and LULAC attorneys, in a case they would take all the way to the US Supreme Court, argued that it was a denial of the Fourteenth Amendment's Equal Protection Clause to try a defendant of a particular race or ethnicity— Mexican American in this case—before a jury where all persons of his race or ancestry have, because of that race or ethnicity, been excluded by the state.

Accepting the view of the *Hernandez* lawyers, in a unanimous opinion delivered by US Supreme Court Chief Justice Earl Warren, the court held that the Fourteenth Amendment protects those beyond the 'two classes' of white or 'Negro' and extends to other racial groups in communities when a plaintiff can factually establish a pattern and practice of group discrimination within that community. The court concluded that the Fourteenth Amendment 'is not directed solely against discrimination due to a "two-class theory"' but in this case covers those of Mexican ancestry. The distinction between whites and Mexican-ancestry (as well as African American) individuals was made clear at the Jackson County Courthouse itself where 'there were two men's toilets, one unmarked and the other marked "Colored Men" and "Hombres Aquí" (Men Here),' and by the fact that no Mexican-ancestry person had served on a jury in 25 years. After *Hernandez*, Mexican Americans were a 'special class' entitled to equal protection under the Fourteenth Amendment.[17]

The *Hernandez* case also highlighted the differences between Mexican American and African American litigation organizing. In the 1950s the comparatively well-funded NAACP Legal Defense Fund (LDF), headed by future Supreme Court Justice Thurgood Marshall, operated from a national office in New York City and managed cases nationwide through a network of staff and volunteer attorneys. The LDF sought to end *de jure* and *de facto* discrimination across all areas of life for African Americans and was in a position to implement a litigation strategy of seeking out test cases nationwide through a network of committed attorneys. Mexican Americans, on the other hand, were not only under the paradoxical disadvantage of being technically classified as 'Caucasians' and considered white, but also comprised a smaller national population at the time. The AGIF and LULAC supported *Hernandez* and other cases, but there was no legal department and few committed philanthropic supporters. Litigation support often amounted to small grants for research and the donation of services by cash-strapped Mexican American attorneys. The AGIF, much as LULAC had done previously, took cases that came to it as the result of grassroots organizing on the part of family members and local communities and lacked the resources for a proactive litigation strategy.[18]

Nonetheless, by the late 1950s the AGIF had established itself as a strong defender of equality for Mexican Americans from Texas to California and across the Midwest. Embracing a strong Cold War Mexican Americanism, the AGIF worked hard not only to expand its membership base in the often difficult-to-organize rural areas of the Southwest but also to stake out territory as a national organization representing the interests of patriotic Mexican Americans distinguished by service in the armed forces. While driven by veterans as members, the organization worked on behalf of migratory agricultural workers, schoolchildren, and those facing unjust criminal prosecution within the Mexican American community. Relying on its pedigree as a veterans' organization, the AGIF adopted an ideology in action more confrontational than that of other organizations and pushed a comparatively militant brand of Mexican Americanism. The AGIF continues today as a civil rights and veterans' assistance organization across the country.

The Community Service Organization (CSO)

In 1947 Fred Ross and longtime political activist Edward Roybal founded the Community Service Organization (CSO) in Los Angeles, California, with assistance from Saul Alinsky's Chicago-based Industrial Areas Foundation (IAF). Roybal, a Los Angeles Mexican American activist, had lost his bid for a seat on the Los Angeles City Council, and to keep the organizational momentum going he decided to transform his campaign organization into a potent service group. The CSO functioned as a 'People's Organization' as it sought input from the community and engaged in social service, citizenship education, voter registration, and political mobilization. Central to the CSO was a belief that participation mattered, and the group spent much of its time engaged in grassroots voter registration in Los Angeles County. These drives succeeded in increasing registrations in East Los Angeles and other Mexican American neighborhoods by tens of thousands of voters. The CSO expanded to other areas of California, educating community members and training a cadre of activists in civic engagement. Driven by a focus on participatory democracy, the CSO brought together a diverse group of Mexican Americans and others in the name of increasing community political engagement.[19]

Mexican Americanism in Southern California

While dedicated to broader participation for all members of the Mexican American community and representing a diverse group of ethnic activists, the CSO focused on Southern California. The first successful CSO-led voter registration drive helped Roybal win a seat on the Los Angeles city council in 1949. Roybal was the first Mexican American elected to this post since the late nineteenth century, and he went on to win election to the United States Congress in 1962. Initially a vehicle for the election of Roybal, the CSO grew to become the most prominent grassroots political organization for Mexican Americans in California.[20] With offices across the state, it became, for a time, an important force in California politics as it registered enough voters in several areas to alter outcomes in elections.

The CSO also pressed for civil rights and opportunity across Southern California in the 1950s. Engaging in direct action, and with assistance from Roybal, it pushed for an end to discrimination and police harassment and called for open housing (equal access) for Mexican Americans and other racial and ethnic minorities in Southern California. The CSO expanded to Northern California under the direction of Fred Ross, who recruited Cesar Chavez and Dolores Huerta to work as organizers for the group. Chavez rose through the ranks to become the national director of the CSO in 1958, a post he held until he resigned in protest in 1962 after the CSO rejected direct involvement in organizing farm workers. After Chavez left to organize, with Dolores Huerta, what became the United Farmworkers Organizing Committee (UFWOC), the CSO continued as a less militant civic engagement organization in California, but much of its leadership and momentum transferred to the farm workers' movement.[21]

The Mexican American Political Association (MAPA)

Edward Roybal's influence in California after World War II cannot be overstated. In 1959 Roybal and other Mexican Americans in the Democratic Party discussed the establishment of MAPA in California as a way to focus the efforts of the Mexican American electorate and develop leadership. A major problem faced by Mexican Americans seeking to enter politics was a lack of support from the Democratic Party of California and Governor Edmund Brown. There was a belief that Mexican Americans were not electable when it came to statewide office. Following primary victories, Mexican American candidates were set adrift without adequate party funding and lost elections they should have won. In 1960, Roybal brought together the leadership of the CSO and AGIF and established MAPA to help elect Mexican Americans to office in California. This effort to end discrimination and push for representation in elected office was part of the broader integrationist movement among minority activists after World War II.[22]

With a mission that overlapped with that of the CSO in California, MAPA entered the political scene as an organization supported by a number of other prominent Mexican American civic engagement groups. Established as a nonpartisan group, officially MAPA worked on behalf of Mexican American interests with both parties, yet it did plan to endorse candidates. Focused on recruiting candidates and registering voters in urban and rural neighborhoods in California as an ethnic-identity organization working on behalf of Mexican Americans, MAPA pressed for support for candidates from the Democratic Party of California. With the aim of becoming the voice of Mexican American politics in California, MAPA was primarily a vehicle for Edward Roybal and other Mexican Americans in Southern California, though it had representatives in San José, Sacramento, and San Francisco to serve these communities as well. MAPA continued to be important as a California-based civic engagement organization well into the mid 1960s, as it promoted an electoral brand of Mexican Americanism.[23]

1960: The Viva Kennedy Clubs

During the 1960 election, the membership and leadership of the AGIF, MAPA, and LULAC supported the Kennedy campaign for the presidency via the independent Viva Kennedy Clubs. In 1960 Democrat John F. Kennedy of Massachusetts was running against Republican Richard M. Nixon of California, formerly Eisenhower's vice-president, in what many expected to be a close election. In need of every possible vote, Kennedy courted the Mexican American community in the United States in a targeted campaign. In some ways, the Viva Kennedy Clubs signaled the zenith of national organizing among Mexican Americans, as the campaign brought national unity among Mexican American political activists in Texas, California, and elsewhere.

The Viva Kennedy Clubs emerged between 1959 and the summer of 1960. Kennedy's staff included Carlos McCormick, an AGIF member, who developed a campaign tailored to the large Spanish-speaking communities of the Southwest. In the summer of 1960 McCormick began to establish the Viva Kennedy Clubs as separate state-level organizations. After the Democratic national convention he organized Viva Kennedy Clubs in nine states with large Spanish-speaking populations and supported large voter-registration and get-out-the-vote drives. In California, MAPA played a leading role under Southern California Director Hank Lopez. Within a short time, elected officials such as Edward Roybal of California and Dennis Chavez and Joseph Montoya of New Mexico came together with activists from Texas, Illinois, and other states to support the Kennedy–Johnson ticket. With Texas Senator Lyndon B. Johnson, former US Senate Majority Leader, on the ticket, the Viva Kennedy Clubs were quite active across Texas. The clubs delivered huge voter turnouts for the Kennedy–Johnson ticket in California, Texas, and elsewhere and showed how a variety of Mexican American organizations could work together toward a single goal. The Political Association of Spanish-Speaking Organizations (PASSO), founded by Viva Kennedy-affiliated organizations in Texas and California, was an effort to extend the life of the Viva Kennedy Clubs following the success of the Kennedy campaign.[24]

The Political Association of Spanish-Speaking Organizations (PASSO)

In Texas, activists led by Bexar County Commissioner Albert Peña Jr. of San Antonio sought to expand upon the base of intercommunity cooperation by establishing an organization to continue what the Viva Kennedy Clubs had begun. Meeting in Victoria, Texas, in early 1961, Peña and others formed Mexican Americans for Political Action (MAPA), Texas—not affiliated with the Mexican American Political Association (MAPA) based in California. Texas MAPA supported Mexican American candidates for office and focused its attention on helping Henry B.

Gonzalez win a Congressional seat in San Antonio. Texas MAPA members soon decided to bring together all the Viva Kennedy activists and supporters to discuss the formation of a national political organization.[25]

Later in 1961, members of the Viva Kennedy Clubs, led primarily by the two separate organizations of MAPA (California and Texas), established the Political Association of Spanish-Speaking Organizations (PASSO). The meeting in Phoenix, Arizona, attended by Kennedy advisor Carlos McCormack, Hector Garcia, and Edward Roybal, stumbled over the issue of leadership, with California and Texas representatives pressing for control. Roybal and others from California argued for leadership over the organization by citing the fact that California had recently surpassed Texas to become the largest population center for Mexican Americans. After much discussion, the group elected Hector Garcia to lead PASSO and Roybal to serve as vice-president. The meeting also included discussions of the lack of political appointments given by Kennedy to Mexican Americans and issues related to the economic and social status of Mexican Americans in the broader society. Despite revealing tensions between Mexican American leadership in Texas and California, and to a lesser extent New Mexico, the establishment of PASSO signaled that Mexican Americans were beginning to look like an organized and organizable minority group in American politics. PASSO sought out a test case, with Texas PASSO taking the lead.[26]

PASSO and the Revolt in Crystal City, Texas: Racial Pride and the Rise of Militant Politics

Texas was a borderland separating the United States from Mexico and the American South from the American Southwest. Not only did Texas share a border with Mexico, its own geography was divided between an Eastern section, where race relations between African Americans and Anglos resembled those of the Jim Crow South, and the South and Western section that bordered Mexico, where race relations reflected Mexican American/Anglo divisions.

This predicament led to complicated political decisions on the part of Mexican American civil rights activists and other groups that pursued civil rights and electoral activism in the early 1960s. Mexican American activist groups lacked the financial and organizational resources of the NAACP, and some perhaps lacked the will to make common cause with African Americans, preferring to pursue a politics of 'whiteness' in the face of discrimination and violence. Some within PASSO sought to embrace a politics of ethnicity and perhaps even race, while other powerful leaders within the organization clung to whiteness politics and feared the untested waters of a politics of confrontation and racial mobilization.

PASSO not only failed to unify the various regional organizations representing Mexican Americans in Texas, California, and elsewhere, but it also failed to unify the increasingly divided community of politicians and organizations in Texas who struggled over the issue of race in politics. In Texas, the AGIF played a significant role in the organization and in many ways provided the architecture for the newly established group. Hector Garcia, Henry B. Gonzalez, and the often overlapping AGIF and LULAC leadership had long won victories by maintaining a color-blind or whiteness approach in Jim Crow Texas and felt uncomfortable embracing a politics of Mexican American race consciousness. This is not to say that Mexican Americans distanced themselves entirely from African Americans or failed to support anti-discrimination laws that attacked Jim Crow. Henry B. Gonzalez fought to create opportunities for both African Americans and Mexican Americans— though he never adopted an outward persona as a 'Mexican American' race leader and in fact attacked those who claimed this mantle. The AGIF supported litigation to desegregate schools and expand civil rights for Mexican Americans, but it also rejected a politics of racial identity and did not join in many African American protests. Likewise, few African Americans joined in efforts aimed at Mexican American equality. On the other hand, some within PASSO, and perhaps many everyday people in the Mexican American community, were slowly moving toward a politics of confrontation and racial identity for Mexican Americans, as they began to see their civil rights struggles as analogous to those of African Americans. Key among these activists in Texas was San Antonio County Commissioner Albert Peña Jr., a longtime supporter of Gonzalez, a member of the AGIF, and a key founder of PASSO, who felt it was time to bring real democracy to South Texas. Peña and his supporters within PASSO sought out a test case to show how powerful PASSO might become if it could tap into the wellspring of Mexican American pride and resistance and use it as the foundation for a political movement.[27]

Working-Class Mexican Americanism

PASSO found its test case in the Southwest Texas farm and ranch city of Crystal City, where a majority of the population was of Mexican ancestry yet had no voice in politics and local society. The Crystal City case both demonstrated the progress of race relations in Texas and gave stark evidence of the durability of discrimination and inequality in the lives of most Mexican Americans in the Southwest. Mexican Americans in Crystal City made up an overwhelming majority of the local population and lived in neighborhoods plagued by poverty in a city and county run by Anglos.[28]

The events that followed in Crystal City led to the collapse of PASSO, yet they succeeded in revealing the deep divisions within Texas society and laying bare the true nature of discrimination in the Mexican-majority regions in the state. Peña and an important group of youth activists in Crystal City faced Anglo Texas head on, and they learned that the veil of accommodation in fact hid deep-seated racial and class antagonisms within the Mexican American community. Removing that veil exposed the failings of the accomodationist social order. Unlike in large cities such as San Antonio and Los Angeles, which had diverse Mexican-ancestry populations and where Mexican Americans and coalitions of voters elected politicians such as Roybal and Gonzalez, a much different and more durable form of oppression limited the political aspirations and life chances of Mexican Americans in many of the segregated agricultural communities, where they comprised a majority of the local population and were a significant local labor force. Accommodationist politicians in PASSO turned away from or actually attacked Peña and other reformers who sought to mobilize working-class Mexican Americans in places such as Crystal City where pent-up demands for civil rights often took on the form of race politics. In the process they pushed many, most importantly young, activists toward a more radical protest politics.

A series of seemingly unrelated events coalesced to bring about the Crystal City revolt. Juan Cornejo, a former migrant worker and veteran who had helped organize the Teamsters union at the Crystal City Del Monte canning plant, visited San Antonio in October 1962 to meet Ray Shafer, president of Teamsters Local no. 657. Shafer agreed to lend Teamster support to a poll-tax drive among the Mexican American majority in Crystal City. The radical idea proposed was that Mexican Americans should register and run their own slate of candidates in a city where they were the overwhelming majority. Cornejo requested help with a voter poll tax and registration drive. One needed to pay a poll tax in order to vote in Texas in 1963. The Teamsters invited PASSO to join the effort. Albert Peña accepted the challenge and sent organizers to Crystal City who helped train a cadre of local activists which included significant numbers of women and young people.[29]

Mainly a civic engagement effort at first, the campaign began with a poll-tax drive to boost Mexican American voter registration and force local officials to adopt a more expansive view of Texas election law. Not only did the $1.75 expense of the tax impose an economic burden on poor people, but Crystal City's Mexican American voters had traditionally been required to complete registration in-person before Anglo city or county officials. In 1963 the Teamsters and PASSO forced the city to appoint Mexican Americans as registrars, as allowed under Texas election law. This change in election practice threatened the very foundation of racial and ethnic politics in South Texas, where Mexican Americans had long been 'voted' by Anglo bosses and coercion played a large role in maintaining Anglo minority control of the borderlands.[30]

Youth Participation and Radicalization

The movement also encouraged high-school-educated young people—who could not vote until they were 21—to play a role in politics. In Crystal City, young people acted as preregistration activists, canvassing neighborhoods and doing much of the work for the registrars. Thus, rather than face an Anglo registrar at City Hall, new voters were greeted by neighborhood kids and a Mexican American official. The working-class Mexican American community in Crystal City quickly came together to support the registration drive. Mothers sponsored tamale sales to get people to register. Much as they did for church events, mothers and children requested donations of supplies from Mexican-owned grocers, monitored which stores made donations, and boycotted those that refused. Mothers gave the tamales to those who paid the $1.75 poll tax. The activists also used the Catholic parish hall for dances and cakewalks; admission required payment of the poll tax. The registration drive took on the form of a community celebration or church fund-raising campaign as registrations skyrocketed.[31]

While the Teamsters and PASSO provided structure to the campaign, Mexican American young people's social networks were crucial to its success. Teen activists assembled an organized core of leaders who encouraged family members, migrants, women, and the elderly to pay the poll tax. The combined efforts of local grassroots organizing and national support and political expertise resulted in a successful poll-tax drive. The Mexican American migrant community outregistered Anglos: a total of 1,139 Mexican Americans versus only 542 Anglos. The Teamsters and PASSO assigned organizers to Crystal City to ensure that the incumbent Anglos ran the election in compliance with state election law.[32]

The Anglo Backlash and Union Response

Local Anglos, following a long tradition in Texas politics, attacked the patriotism of the candidates and brought in the Texas Rangers. Local Anglo media branded the campaign a movement of outside agitators and Communists and worked to weaken middle-class Mexican American support by appointing token middle-class Mexican Americans to government posts. The men selected as candidates, soon dubbed 'Los Cinco,' reflected the majority of the adult Mexican American population, in that they had limited education and had been migrant workers. The Texas Rangers soon flooded the city to keep the 'peace.' Ranger Company D Captain Alfred Y. Allee, a fourth-generation Texas Ranger and former Zavala County sheriff stationed in nearby Carrizo Springs, militarized the city on orders from Governor John Connally.[33] The Rangers were a disruptive force that harassed youth activists and community members and even accosted the Teamster and PASSO organizers.[34]

The Teamsters/PASSO coalition protected registered voters from intimidation at the hands of the Texas Rangers and local employers. Teamster President James R. Hoffa worked to make sure that local Teamster union employers allowed their workers to vote and participate in politics.[35] On April 2, 1963, Mexican Americans voted overwhelmingly for Los Cinco and defeated all five Anglo incumbents. Cornejo ran for and got the largely honorific post of mayor.[36] PASSO had won.

It had organized a Mexican American-majority city and had helped local people elect a representative city council for the first time in the history of South Texas. This victory was, however, short lived.

The election of Los Cinco revealed class divisions within the Mexican American community both at the local and state levels. Some PASSO leaders questioned the efficacy of an explicitly racial strategy for Mexican Americans, and the controversy over tactics and rhetoric weakened the organization, whose very purpose was to act as a unified force in Mexican American politics. Militants within PASSO, led by Albert Peña Jr., faced direct and open hostility, and Peña himself faced reprisals in San Antonio. Congressman Henry B. Gonzales of San Antonio, a leading moderate, strongly criticized the Peña-backed PASSO effort in Crystal City for alienating moderate Anglo voters statewide. The arrival of a more radical and confrontational Mexican Americanism exposed deep fissure between those who saw Mexican American politics as primarily Americanist and color-blind and a new group of militants who sought to define a new politics driven by a radical commitment to citizenship rights and racial and ethnic consciousness.[37] Although short lived, the Crystal City revolt demonstrated that Mexican Americans, especially the poor, and farm workers were organizable. For the young people who participated in the campaign, the election represented the beginning of a new movement. According to one youthful protester, 'We did realize one thing—that if we were going to succeed against the Gringo, we had to educate ourselves in the Gringo world—to know how to use this new power that we could gain.'[38]

The PASSO effort in Crystal City was the first and last major effort led by the organization. Often considered a precursor to the 1969 Crystal City revolt that led to the rise of La Raza Unida Party, the Los Cinco movement—both its successes and its failures—changed the way in which Mexican American youth, the poor, and farm workers viewed their place within American political life, even as it forced the collapse of PASSO.[39] After 1963, the dream of a national PASSO that would organize and field Mexican American candidates died. Texas, California, and New Mexico PASSO leaders never worked together again, and PASSO only functioned, albeit briefly, in Texas. Following the landmark effort in Crystal City, PASSO fell apart, though its member organizations continued to function. The next Mexican American organizing effort to attract national attention and support began among farm workers (like the working-class people of Crystal City), not politicians.

The United Farm Workers: The California Grape Boycott and the National Protest Architecture

In the late 1950s the perennial effort to organize California's farm workers continued with greater organizational success yet few sustained victories. The constant issue in organizing farm workers is that of transforming grassroots organizational success into a stable collective bargaining process that will last more than a single season or harvest. All unions seek to represent workers as their collective bargaining agent. Without this status, the union effort dies on the vine. The American Federation of Labor and Congress of Industrial Organizations (known as the AFL-CIO after the Federation and the Congress merged in 1955) built upon past efforts of older defunct unions and in 1959 established the Agricultural Workers Organizing Committee (AWOC) to organize the 150,000 agricultural harvest workers in California, attack the Bracero guest worker program, discredit the image of farmers as individual yeomen rather than large corporations, and organize domestic farm workers as voters. With support from the United Packinghouse Workers of America (UPWA), the AWOC attempted to unionize lettuce workers in the Imperial Valley of California in 1961 through a series of pickets, protests, strikes, and a media campaign led by experienced AFL-CIO organizers. Foreshadowing tactics to come, the AWOC challenged the Bracero Program by demonstrating that there were domestic workers available for work and pushing for a ban on foreign workers.

Guest Workers and Mexican American Labor

The Bracero Program, formally known as 'Public Law 78,' emerged from prior labor agreements between the United States and Mexico, and by the early 1960s it had served to depress wages for domestic farm workers. Under the provisions of the law Mexican workers were recruited when there was a labor shortage and domestic workers were not available. In practice, employers recruited these guest workers to harvest agricultural crops in places where large populations of domestic workers lived or to which they had traditionally traveled for the harvest. Abused by the agricultural industry, the Bracero Program created a labor situation where domestic workers often labored at wage rates below those of the contracted Mexican workers in a complicated employment environment that effectively pitted domestic workers, undocumented workers, and Braceros against one another in competition for employment. Farm workers in California were a diverse group: Mexican Americans and Mexicans were in competition with each other and with domestic workers of Filipino, African American, Anglo, and other backgrounds. Despite significant investment from the AFL-CIO, the AWOC's efforts had had limited success in the years prior to the end of the Bracero Program, but in 1964 the Bracero Program was cancelled as a result of sustained opposition from unions. The AWOC planned to use the opportunity to organize domestic workers in California across ethnic and racial groups.[40]

Meanwhile, Cesar Chavez and other CSO alumni were trying to build a farm laborers' association in Delano, California. Having failed to convince the CSO to organize farm workers directly, Chavez resigned as the executive director of the organization in 1962 and began work on the National Farm Workers Association (NFWA). Chavez envisaged the association as a worker-supported and -funded operation whose leaders would work mainly as volunteers. This notion of personal sacrifice went against the paid-organizer model used by most labor unions. While Chavez was building his association's base of dues-paying members through the early 1960s, the AWOC was gaining a significant base of support among Filipino agricultural workers. Filipino laborers had established their own ethnic labor unions in the 1930s, but by the late 1930s they had realized that any successful union would need to welcome all farm workers. The resulting AFL-supported National Farm Labor Union (NFLU) in the early 1950s concentrated on the divisive role of the Bracero Program in creating a surplus labor supply, yet despite the committed activism of leaders such as Dr. Ernesto Galarza, the union failed to survive. As Chavez, Dolores Huerta, and other former CSO organizers built the NFWA in the early 1960s, Larry Itliong organized workers along traditional lines within the AWOC. These two struggles soon merged as the AWOC pressed the issue of grape harvesters' rights in the summer and early fall of 1965.[41]

A New Effort to Organize Farm Workers in California

In the summer of 1965, the AWOC led a series of walkouts in an effort to bring about wage parity with what Bracero workers had been paid in 1964 (the last year the program operated) and to win recognition for the union. Mexican- and Filipino-ancestry workers labored side by side in the grape harvest and walked out together in the Coachella Valley in Southern California. As in past efforts, the AWOC led a successful organizing drive and succeeded in gaining a wage increase, but official recognition of the union as a collective bargaining agent remained elusive. Building upon this active summer of organizing, Filipino workers in Delano walked out in September, demanding $1.40 an hour—similar to the wages paid to foreign workers in the final year of the Bracero Program. Mexican American workers affiliated with the NFWA wanted to join the effort led by the AWOC and pressed Chavez to act. Realizing that the strike could not succeed without support from the NFWA, Itliong convinced Chavez to join, despite reservations and concern that the NFWA was not ready for a labor action. Chavez, who had hoped to spend several more years building the NFWA, found himself in a cooperative agreement with the AWOC and in the middle of a strike long before he thought the NFWA would be ready for such endeavors. On Diez y Seis de Septiembre (September 16), 1965, Mexican Independence Day, the NFWA voted to join the AWOC in their strike of the two largest grape growers in California, Schenley Industries and the DiGiorgio Corporation.[42]

In the struggle that followed, the NFWA led the most successful consumer boycott on behalf of labor unionization in US history. This struggle made Cesar

Chavez a household name in the United States due to his commitment to non-violent protest on behalf of farm workers in the face of massive grower resistance. The AWOC and the NFWA merged in 1966 and became the United Farmworkers Organizing Committee (UFWOC) with an AFL-CIO union charter and a mission to organize domestic farm workers. Chavez's unique vision of a union that operated much like a civil rights movement organization rejected several basic premises of union organizing and forced many of the AWOC organizers out of the union. In place of paid organizers, Chavez, Itliong, and Huerta relied on volunteers who committed themselves to work long hours for little pay, and thus tended to recruit youth and university students for much of the organizing infrastructure. This commitment to the UFWOC as a social movement union organization created opportunities nationwide, not just for official organizers but also for the Mexican American community and campus activists from coast to coast who aided the UFWOC grape boycott.

Marching for Labor Rights

Perhaps the signal event in the development of the UFWOC was a pilgrimage to Sacramento, which began in March of 1966. The march, led by Chavez, mirrored the well-known civil rights marches of the Southern Christian Leadership Conference (SCLC), led by Dr. Martin Luther King, Jr. and struck the leadership of the AWOC as nontraditional at best. In a religious expression of activism tied to the Catholic faith, the march featured the Virgin of Guadalupe in addition to displays of the US and Mexican flags—the black and red UFWOC Aztec eagle flag, which for many participants and observers came to represent the movement. Chavez and his organizers linked the struggle for farm workers' rights to the Mexican independence movement and the Mexican Revolution of 1910. Playwright Luis Valdez drafted 'El Plan de Delano' which drew on past practice among Mexican and Mexican American revolts. The march and the support it generated within the Mexican-ancestry community nationwide moved many moderate Mexican American organizations to support the farm workers' struggle and side with a more radical view of citizenship rights, as young people saw in Chavez and the marchers a new example of militant leadership. The Mexican, American, and religious symbolism and rhetoric deployed during the 300-mile 25-day march on California's capitol building foreshadowed much of what became the Chicano Movement for civil rights among Mexican Americans. As the workers rallied at the California state capitol, the farm workers' movement permanently transformed the dynamics of Mexican American politics and civic engagement.[43]

The Sacramento trek, which inspired sympathy marches on the part of farm workers in Texas and Wisconsin, also stimulated nationwide interest in the struggle of farm workers for rights. Keenly aware of the importance of media perception during the Cold War, Chavez and other UFWOC organizers, themselves committed Cold Warriors, highlighted the family- and faith-centered nature of the workers' lives and found support in Catholic doctrine for their demands for the right to organize. From the early days of the NFWA, Chavez, Huerta, and others sought to build the movement as a community-based effort, and the emphasis on providing services (such as a credit union and other cooperative ventures) became part of the social justice unionism model. The consumer boycott itself created a framework for grassroots movements among urban Latinos and Chicanos from coast to coast. The UFWOC was a radically different type of union—more a social movement than a bureaucratic union, and this fact drew young people to its banner.[44]

Within its first year, the UFWOC won a contract with one of its targeted growers. Schenley Industries agreed to recognize the UFWOC as the grape harvesters' bargaining representative soon after the march on Sacramento. Dolores Huerta negotiated the union contract with the winery, and the young union had its first victory. The strike, however, continued as many large growers continued to reject calls to begin collective bargaining and politicians accused the strikers of 'red' or Communist ties. As the UFWOC set up its hiring hall and continued to expand its social movement unionism model, it also intensified its boycott focused primarily on the DiGiorgio Corporation, the largest grower and landowner in the San Joaquín Valley, whose owners engaged in tactics meant to stifle unionization while giving the impression that they were open to bargaining. Founded by an immigrant with roots in Sicily, DiGiorgio had a personal story that embodied the 'American Dream' of immigration, hard work, and upward mobility. Perhaps because of this narrative, the family-controlled company fought off the UFWOC, thus becoming the focus of a national and international boycott of all of California's table grapes. Despite the patriotic symbolism of the UFWOC's activities, in the struggle that followed, DiGiorgio supporters persistently and stridently accused the union of having Communist or 'red' influences, while local police officials used questionable control tactics and conservative California politicians supported the growers. Chavez, with solid anti-Communist credentials, declared the charges of Communist influence a 'lot of garbage.'[45]

The Grape Boycott

In 1966 and into 1967 the struggle for recognition of the union from the DiGiorgio family proceeded slowly. The International Brotherhood of Teamsters competed with the UFWOC for the right to represent the workers, which led to a contested election that the UFWOC won. DiGiorgio and the union finally entered contract negotiations and the union was recognized. However, soon after the parties signed the contract, DiGiorgio then announced that it was making a business decision to leave the table grape business and began to sell off its farm interests in California. In a process that would become common, the union won contracts, then growers sold off, shifted into new businesses or reincorporated, and thus escaped the contracts bargained for with the UFWOC. Nonetheless, victory was in the air in 1967: the first two targets of the boycott had signed contracts. Instead of concluding the boycott with the successful negotiating of contracts with the two primary targets, the UFWOC soon extended it to cover all table grapes. The grape boycott, which had garnered national support, was expanding rather than ending.[46]

The national boycott required that the UFWOC have boycott committees in every major city in the United States. Begun in 1966 and expanded significantly in 1968, 'La Huelga' (the strike) became 'La Causa' (the cause). Not only did organizers travel from Delano but activists in Texas, the Southwest, Southern California, the Pacific Northwest, and the Midwest became UFWOC-affiliated boycott representatives. In this way, young Mexican Americans, as they increasingly participated in the boycott, learned the basics of community engagement and grassroots organizing. Participants from a variety of racial and ethnic backgrounds organized pickets and outreach efforts and educated the press, college students, and consumers on the plight of the American farm worker. Whether leading protests, marches, or demonstrations in New York City, Austin, Berkeley, or Milwaukee, Chicano youth activists began to tie the demands of the farm workers of California (as well as Texas and the Midwest) to the broader civil rights demands of Chicanos nationwide. While Chavez and his vanguard leadership circle were older than most youth volunteer activists, through cross-pollination with other Mexican American and 1960s-era social movements the youth brought skills learned in other movements to the farm workers' struggle. Through volunteer activism in the UFWOC they learned new tactics that they put to good use— often simultaneously—in other areas of the Chicano Movement.[47]

The national boycott involved grocers, families, and everyday people in an evaluation of working conditions, as empathy for farm workers led many to respond favorably to the boycott. The cause gained pledges of support from the mayors of New York, San Francisco, and Detroit, and many college campuses followed suit. Although the strike gained national attention after 1966, negotiations between growers and the UFWOC remained stalled. Three years into the boycott, California grape growers showed that they were feeling the impact by bringing suit against the UFWOC and five other unions for losses of $25 million because of union efforts to prevent major cities from purchasing nonunion California grapes. The lawsuit revealed that the boycott was working at the national level and altering consumer patterns of purchasing.[48]

Cesar Chavez, in the effort to establish the UFWOC as a viable union, became a national civil and labor rights figure. Certainly, Larry Itliong and Dolores Huerta were central to the operation and success of the union, but for most Americans, and for many Chicano activists, Chavez became the iconic leader of the movement. Fashioning his efforts on the social movement and nonviolent tactics of Martin Luther King, Jr. and Mohandas Gandhi, Chavez convinced Americans that farm workers were noble, Christian, hardworking people who, through the UFWOC, sought to earn a living wage for providing food for the nation. This attention to image and the American consumer's conscience brought success. Following the example of Gandhi, Chavez began a hunger strike that lasted 25 days to demonstrate the farm workers' commitment to nonviolence during a period of increased grower opposition, union tension, and urban unrest in American cities. The fast came to an end on March 10, 1968, when Chavez broke bread with Robert F. Kennedy. The image of the weakened Chavez (he had lost 35 pounds) breaking his fast by sharing bread with Kennedy, a staunch Catholic and a strong supporter of the UFWOC, became one of the iconic images of the 1960s. Chavez became a delegate for Kennedy at the Democratic national convention, and the farm workers registered voters and worked on behalf of the Kennedy campaign. Sadly, after delivering a victory speech on winning the California primary, in which he thanked Cesar Chavez and Dolores Huerta, Kennedy was assassinated by a gunman as he exited the Ambassador Hotel in Los Angeles. The death of Robert F. Kennedy hit young people particularly hard in the spring of 1968. The connection between Kennedy and Chavez was one that excited many young Chicanos who saw the youthful Kennedy as a person who understood them. The UFWOC mourned his death as the loss of a 'friend' who was a 'beacon of hope for the farm worker.'[49]

The boycott entered 1969 with grower resistance weakening in the face of significant drops in the demand for table grapes. With table grape sales off by 30–40 percent, growers began bargaining with the union for recognition. The strike had entered the mainstream, as suburbanites refused to purchase grapes, and wholesale purchasers, under union pressure, refused likewise. In addition to the success of the consumer boycott, the effort had succeeded in unifying much of the Mexican-ancestry community and was proof positive that Mexican Americans were organizable. The grape boycott had mobilized Mexican Americans from coast to coast and linked the efforts of activists to those within the antiwar, New Left, and Old Left movement communities nationwide. Moreover, where the grape boycott took root, Mexican Americans participated in La Causa—a movement that expanded to include civil rights, educational rights, community control, and affirmative action for Latinos.[50]

By 1970 the boycott had won the support of major organizations and individuals across the United States and the world, facts that brought growers to the bargaining table. Major grocers, in response to pickets, discontinued the purchase of table grapes. National leaders within the Catholic Church put their weight behind the strike and were key players in bringing about the first contracts for the fledgling UFWOC. The efforts of Los Angeles Archbishop Timothy Manning and others led to negotiations between the union and ranch owners, including the Freeman Ranches. The Freeman Ranches were the first to sign contracts with the UFWOC, and others soon followed as grapes shipped from the ranch with the union label on the boxes. The contract gave the workers a 6 percent raise, bonuses on harvested grapes, and union representation. Other ranches followed suit. With some of the growers under contract, grapes began appearing on grocer's shelves again—but in most cases only those with the union label.[51]

As union-labeled grapes began hitting the shelves in the United States and worldwide, other growers began negotiations with the UFWOC in the early summer months of 1970. Even some agricultural industries outside of grapes began negotiations with the UFWOC. The notion that having a UFWOC label on one's products would improve sales was not lost on perceptive agricultural producers, who began to sign contracts with the union. By June of 1970, the UFWOC had won contracts and was negotiating with other growers. The victories also brought reflection, as some considered the utility of nonviolence during a period where young people were rejecting the concept, and others considered the similarities between African American struggles and those of the Mexican American people. As union grapes hit the shelves, some grocers had to fight off angry housewives who asked why they were selling grapes. The growers then showed the union labels on the boxes and explained that some growers had signed contracts. Many grocers, rather than packing the grapes in bags, placed the boxes out in open to display the 'black Aztec emblem' of the union for all to see. The boycott had won the support of American consumers who did not want scab-harvested grapes.[52]

Rather than manage the union effort from Delano, Chavez entered the organizing field once again. With unions organized in the grape-growing industry, the UFWOC and its organizers went after the lettuce harvest in California and soon found themselves managing a strike action, calling for a national boycott, and fighting a jurisdictional dispute with the Teamsters. The UFWOC won contracts in lettuce. For much of the 1970s, the UFWOC had difficulty managing its contracts as it battled against its rival the Teamsters and struggled to maintain its status as bargaining agent for farm workers. Despite its shortcomings after 1970, the UFWOC had become a powerful symbol, and the many boycott centers across the nation became key grassroots training grounds for Chicano and Chicana activists.[53]

Conclusion

By the 1960s, Mexican American activists increasingly rejected the accomodationist or assimilationist approach advocated by established civil rights organizations. Throughout the 1950s, as Mexican Americans pressed for greater opportunity and access to civil rights long denied them, the resistance of Anglos in Texas, the ranchers in California, and persistent racism led many to consider abandoning older understandings of ethnicity in favor of an increasingly racially and ethnically defined identity. This shift from accommodation to radical praxis on the part of Mexican American movement leaders created tensions between establishment Mexican Americans and the group of activists influenced by the African American civil rights movement, who increasingly sought to highlight a distinct ethnic identity as they rejected traditional 'whiteness' politics.

The transformation from accomodationist politics did not result in a complete rejection of longstanding demands. Rather, movements like those in Crystal City, Texas, and Delano, California, were in line with prior efforts led by Mexican American political and labor leaders. The shift was in the tone and rhetoric of protest. Where past movements played on the Americanism and whiteness of Mexican Americans seeking rights guaranteed under the constitution, labor laws, and local statute, the UFWOC and Los Cinco made demands as Mexican Americans, utilized the symbolism of Mexican radicalism, and blended these with the iconography of Cold War Americanism. This embrace of a hybrid politics startled many Mexican American leaders who had invested much in color-blind or 'Caucasian' politics in Texas and elsewhere and resulted in divisions between the old-style leaders and those who eventually embraced Chicanismo and a politics that drew from those things that made Mexican Americans exceptional, different, and uniquely 'American' in the broadest sense of the word.

Notes

1 Certainly, there were radical organizations that proposed militant solutions prior to the Chicano Movement, yet these often short-lived groups had few members and limited long-term influence. The aim here is not to provide an encyclopedic survey of all the organizations serving Mexican-ancestry people in the United States but to detail key organizations and provide a foundation for understanding Mexicanist and Mexican Americanist views as predecessor ideologies to the Chicano Movement.

2 For insightful new work on the Farm Workers, see Frank Bardacke, *Trampling Out the Vintage: Cesar Chavez and the Two Souls of the United Farm Workers* (New York: Verso Press, 2012); Matt Garcia, *From the Jaws of Victory: The Triumph and Tragedy of Cesar Chavez and the Farm Worker Movement* (Berkeley: University of California Press, 2012). For histories of Crystal City, Texas, see Armando Navarro, *The Cristal* [sic] *Experiment: A Chicano Struggle for Community Control* (Madison: University of Wisconsin Press, 1998); Marc S. Rodriguez, *The Tejano Diaspora: Mexican Americanism and Ethnic Politics in Texas and Wisconsin* (Chapel Hill: University of North Carolina Press, 2011).

3 In this text I use the term Mexicanist to identify those institutions such as the Mexican consulates, and consulate-supported groups, as well as individuals who sought to maintain Mexican citizenship and a nationalist orientation among the immigrant population as well as support Mexican patriotic celebrations. As the United States sought to Americanize immigrants, the Mexican consulates sought to Mexicanize its citizens residing in the United States simultaneously. I use Americanist to describe those aspects of political and social ideology that tended to reflect a strong connection to ideals and ideology considered the foundation of political life in the United States

such as free speech, equal rights, and other rights enshrined in the US Constitution, yet often not adhered to when it came to minorities. I use the term Mexican Americanist to refer to those Mexican Americans who through their civil rights efforts embraced the ideals of the US Constitution's rights guarantees and sought to implement them wherever Mexican-ancestry people lived or worked. On Americanism see generally Michael Kazin and Joseph Anthony McCartin, *Americanism: New Perspectives on the History of an Ideal* (Chapel Hill: University of North Carolina Press, 2006). On the role of the consulates in creating what I refer to as a Mexicanist worldview see Gilbert G. Gonzalez and Raul A. Fernandez, *A Century of Chicano History: Empire, Nations, and Migration* (New York: Routledge, 2003).

4 For a critical comparison of Mexican Americanist and Mexicanist organizations, see David G. Gutiérrez, *Walls and Mirrors: Mexican Americans, Mexican Immigrants, and the Politics of Ethnicity* (Berkeley: University of California Press, 1995), 87–107; for an interesting exploration of the elite and middle-class impulse among mutual benefit societies in the Midwest, see Juan R. García, *Mexicans in the Midwest: 1900–1932* (Tucson: University of Arizona Press, 1996), 159–90. For a detailed study of mutual benefit and labor organizations in early twentieth-century Texas, see Emilio Zamora, *The World of the Mexican Worker in Texas* (College Station: Texas A&M University Press, 1995). In Zamora's book, photographs show that Mexicanist organizations displayed both the US flag and the Mexican flag, along with the banners and coat of arms of the organization, blurring the lines of membership and intent.

5 See Gutiérrez, *Walls and Mirrors*, 95–6; Zaragosa Vargas, *Crucible of Struggle: A History of Mexican Americans from Colonial Times to the Present Era* (Oxford: Oxford University Press, 2011), 201–3.

6 See Benjamin Heber Johnson, *Revolution in Texas: How a Forgotten Rebellion and Its Bloody Suppression Turned Mexicans into Americans* (New Haven: Yale University Press, 2003). The term 'hyphenated American,' which is no longer obvious from current usage, represented the in-between nature of describing one's self as Mexican-American or Italian-American (hyphen included) rather than as 100 percent of one group or another. The notion of in-between status is less relevant in the twenty-first century since the practice of hyphenating descriptors such as 'Mexican American,' 'Asian American,' 'African American' has been abandoned. On this issue in a specific setting see John Horton, *The Politics of Diversity Immigration, Resistance, and Change in Monterey Park, California* (Philadelphia: Temple University Press, 1995), 185–214.

7 For a concise history of the development of LULAC, see Benjamin Márquez, *LULAC: The Evolution of a Mexican American Political Organization* (Austin: University of Texas Press, 1993); and for a policy history of LULAC, see Craig A. Kaplowitz, *LULAC, Mexican Americans, and National Policy* (College Station: Texas A&M University Press, 2005). For criticisms of LULAC as a presumably assimilationist, integrationist, and sometimes racist organization, see Gutiérrez, *Walls and Mirrors*, 69–116, and Neil Foley, *Quest for Equality: The Failed Promise of Black-Brown Solidarity* (Cambridge: Harvard University Press, 2010). Two points are worthy of note here. Gutiérrez, in his landmark study, engages in theoretical gymnastics to make the case that LULAC did not represent the majority view among Mexican-ancestry people in the United States, yet he posits that organizations that represented far fewer people than LULAC—and had extremely limited organizational life spans—represented the working-class majority of the Mexican-ancestry people in the United States, and the evidence he presents

is far too thin. If one looks to the goals and platforms of all of these organizations, there is little that separates them in practice—radical and or middle-class ideology notwithstanding. Foley's text is a timely corrective to his earlier work which located what appeared to be a racist tendency among some individual leaders and by extracting language from court cases meant to defend the rights of 'Caucasians' under the law, Foley initially engaged in over-reach. Foley's latest book shows that there were many reasons why LULAC leaders chose to push for citizenship rights within the context of their 'Caucasian' legal status. Perhaps the analogy—not made by either scholar—between Mexican Americans and other so-called hyphenated ethnic/immigrant groups would have long ago situated LULAC at the center rather than the margin of organized ethnic politics in the twentieth century.

8 See Márquez, *LULAC*; Patrick James Carroll, *Felix Longoria's Wake: Bereavement, Racism, and the Rise of Mexican American Activism* (Austin: University of Texas Press, 2003); Cynthia E. Orozco, *No Mexicans, Women, or Dogs Allowed: The Rise of the Mexican American Civil Rights Movement* (Austin: University of Texas Press, 2009).

9 *In re Rodriguez* is a landmark court case which upheld the naturalization rights of Mexican immigrants and the right of Texas Mexicans to vote. In this case, Rodriguez, clearly of native ancestry, was determined to be 'white' or 'Caucasian' as a result of the provisions of the Treaty of Guadalupe Hidalgo (1848), which brought to an end the widespread effort to disenfranchise Mexican-ancestry people and deny them naturalization based on race. See Fernando V. Padilla, 'Early Chicano Legal Recognition: 1846–1897,' *Journal of Popular Culture* 13, no. 3 (Spring, 1980): 564–74.

10 See Arnoldo De Leon, '*In Re Ricardo Rodríguez*: An Attempt at Chicano Disenfranchisement in San Antonio, 1896–1897,' in *En Aquel Entonces: Readings in Mexican-American History*, ed. Manuel G. Gonzalez and Cynthia G. Gonzales (Bloomington: Indiana University Press, 2000), 57–63. On whiteness, see Emilio Zamora, *Claiming Rights and Righting Wrongs in Texas: Mexican Workers and Job Politics during World War II* (College Station: Texas A&M University Press, 2009), 9–12.

11 See Mario García, *Mexican Americans: Leadership, Ideology, and Identity, 1930–1960* (New Haven: Yale University Press, 1991), 45–61.

12 On the Cold War, see David K. Johnson, *The Lavender Scare: The Cold War Persecution of Gays and Lesbians in the Federal Government* (Chicago: University of Chicago Press, 2006); Shelton Stromquist, ed., *Labor's Cold War: Local Politics in a Global Context* (Urbana: University of Illinois Press, 2008); Landon R.Y. Storrs, *The Second Red Scare and the Unmaking of the New Deal Left* (Princeton: Princeton University Press, 2012).

13 On labor and the Cold War, see Robert W. Cherney and William Issel, eds., *American Labor and the Cold War* (New Brunswick: Rutgers University Press, 2004). On the wartime and postwar experiences of Mexican Americans, see Richard Griswold del Castillo, ed., *World War II and Mexican American Civil Rights* (Austin: University of Texas Press, 2008).

14 See Carroll, *Felix Longoria's Wake*; Henry A.J. Ramos, *The American GI Forum: In Pursuit of the Dream, 1948–1983* (Houston: Arte Público Press, 1998), 1–18.

15 See Ignacio M. García, *Hector P. Garcia: In Relentless Pursuit of Justice* (Houston: Arte Público Press, 2002), 172–207.

16 For a detailed examination of the *Hernandez* case, see Ignacio M. García, *White But Not Equal: Mexican Americans, Jury Discrimination, and the Supreme Court* (Tucson: University of Arizona Press, 2008).

17 *Hernandez v. Texas*, 347 US 475 (1954).

18 On the NAACP in the 1950s, see Mark V. Tushnet, *Making Civil Rights Law: Thurgood Marshall and the Supreme Court, 1956–1961* (New York: Oxford University Press, 1996), 311–15. On 1950s Mexican American litigation, see Michael A. Olivas, '*Hernandez v. Texas*: A Litigation History,' in '*Colored Men*' *and* '*Hombres Aquí*': *Hernandez v. Texas and the Emergence of Mexican American Lawyering*, ed. Michael A. Olivas (Houston: Arte Público Press, 2006), 209–24.

19 See Juan Gómez-Quiñones, *Chicano Politics: Reality and Promise 1940–1990* (Albuquerque: University of New Mexico Press, 1990), 53–5.

20 See Shana Bernstein, *Bridges of Reform: Interracial Civil Rights Activism in Twentieth-Century Los Angeles* (New York: Oxford University Press, 2011), 139–45.

21 Gutiérrez, *Walls and Mirrors*, 168–72.

22 Gómez-Quiñones, *Chicano Politics*, 67–9.

23 Gutiérrez, *Walls and Mirrors*, 181–2.

24 On the growth and importance of the Viva Kennedy Clubs, see Ignacio M. García, *Viva Kennedy: Mexican Americans in Search of Camelot* (College Station: Texas A&M University Press, 2000).

25 García, *Viva Kennedy*, 44–88; Luis DeSipio, 'The Pressures of Perpetual Promise: Latinos and Politics, 1960–2003,' in *The Columbia History of Latinos in the United States since 1960*, ed. David G. Gutiérrez (New York: Columbia University Press, 2004), 422–5.

26 García, *Viva Kennedy*, 124–33; Brian Behnken, *Fighting Their Own Battles: Mexican Americans, African Americans, and the Struggle for Civil Rights in Texas* (Chapel Hill: University of North Carolina Press, 2011), 85–7.

27 Teresa Palomo Acosta, 'POLITICAL ASSOCIATION OF SPANISH-SPEAKING ORGANIZATIONS,' Handbook of Texas Online. Retrieved from: www.tshaonline. org/handbook/online/articles/vep01 (accessed May 9, 2014); Ignacio M. García, *Chicanismo: The Forging of a Militant Ethos Among Mexican Americans* (Tucson: University of Arizona Press, 1997), 23–5; Behnken, *Fighting Their Own Battles*, 72–101.

28 See John S. Shockley, *Chicano Revolt in a Texas Town* (Notre Dame: University of Notre Dame Press, 1974).

29 See Navarro, *The Cristal Experiment*, 25–8.

30 See Rodriguez, *The Tejano Diaspora*, 49–50.

31 José A. Gutiérrez, *The Making of a Chicano Militant: Lessons from Cristal* (Madison: University of Wisconsin Press, 1998), 62–8.

32 Rodriguez, *The Tejano Diaspora*, 50–51.

33 On Ranger captain Allee, see Handbook of Texas Online, s.v. 'Allee, Alfred Young.' Retrieved from: www.tsha.utexas.edu/handbook/online/articles/AA/fal97. html (accessed July 19, 2006); Julian Samora, Joe Bernal, and Albert Peña, *Gunpowder Justice: A Reassessment of the Texas Rangers* (Notre Dame: University of Notre Dame Press, 1979); Beatriz de la Garza, *A Law for the Lion: A Tale of Crime and Injustice in the Borderlands* (Austin: University of Texas Press, 2003); O.W. Nolen to John Connally, May 1, 1963, Zavala County File, Connally Papers; H. Joaquín Jackson with David Marion Wilkinson, *One Ranger: A Memoir* (Austin: University of Texas Press, 2005).

34 Albert Peña Jr., interview by José Angel Gutiérrez, CMAS 15, TVOH, July 2, 1996.

35 Shockley, *Chicano Revolt*, 38; US Senate, Committee on Commerce, Federal Trade Commission Oversight, 104–5.

36 'Latin Ticket Wins Council Race,' *Zavala County Sentinel*, April 5, 1963; 'New Council Takes Office Apr. 16,' *Zavala County Sentinel*, April 5, 1963; Robert A. Cuellar,

'Social and Political History of the Mexican American Population, 1929-1963,' Master's thesis, North Texas State University, 1969, 59; Larry Goodwyn, 'Los Cinco Candidatos,' *Texas Observer*, April 18, 1963, 7.

37 'Crystal City Expected to Affect More Elections,' *Dallas Morning News*, May 9, 1963; 'Dissenting Passo Group Scores Crystal City Coup,' *Alamo Messenger* (San Antonio), April 19, 1963; 'Pena, Ploch Trade Oral Jabs over Crystal City,' newspaper clipping dated May 10, 1963, Zavala County Folder, Connally Papers.

38 Quoted in Rodriguez, *Tejano Diaspora*, 58.

39 García, *Viva Kennedy*, 146–56.

40 Howard Kennedy, 'Lettuce Farm Strike Part of Deliberate Union Plan,' *Los Angeles Times*, January 23, 1961.

41 Gladwin Hill, 'Big Farms Blamed for Migrant Woes,' *New York Times*, August 13, 1950; Gladwin Hill, 'Penalty for Hiring "Wetbacks" Hailed,' *New York Times*, May 6, 1951; 'Union Accuses U.S. on Wetback Pact,' *New York Times*, February 14, 1952.

42 Harry Bernstein, 'Yule Gifts for Grape Strikers Called Stunt,' *Los Angeles Times*, December 24, 1965; Harry Bernstein, 'Benefits in End of Bracero Plan Told by Brown,' *Los Angeles Times*, March 15, 1966.

43 'Bishop Pike Backs Farm Workers Strike,' *Chicago Daily Defender*, March 24, 1966; Lawrence Davies, 'Religion Inspires Grape Marchers,' *New York Times*, March 25, 1966; 'Grape Pickers Call off Strike against Schenley,' *Chicago Daily Defender*, April 7, 1966.

44 Art Berman, 'Chavez a Modern Zapata to Grape Strikers,' *Los Angeles Times*, May 6, 1966; Nicholas Chriss, 'Texas Farm Laborers March to Protest Pay,' *Los Angeles Times*, July 12, 1966; 'Wisconsin Migrants March to Capital to Protest Pay,' *New York Times*, August 16, 1966; Frank Del Olmo, 'Cesar Chavez—Out of Sight but Still in Fight,' *Los Angeles Times*, February 14, 1972.

45 Lawrence Davies, '2d Grape Grower Agrees to a Union,' *New York Times*, April 8, 1966; 'Grape Strikers, Nearing End of Walk to Capitol, Rap Brown,' *Los Angeles Times*, April 10, 1966; 'Workers Reach Destination,' *Chicago Tribune*, April 11, 1966; 'Protest March Stirs up New Boycott, Wine Grower to Talk Union,' *Pittsburgh Courier*, April 23, 1966; 'Teamsters Quitting Drive to Organize DiGiorgio Workers,' *Los Angeles Times*, June 8, 1966; 'Red Influence in 1966 Grape Strike Seen by Burns,' *Los Angeles Times*, June 9, 1967; Ray Zeman, 'Reds Accused of Role Win Delano Grape Strike,' *Los Angeles Times*, September 8, 1967; 'Chavez Declares Senate Report "Lot of Garbage",' *Los Angeles Times*, September 8, 1967.

46 'Teamsters Quitting Drive'; Lawrence Davies, 'Farm Union Vote Set on the Coast,' *New York Times*, August 28, 1966; 'Vast Di Giorgio Farm Empire Nearing End after Many Woes,' *New York Times*, December 25, 1968; Garcia, *From the Jaws of Victory*, 57–62.

47 Harry Bernstein, 'Grape Growers Sue Unions for $25 Million over Boycott,' *Los Angeles Times*, July 12, 1968; Dick Meister, '"La Huelga" Becomes "La Causa",' *New York Times*, November 17, 1968; 'The Grape Boycott,' *Los Angeles Times*, September 23, 1968; Richard Orr, 'Chicago Labor Backs Grape Boycott,' *Chicago Tribune*, November 13, 1969; 'Humphrey Backs Farm Union's Grape Boycott,' *Los Angeles Times*, August 8, 1968; 'Hatcher Backs Grape Boycott,' *Chicago Daily Defender*, October 31, 1968; 'Here to Spur Boycott of Lettuce, Farm Workers Urge: Remember the Grape,' *New York Times*, October 9, 1970; 'Grape and Lettuce Boycott to Widen,' *New York Times*, November 10, 1973.

48 Jack Fox, 'Grape Boycott: Small, Soft-Spoken Cesar Chavez Leads Quietly Determined Drive to Unionize Agricultural Workers,' *Washington Post*, November 14, 1968; Harry

Bernstein, 'Grape Growers Sue 6 Unions for $25 Million in Damages,' *Los Angeles Times*, July 12, 1968.

49 'The Fast,' *El Malcriado* (Delano), March 15, 1968; Jean Stein, *American Journey: The Times of Robert F. Kennedy* (New York: Harcourt, Brace, Jovanovich, 1970), 281–4; 'Kennedy Chooses Chavez,' *El Malcriado*, April 1, 1968; 'Paid Political Advertisement,' *El Malcriado*, June 1, 1968; 'Kennedy Wins Race,' *Los Angeles Times*, June 5, 1968; 'Triumph and Tragedy' and 'Our Friend, May He Rest in Peace,' *El Malcriado*, June 15, 1968.

50 'Awake Freedom,' *Chicano Times*, August 21, 1970; Harry Bernstein, 'Massive Boycott Mounted against State's Grapes,' *Los Angeles Times*, August 12, 1968; Cynthia Crossen, 'Against All Odds: 1960s Grape Pickers Won Right to Bargain,' *Wall Street Journal*, May 1, 2006.

51 Richard Orr, 'Shuman Raps Jewel's New Policy on Grapes,' *Chicago Tribune*, May 7, 1970; Robert Wright, 'Farm Workers Union Signs First Table-Grape Contract with Two California Growers,' *New York Times*, April 2, 1970; Harry Bernstein, 'Catholic Bishops Help Union, Grape Growers OK Pact,' *Los Angeles Times*, April 2, 1970; Harry Bernstein, 'Grape Growers in Delano Sign Union Contracts,' *Los Angeles Times*, May 21, 1970; Steven Roberts, 'First Grapes with Union Label Shipped to Market from Coast,' *New York Times*, May 31, 1970.

52 Harry Bernstein, 'Chavez Scores Major Victory, Signs Pact with Huge Farm,' *Los Angeles Times*, June 11, 1970; Harry Bernstein, 'Chavez Revolt Catching Fire across State,' *Los Angeles Times*, June 14, 1970.

53 Harry Bernstein, 'Talks between Teamsters and Chavez's Farm Union Collapse,' *Los Angeles Times*, December 25, 1970; Kenneth Fanucchi, 'Lettuce Boycott Ends with Pro-Chavez Vote,' *Los Angeles Times*, January 8, 1971; Del Olmo, 'Cesar Chavez–Out of Sight but Still in Fight.'

2

THE NEW URBAN POLITICS

Chicanos and the War on Poverty

Introduction

This chapter explores the genesis of the Chicano Movement through a consideration of community activism and the development of organizations focused on community control during the War on Poverty era in several important urban *barrios* and rural *colonias*.[1] As the various Chicano Movements of the 1960s developed locally in cities and *barrios*, the influence of anti-colonial rhetoric and cultural nationalism led many young people to seek community control of their neighborhoods and institutions. The War on Poverty included several programs funded by outside governmental bodies and administered or founded by religious groups such as the Catholic Church. Rather than allowing these organizations to provide experience for appointed bureaucrats and Anglo volunteers from other communities, however, Chicano activists sought to remake the institutions of the *barrio* as training centers for local activists, young people, and *barrio* residents, often with the help of supportive Anglos and religious leaders. In very real ways, the demand for community control fit within accepted frameworks of mainstream Americanism, as Chicanos sought to use the resources of the state, business, and the *barrio* itself to repair and heal the social trauma caused by a long history of neglect and discrimination. From Denver to Milwaukee, and Los Angeles to Crystal City, Chicano activists demanded control of their communities, often refashioning them as homelands or mini versions of Aztlán.[2]

Both radical and reformist, a variety of organizations took shape to press for change in Mexican American neighborhoods, many of them challenging the relationship of their community to the state as they demanded a stakeholder position in determining how resources were allocated across a variety of areas of concern, including schools, job training, gang prevention, and well-being programs. Some organizations focused on securing formal Office of Economic Opportunity (OEO) federal and state funding for community services, whereas others saw community engagement, self-help, and ethnic pride as their central mission. OEO or 'War on Poverty' funds were sometimes directed to organizations run by city- or state-wide groups; in these cases, Chicanos often pressured successfully for the appointment of Mexican American staff, employees, and directors of the programs. Some groups, such as the Crusade for Justice based in Denver, Colorado, grew out of the War on Poverty but quickly rejected its acculturationist bent. The Crusade for Justice and its charismatic leader, Rodolfo 'Corky' Gonzales, came to define a new 'Chicano' identity, as Gonzales embraced a new form of cultural nationalism and the rhetoric of irredentism (independence for the US Southwest as Aztlán), based on the frameworks of the Black Power Movement and anti-colonialism. Some, such as Reies López Tijerina, led armed community efforts to take land back from the government and those they accused of land grant chicanery in New Mexico.[3] Thus, *barrios* and *colonias* in the US Southwest became the 'homeland' for Chicanos seeking self-determination. Others, in Los Angeles, Chicago, and San Antonio, took different approaches to the problems of the urban environment, yet to different degrees also embraced a Chicano identity and a cultural nationalist worldview. La Raza Unida Party (RUP) in challenging the one-party system in South Texas also embraced cultural nationalism and community control, as it likewise sought to benefit from federal funds in attempting to remake society for residents of Crystal City, Texas, and other South Texas *colonias*. Briefly shining as a national third party, the RUP embodied, as did the Crusade for Justice, the potentials and limits of cultural nationalism. Throughout this era, Mexican Americans remade themselves as Chicanos, and even if they failed to adopt the Chicano appellation, they incorporated elements of cultural nationalism into their repertoire.[4]

The War on Poverty had a great impact on the Chicano Movement in the 1960s and 1970s. The OEO provided the framework for solutions and responses to urban problems for Mexican Americans and other minority groups. The OEO grew from efforts to end poverty at the state and federal level and targeted the social problems that appeared to lock people in poverty. In an effort to end poverty in cities and rural areas alike, the United States committed itself to bring all Americans into the mainstream by funding programs to help the poor help themselves. For its primary architect President Lyndon Johnson, the War on Poverty was an extension of the New Deal. A large package of progressive measures was passed after the assassination of President John Kennedy, and Johnson pushed for revolutionary reforms in the areas of voting rights, education, immigration, and poverty. The Cold War effort to convince underdeveloped nations to align with the United States and the recent death of President Kennedy created a unique opportunity for Johnson, a talented politician with significant experience as a former Senate Majority Leader, to pass legislation quickly in 1964 and 1965. The Economic Opportunity Act (EOA), which created the OEO, was part of this reform package, and with it many African Americans, rural whites, and Mexican Americans saw real opportunities for community betterment and upward mobility.[5]

Mexican American community activists and other concerned citizens greeted the creation of the OEO with guarded optimism as they looked for creative ways to remedy the worst problems faced by poor people in the United States. From Los Angeles to New York and points in-between, political machines, social reformers, community activists, and everyday people developed plans for the creation of Community Action Agencies (CAA) to help inner-city residents, Appalachian villagers, and migrant farm workers enter the mainstream through programs that sought to provide education and training and allow for personal and societal transformation. The OEO was nothing short of a revolutionary reform model, but its aims were not an overthrow of the status quo, but rather an expansion of opportunity within the framework of American capitalism. Upward mobility within cities, small towns, and mountain hamlets and prosperity for the less privileged was the goal rather than social revolution. In fact, many argued that the OEO would help reduce the number of urban rebellions and assuage discontent in the *barrios* and ghettos of the United States. By trying to bring about even these moderate changes, however, the OEO was often deemed radical by urban machine and rural politicians nationwide. The War on Poverty was itself a challenge to the established class structure of American society, politics, and economics, and CAAs often attracted young minorities and committed leftist youth to the mission of social reform. Chicanos responded to the call and engaged the OEO by participating in, managing, and agitating for community control of the War on Poverty organizations serving their neighborhoods. Often the War on Poverty led to conflict between African Americans and Chicanos, but it also led to coalitions and cooperation. Some Mexican Americans would strike out on their own path without aid from the OEO, as others sought ways to balance a commitment to the Chicano Movement with accepting support from government funded programs for uplift.[6]

This chapter explores the main activist developments of the Chicano Movement's protest phase with an eye to understanding the complex origins of the movement, as well as the many parallels across social movements. When considering the Chicano Movement through the web of support structures such as the War on Poverty, as well as the institutions that sought to undermine it such as the police and FBI, one sees that the state response was varied and complex and that the movement itself, while militant and radical, also focused on the specific demands of participatory democracy, ethnic pride, and an ever more expansive view of economic and educational opportunity. The revolutionary aspect was embodied in the many examples of upwardly mobile and often acculturated youth rejecting the proscribed model of mobility without ethnic identity in favor of an Americanism that allowed them the liberty to define and shape a new identity as Chicanos and call attention to the many injustices of the past, as well as the ongoing discrimination against and persecution of their people by the police, educational system, and the broader society. Chicano nationalism was in this view, for all but the committed irredentists, a radical refashioning of Americanism.

Denver and the Urban Chicano: Rodolfo 'Corky' Gonzales and Chicano Nationalism

Rodolfo 'Corky' Gonzales was an unlikely civil rights activist. The son of Mexican American beet harvesters, he was a former professional boxer, bar owner, bail bondsman, and Democratic machine operative in Denver, Colorado. In the late 1950s and early 1960s he appeared to be on his way to elective office in Denver. Through voter education and registration drives, especially the 1960 Viva Kennedy drives (see Chapter 1), Gonzales had proved his effectiveness as a Democratic Party political operative in Denver. Gonzales was known for speaking his mind, but the success of his registration drives ensured his place within Democratic Party circles. When elections came, he could be counted on to do his part to bring Mexican Americans to the polls in support of Democrats. His past as a boxer, his role in the bail bond business, and participation in local Mexican American fraternal organizations earned him a place in middle-class and working-class networks alike.[7]

In the early 1960s this boxer and bail bondsman grew increasingly concerned with issues in the community. As a bail bondsman, he earned an income by providing funds to those facing criminal charges who were unable to pay their own bail, and he served as bondsman to several young people whom many felt had been abused and brutalized by the Denver Police Department. In several cases that became controversial, Denver Police officers, sometimes off-duty and working second jobs as security guards, used deadly force against Mexican American young men in incidents that were minor altercations at worst. This use of deadly force for minor infractions angered the Mexican American community and Gonzales personally, and led to protests in Denver when the officers were not reprimanded or punished following the death of Mexican American teens. These cases of police brutality spurred Gonzales to begin a transformation from former boxer and bail bondsman to leading Chicano activist.[8]

Police Brutality

Gonzales, like many Mexican Americans, had had contact with the police department of Denver that resulted in arrest. In 1958 he and a police officer got into a fight, and it was reported that he had eventually beaten the officer with his own night stick. The arrest and trial that followed revealed his well-developed political connections. At trial, former elected Democratic officials, including a Colorado Supreme Court justice and the county Democratic chairman, testified on Gonzales's behalf. The case was a spectacle that highlighted Gonzales's connections to the political machine and his past fame as a celebrated local boxer. A hung jury followed, and later the case was dismissed by the prosecutor. It was clear that Gonzales was being groomed by powerful politician patrons, but even so, he endured direct contact with the Denver police.[9]

For other young men, who lacked the backing of the Democratic machine and did not overpower their police attackers, the result in some cases was death. Between 1962 and 1964, police brutality became a significant issue for Mexican Americans in Denver and was the spark that ignited community activism. Several young men had had interactions with the police, and what should have been no more than minor skirmishes led to the young men's deaths. These attacks and killings led to significant political mobilization. Gonzales and other concerned community leaders organized Los Voluntarios (the volunteers) to advocate on behalf of Mexican Americans in Denver. The group drew its leadership from the Mexican American mainstream which, like Gonzales, played a role in Democratic machine politics in Denver, yet challenged the police department and the status quo.[10]

Struggles within the War on Poverty

In addition to his political work, Gonzales was involved in antipoverty work across the Southwest. He was involved with the Service Employment Redevelopment (SER)-Jobs for Progress, a program founded through cooperation between the American GI Forum (AGIF), the League of United Latin American Citizens (LULAC), and local employment-training programs in 1964. As a result of his activism and role as a political operative, Gonzales was appointed by the mayor of Denver to direct the city's Neighborhood Youth Corps (NYC) in the summer of 1965. After several months at the NYC, Gonzales was chosen to serve as the chairperson of the Denver War on Poverty board. In subsequent interviews Gonzales opined 'I'm an agitator and a trouble maker,' before going on to say, 'they didn't buy me when they put me in this job.'[11] His short tenure as the administrator of the NYC was plagued by charges of favoritism and mismanagement, yet the OEO itself defended him against such charges. In a style that would become characteristic, Gonzales met criticism of his management with personal attacks on the individuals involved, including his subordinates, and called for a boycott of the newspaper that reported on problems within the NYC. Though he was criticized for purportedly favoring Mexican American applicants, it appears that the ranking of candidates was done based on family income. Whatever the internal issues, Denver's mayor fired Gonzales, and he attacked the mayor personally and organized a protest that called for a 'crusade for justice.'[12]

In the protests that ensued following his dismissal, Gonzales burned his connections to the Democratic machine of Denver. He lashed out at the mayor for his lack of 'courage' and then attacked the Democratic Party chair for pursuing policies aimed at the 'emasculation of manhood' and the 'sterilization of human dignity.'[13] For Gonzales, the notion of male sexuality and power often defined his outlook. In Denver, as was the case in many cities, tensions arose between African

Americans and Mexican Americans when it came to fairness in program delivery and jobs within the programs. By giving the appearance of favoritism toward Mexican Americans, Gonzales opened himself up to attacks from African Americans, the press, and elected officials. The former boxer was not used to defeat, and poverty politics often required nuance and compromise with all the groups involved rather than clear-cut lines between the victor and vanquished. After his dismissal, Gonzales attacked the very people who had supported his rise within Democratic Party circles throughout the 1950s and early 1960s and struck out on his own increasingly radical path. This episode defined an approach to confrontation that would become a hallmark of Gonzales's career as a leading activist of the Chicano Movement. When he faced criticism or confrontation, Gonzales usually rejected cooperation and used sharp, often hyper-masculine language to criticize his detractors. When Gonzales left the OEO in Denver, he set out on a path that would define the rhetoric and philosophy of the Chicano Movement, as he shaped what became cultural nationalism.[14]

Chicano Nationalism

Gonzales's Chicano nationalism was not made of whole cloth but rather was a product of his understanding of Mexican and Mexican American history and his engagement with national and international radicalism. By 1966, Gonzales had embraced a politics that reflected that of other movements, including Black Power, anti-colonialism, and the antiwar movement, as he formulated his own critique of American society and the role of Mexican Americans in North American history. By dramatically rejecting the notion of upward mobility through machine politics and public funds in his own case—a well-worn path to assimilation taken by many ethnic leaders in American cities—he made a choice to embrace an ethnic and racial identity as a Chicano. Although, very few people of Gonzales's age would have referred to themselves as Chicanos in 1966, he and others like him soon became the vanguard of the Chicano Movement.[15]

In the spring of 1966, Gonzales formally established what would become his signature organization, the Crusade for Justice, based in Denver, Colorado. Adopting many of the goals of the War on Poverty programs yet rejecting governmental support, the Crusade embraced self-help, community development, a militant focus on ethnic pride, and a form of hyper-masculinity, while seeking to help remedy the problems faced by urban youth in Denver. The organization was attractive to *barrio* men, and as Gonzales expressed his frustration with the status quo, he increasingly came to define the key concepts of Chicano nationalism. To express his concerns with the negative impact of American society on Chicanos, Gonzales penned 'I am Joaquín/Yo Soy Joaquín' in 1967. This expression of male angst, the search for identity, and a framework for Mexican American history was widely circulated and performed throughout the late 1960s and became a defining text of the Chicano Movement. Covering much of the history of the Aztecs, Mexico, the Southwest, and Mexican Americans in the United States, the poem reads like an outline of Mexican American history, as it defines the Chicano as both a victim and a creative force with a long history in North America. Chicanos were hybrids with a long and proud history in North America—they built pyramids, proved their valor on battlefields as Aztec, Spanish, Mexican, Native, and Mexican American warriors, and in the face of opposition built strong and vibrant communities. Their history pre-dated that of the British colonists or the European immigrants who peopled the Eastern United States. Mexican Americans as a new Raza (people or race) in the New World had links to both Europe and Native peoples. Chicanos therefore had deeper roots in North American history than those of European Americans. The poem celebrated the maintenance of community and culture in spite of exploitation, violence, and discrimination at the hands of American society. By rejecting assimilation, Chicanos were engaged in the epic process of self-fashioning and self-definition in the face of injustice. The world presented by Gonzales was clearly defined by bright lines of demarcation between Anglos/mainstream society and Chicanos/minority society, and an emphasis on masculinity. There were few references to women in the text. Masculinity was central to Gonzales's worldview, and the poem was an effort to express and reclaim dignity for Chicanos in the face of debasement and exploitation, yet women were left on the margins of this world. Women were the 'black-shawled' and 'faithful' people who 'die with me [o]r live [d]epending on the time and place.' Rather than makers of history, women were constructed as mere appendages to the lives of men. Even with its limited view of the role of women in history, 'I am Joaquín/Yo Soy Joaquín' had an enormous impact in shaping common understandings of the Chicano view of history.[16]

The Poor People's Campaign

In 1968 after the murders of Martin Luther King, Jr. and Robert F. Kennedy, Gonzales and the Crusade for Justice joined the thousands of people heading to Washington to participate in the Poor People's Campaign. Following King's assassination, the Southern Christian Leadership Conference (SCLC) decided to continue with his plan to hold a Poor People's March on Washington. Bringing together African Americans, Mexican Americans, Native Americans, Puerto Ricans, and poor whites, the idea was to unify the poor people in the United States on behalf of social change. What resulted was a splintered organization of segregated encampments—with some living in the tent city dubbed 'Resurrection City' and others camped out at churches and a local elementary school. African American organizers dominated the event, despite King's desire to create bridges between all the various communities of poor people in the United States, which led Mexican American and Native American activists to demand greater input. The resulting negotiations failed to end the spatial separation among the rank and file, yet Gonzales together with members of the Crusade for Justice had positive encounters with Appalachian whites, activist Anglo priests such as Milwaukee's Father James Groppi, and Native Americans. Many of the interracial and interethnic relationships made in Washington in the chaotic days of the Poor People's Campaign proved durable for Gonzales and Crusade members as they sought to strengthen their own community. For some, the Poor People's Campaign marked the dramatic end of the King era in civil rights history. The discord, intergroup conflict, and eventual bulldozing of Resurrection City did appear to alter the landscape of civil rights politics, yet it also brought people together, and in Gonzales's case led him to consider alliances beyond the *barrio*.[17]

Gonzales became a leader, recognizable on the national stage following the Poor People's Campaign. By opening his door to Chicanos and others and serving as a rational counterweight to Reies López Tijerina, a land grant activist representing Hispanos from New Mexico, whose efforts to find the media spotlight and his singular focus on land grants increasingly made him marginal to the experiences of young Chicanos, Gonzales clearly became a leader whose community involvement and Chicano nationalist rhetoric appealed to the many Chicanos from California, Texas, the Great Lakes, and the Pacific Northwest who spent time getting to know him. He made important connections as he gained real-world experience of the difficulty of cross-racial and cross-ethnic movement building.[18]

Youth Liberation Conferences

Gonzales came away from the Poor People's Campaign dedicated to making the Chicano nation he dreamed of a reality. To build and celebrate the proud community imagined in 'Yo Soy Joaquín' in 1969, Gonzales hosted the first Chicano Youth Liberation Conference in Denver. This event, which spanned several days in March 1969, brought together Chicanos and Chicanas from Texas, the Southwest, California, the Great Lakes, and the Pacific Northwest, as well as small groups from other locations nationwide. The event informed and educated Chicanos, offered seminars and panels on the basics of organizing, protest, and self-defense, as well as on Chicano art, literature, journalism, women's issues, and culture. Most of the newly organized Mexican American student groups sent representatives, and urban political groups, Chicano labor organizers, and community activists attended the event alongside members of the Puerto Rican Young Lords (a self-defense and community activist group based in Chicago and New York City). While the conference highlighted the political philosophy and rhetoric of Gonzales, it also became a key training ground and workshop for Chicano activists from across the nation—like Washington, Minnesota, and Michigan—to network, brainstorm, and learn from one another. In many ways, the Black Power Movement set the tone as Mexican Americans sought to define their own anti-establishment self-help model of political engagement. Once at the conference, young people painted, read poetry, debated politics, argued, made new friends, and discovered that within the Chicano nation there were many different types of people: the folkways, outlooks, and cultural heritage were similar, but different regional influences shaped the many peoples of the Chicano world.[19] For many attendees, the conference was a transformative event. Some 'batos locos' (crazy guys, or tough guys) rebelled from what they felt was a '50-cent-word ideology' and demanded more focus on the *barrio* and its problems rather than ideology. Others drew different, more positive lessons from the event.[20]

The conference resulted in the creation of another important document that sought to express the political and cultural philosophy of the Chicano Movement, El Plan Espiritual de Aztlán (El Plan). El Plan embraced the idea of Aztlán, the mythical homeland of the Aztecs, and refashioned it as the American Southwest. This remaking of the American Southwest as Aztlán gave Chicanos a homeland— part of, yet separate from, both the United States and Mexico. Chicanos, with their varied histories as mestizos, colonizers, conquerors, immigrants, natives, and vanquished settlers, were a unique and hybrid people with a long, proud history and claims to nationhood. Chicanos sought to claim a space for themselves and to reclaim their nation. Chicano activists had to commit themselves to the unification of all segments of Mexican American society, regardless of class, under the Chicano nationalist banner. Reflecting but at the same time rejecting the ideology of the War on Poverty, El Plan called for Chicanos to strengthen and build vital centers of culture in the urban *barrios* and rural *colonias* of the nation; they were to make these spaces their own through self-help and hard work and the expression of a unique Chicano culture and pride rather than through passive acceptance of government financing. The rebuilding of the *barrio* as a refuge from American society meant that Chicanos had to do the work themselves. El Plan embraced a rhetorical mix that reflected elements of Black Nationalism, college level anti-colonialism, Mexican nationalism, and the community-building and institution-building language of the War on Poverty.[21]

Chicana women attended the 1969 conference and played a significant role in the many meetings and panels held in Denver. Women's issues, however, much as was true in other civil rights movements, the New Left, and the antiwar movement of the era, were not central to the vision of male leaders or that of many rank-and-file Chicanos and even certain Chicana women. For the Chicana feminists who labored at the event's Chicana caucus, the conference proclamation that the 'Chicana woman does not want to be liberated' was a shocking betrayal to the cause of human freedom.[22] Chicana women, like other women in the social movements of the 1960s and 1970s, found that political progressives were often still committed to 'machismo' and traditional gender roles and gender norms. Revolution was, from their perspective, not that revolutionary when it came to women's issues.

The second Chicano Youth Conference of 1970 was an even larger and more diverse affair, which brought more people from the national Chicano world to Denver and showed the diversity of worldviews within that community. As the Crusade for Justice entered the 1970s, the second conference, while larger and broader in focus than the first, also saw Gonzales and others increasingly embracing irredentist rhetoric, and due, perhaps, to Gonzales's strong personality, he became the dominant leader of the movement, albeit briefly. Following his leadership defeat at the National La Raza Unida Party Conference in 1972, and later quixotic armed conflicts with the Denver Police Department, Gonzales increasingly withdrew to Denver. Despite his many shortcomings, Gonzales for a time gave voice to the dreams and desires of many Chicanos nationwide, as he defined and expressed the foundational rhetoric of Chicano nationalism and, through the Denver-based youth conferences, brought people together to discuss its meaning and future.[23]

Chicanos and Urban Communities in Los Angeles

Like many large American cities, Los Angeles ushered in the War on Poverty with an emphasis on the African American community. This was not a surprising development considering the community revolts in Watts in the summer of 1965.[24] There was clearly an urgent need to remedy the worst manifestations of poverty in an African American community that required physical and social rejuvenation following the revolts.[25] As was also true in many other cities where the minority community was diverse, the creation and functioning of the government-led poverty programs tended to focus on African American problems, and the development of leadership within those programs meant that the agencies tended to hire African Americans. This situation caused tension between African Americans and Mexican Americans over resources and program administration and management in the early years of the OEO nationwide. As Chicanos increasingly demanded that poverty programs, and the community at large, no longer ignore and neglect Mexican Americans, activists in Los Angeles came up with creative ways to approach the needs of their community.[26]

In Los Angeles the 1960s witnessed the rapid expansion of the Mexican American population on that city's East Side. The post-World War II era between 1950 and 1960 saw California surpass Texas as the state with the largest Mexican-ancestry population in the United States, with Los Angeles also overshadowing San Antonio as the largest population center for Mexican-heritage people north of Mexico City. This trend continued throughout the 1960s as California became a gateway state for Mexican immigrants (many of whom were Mexican guest workers or Braceros) and Tejano and other Southwestern migrants of Mexican ancestry. By 1970, the Spanish-surnamed population of California reached 2.4 million people, surpassing Texas's population of 1.8 million.[27] This transformation meant that Los Angeles, a city established by eighteenth-century Spanish colonization and subsequent Mexican settlement prior to 1848, entered a period of expansion of Mexican American neighborhoods as migrants and immigrants made the city home and redefined it as a Mexican cultural space.[28]

The 1960s witnessed increasing local and national attention to the problems of the poor in Los Angeles County. With the establishment of antipoverty programs geared toward the needs of African Americans, the history of the War on Poverty, and Chicano activism in Los Angeles, as was true in many places, is a story about interracial conflict and competition rather than cooperation. While African Americans and Chicanos certainly learned from one another, at the level of poverty program management and community engagement the two groups were mainly competitors. The focus of contention became the Neighborhood Adult Participation Project (NAPP), a unit of the Economic and Youth Opportunities Agency (EYOA), established in 1965 and headed by Opal Jones, an African American woman with impeccable liberal credentials and a commitment to community action. Through a large number of neighborhood centers, the NAPP focused on helping the poor help themselves, but as Chicanos soon realized, the centers were predominantly in African American neighborhoods, and there were very few Chicanos in management positions. From the start, tensions arose over resource allocation and a perception of unfairness in the establishment of a small number of neighborhood centers in a county where Mexican Americans were the dominant low-income minority group. The NAPP became the focus of protests on the part of staffers and community members.[29]

Interracial Conflict and Cooperation

Los Angeles demonstrated both the possibility and problems of interracial cooperation between Mexican Americans and African Americans. The EYOA, the larger umbrella War on Poverty group, was directed by a Mexican American who fired Jones, and after African American protests Jones was reinstated. The NAPP became the focus of Mexican American protests in 1966 after Jones fired Mexican American staffer Gabriel Yanez, who ran the NAPP Center in Boyle Heights, accusing him of leading efforts to divide Mexican Americans and African Americans. Protest followed involving both street-level activism and lobbying efforts on the part of established Mexican American leaders.[30] This pattern continued for the life of the NAPP as Chicano and African American staffers fought battles over jobs and authority. After Chicano protests in 1966 forced Jones to reinstate Yanez, many feared the scene had been set for continued hostility. African American and Mexican American leaders increasingly came to think that solutions to the problems of their communities had to be accomplished not through interracial cooperation but through neighborhood- and group-specific targeted programs. As one NAPP protester opined, '[W]hat's good for Watts and the civil rights movement is not necessarily good for the Mexican American community.'[31] Throughout the existence of the War on Poverty in Los Angeles, tensions arose between grass-roots Chicano activists and Mexican American administrators and African Americans, even over programs such as Head Start and nutrition programs for children.[32]

As African Americans and Mexican Americans struggled to work together and find solutions to the problems of their respective communities, some Mexican American youth, increasingly altering their worldview and embracing a Chicano identity and outlook, sought other avenues for community improvement and revitalization. Oddly enough, the Black Power Movement became a template upon which they built their own iteration of a cultural nationalist platform and worldview, influenced, of course, by the long history of Mexican American resistance and community preservation. The youth who would have the biggest impact on the shape of the Los Angeles Chicano Movement in 1966 established Young Citizens for Community Action, which soon became Young Chicanos for Community Action (YCCA). Through the establishment of a coffee shop, La Piranya, in 1967 and the open-forum discussions and rap sessions that took place there, young Chicanos from East Los Angeles, many already attending local colleges and universities, came together to discuss politics, education, and access to opportunity in a safe space that they had made for themselves. The coffee house also brought leaders of the Black Power Movement and nascent Chicano and Farm Workers Movement to speak. H. Rap Brown, Stokely Carmichael, and Ron Karenga all spoke there, as well as Cesar Chavez, Corky Gonzales, and Reies López Tijerina. Like other Chicano youth nationwide, the Los Angeles-based YCCA members were embroidering a new cultural identity through an interactive exposure to Black Power and Mexican American radical influences. By gaining a reputation as a welcoming space, La Piranya became the foundation for networks in East Los Angeles high schools, colleges, and even among gang members willing to reject intraethnic competition and violence in favor of community action and, increasingly, a Chicano worldview. While initially begun as an effort to engage the concept of Community Action and the spirit of the War on Poverty, focused on 'civic participation, education, and voting,' the YCCA, as it evolved to become the Brown Berets, did what many young people did in the 1960s: it became outwardly radical in rhetoric and paramilitary dress, yet often made demands that fit within the framework of a militant Americanism rather than anti-Americanism.[33] Gradually Brown Berets moved from reform politics to radical cultural nationalist politics, yet in many cases, their demands were for things that resonated with the deepest traditions of Americanism: strong communities, democracy, education, equality, freedom, and opportunity.[34]

Student Activism and the East Los Angeles Walkouts

Chicano students were also on the move in 1967, holding meetings and developing plans of action in Southern California. Key among these groups was the

United Mexican American Students (UMAS) founded in the summer of 1967 and soon focused on education and activism both on campus and in the community. While there certainly was some overlap with the Brown Berets and significant coordination and participation with the Berets and the student groups in East Los Angeles schools where many UMAS students had their origins, UMAS was a college students' group, based at the University of California Los Angeles, the University of Southern California, and other campuses in the city. One meeting in 1967 focused on creating a 'leadership revolution' among the members. This workshop brought together Chicano student activists from Los Angeles with those from San Francisco and other areas of California. These meetings helped to educate Chicanos on the many issues and problems faced within their communities and the fact that these issues were not merely local but were shared concerns for Chicanos in California and the Southwest and for the small group of Black Student Union members who attended. Education reform was a focus of the 1967 meeting, and plans were made to find ways to press the issue of school reform in California. The meeting included a demonstration at the Los Angeles Coliseum during a football game between the Rams and the Colts, where students held signs that read 'Chicano Power.' In just a few months these meetings and the growth of a leadership cadre in Los Angeles would provide the foundation for Chicano civic action in the area of school reform.[35]

A year after the establishment of the La Piranya coffee house, the Brown Berets and student groups from local colleges had spent a significant amount of time considering the problems faced by Chicanos in high school. With student activists already participating in events at La Piranya and developing their own student organizations, there was a critical mass for protest.[36] The efforts of the students and activists were reformist in nature, even as their coffee shop meetings were disrupted by police harassment, flood lights, and threats of violence with one police officer reportedly saying, 'Take a picture of me Mexican so I can shove that f—king camera up your a—.'[37] Sal Castro, a high school teacher who had adopted a Mexican Americanist worldview in his youth, was increasingly alienated by a school system that he felt failed Mexican American students. Castro developed a growing sense that something should be done for students in East Los Angeles, where he taught at Lincoln High School.[38] Others involved in or inspired by War on Poverty programs, as many founding members of the Brown Berets were, also became directly involved in assisting students prepare to voice their concerns with the district. The student concerns were mainly reformist: fair treatment, an end to discriminatory policies, and the expansion of the curriculum to address the history of Mexican Americans in Los Angeles schools.[39]

Educational improvement had long been a concern for Mexican American parents in Los Angeles and the Southwest generally. California and Texas were home to long-standing efforts to end discrimination against Mexican-ancestry students and provide quality educational opportunities. In the 1960s some parents began to press for better and more effective elementary schools for their children, better middle and high schools, and an end to the discrimination within the schools and among the teachers who taught their children. High dropout rates plagued the East Los Angeles high schools, with rates that came close to 50 percent in some cases. Parents, students, and community leaders had long sought to understand and remedy the educational problems in Los Angeles schools. Young people in the late 1960s would take the lead in the fight for an equal education and schools that provided opportunities.[40]

On March 3, 1968, students at Lincoln High School in East Los Angeles, led by Sal Castro, a Lincoln High faculty member, walked out of classes, and began the 'Blowouts' or East Los Angeles 'walkouts.' This movement brought many emerging strands of the Chicano Movement together, as nearly 10,000 Chicano students walked out, crippling the school district, making the rise of 'Brown Power' a national event, and establishing the Brown Berets as a symbol of Chicano resistance.[41] As students from Roosevelt High School joined the walkouts, the Los Angeles Police Department increasingly adopted aggressive tactics. Other schools joined and African American students made demands as well, even asking for an end to prohibitions on 'natural' hair styles. Efforts were made to lock students in the schools, and eventually students were physically beaten by the police. Many of these beatings were caught on film. Students struggling on the ground, women being attacked, and young men trying to avoid violence being brutally beaten to their knees soon became the image of Los Angeles' police reaction to student protest and made police brutality a central concern of the Chicano Movement. Yet despite police brutality and administrative intransigence, the demands of the students were calls for reform rather than revolution.[42] While it is true that the students called for a more humane learning environment and an end to discrimination, many of the things they wanted showed a desire for upward mobility as well as a commitment to a greater understanding of Mexican American history and culture. Thus, in a defining moment of the Chicano Movement, the dual desire of the new militancy was revealed. The student demands were reformist—and the call for immediate reforms to the status quo was in itself radical.[43] While the goals were often in line with an Americanist understanding of ideology and civil rights, the reaction on the part of the schools and the Los Angeles Police Department were not.[44] As one hopeful student put it, 'We don't have to walk out . . . Once they listen they will agree with what we want.'[45] As the student seemed to imply, there was nothing particularly radical about their demands—except for the fact that Mexican American students were making them.

The East LA 13

The reaction led to the prosecution of the adult leaders of the movement, soon dubbed the 'East LA 13' (ELA13), a group that included student activists, Brown

Berets, War on Poverty workers, Chicano journalists, and Lincoln High School teacher Sal Castro. They were indicted for conspiracy to disturb the peace and faced tough jail sentences. The police and school board branded adult supporters 'outside agitators'—a common tactic in Cold War America—but they were mainly recent graduates from East Los Angeles described as *'our people*, the *cream of the crop.'*[46] The adult protesters and Sal Castro were charged with conspiracy to disturb the peace. The crime was a misdemeanor, but the conspiracy was a felony and the felony charge had serious implications for the ELA13, especially Sal Castro who was barred from teaching after his indictment. Defended by Chicano activist Oscar Zeta Acosta, the case demonstrated the lengths to which the police and prosecutor, with assistance from the Federal Bureau of Investigation, would go to attack reformist movements among Mexican Americans.[47] The indictments led to protests against the Los Angeles Police Department and supportive demonstrations for the ELA13, which brought thousands of Chicanos and supporters to the streets.[48] In the process of confronting police repression and a school system unwilling to change or treat Sal Castro with respect, the self-definition of Chicano took on meaning as activists and community members developed a clear oppositional consciousness—an understanding that the institutions of the state (schools, police, and courts) were not functioning to protect their rights.[49] They were clearly being marked out as a racial minority and the police were singling them out as such, and the attack on their efforts to claim civil rights was nothing short of counterrevolutionary. No longer merely pressing for school reform and curricular change, Chicanos realized that the police, the legal system, and the political system—not entirely new revelations to be sure—were aligned to limit their freedom and safety and weaken the bonds of community in the face of any effort on the part of Mexican Americans for reform. These institutions were violating the ethical foundations of Americanism. Chicanos like Sal Castro were no longer afraid to protest and complain of mistreatment publicly and forcefully, as they demanded that institutions function fairly and democratically.[50] Chicanos dedicated themselves to claiming a new identity as 'Brown,' 'Chicano,' or members of 'La Raza' and to fighting for their community in opposition to the police and others who falsely claimed to protect American society yet in fact rejected the very premise of Americanism. As was the case with the ELA13, the fight took place as social protest and legal defense, but it was all cast in light of a new understanding—a worldview that placed Chicanos in opposition to the architecture of racial repression of brown (and black) peoples and in defense of cultural nationalism and, interestingly, many key components of Americanism.[51]

Reformist movements led to state-sponsored attacks on the Chicano community. As would become clear across the Southwest, militant demands for equality were met with often violent repression by the police and legal attacks by the state. One must remember that the East LA Walkouts were driven by a concern on the part of young students, young adults, and a dedicated teacher that Mexican Americans needed better schools. At heart it was a call for respect, better education for low-income minority students (these schools included Mexican American, African American, and Anglo students in significant numbers), and upward mobility without regard to race or ethnicity. It was revolutionary for young Chicano women and men to ask for an end to discrimination and for cultural education and schools that prepared Mexican American, or any minority students for that matter, for a future in modern society outside of proscribed roles among the underclass. It is not surprising that the leaders of the student movement, many of whom were female, and the adults who helped students organize the protests were themselves upwardly mobile.[52] The Brown Berets in LA were high school and college students dedicated to self-improvement, and in some ways they embraced the 'American Dream' though they opposed the structural forces that limited opportunities for the vast majority of Chicanos at every turn.[53] While it is clear that not all Mexican Americans in Los Angeles supported the tactics, rhetoric, or Chicano nation-building that many activists embraced, and some Mexican Americans served as judges, prosecutors, and even agents provocateurs for the Los Angeles Police Department in its efforts to weaken the movement, the attack on the individuals behind the student protest and the denial of First Amendment protections for speech and assembly led many within the movement to question the commitment of state institutions to the US Constitution and to Americanism.

As the Brown Berets and other militant Chicanos claimed space as a racial minority and as a separate class of people, they continued to press claims for civil rights and opportunity within the system. Even in the face of police harassment, youth activists cited the US Constitution in Los Angeles and across California.[54] The notion of Chicano Liberation grew in Los Angeles and elsewhere and spread from *barrios* to *colonias* across the state as young people drew connections between the Black Power Movement and the Chicano Movement.[55] The walkouts also stimulated activism among other Chicano students in California and the Southwest and even sparked African American walkouts in Southern California. The walkouts demonstrated that minority teens had an interest in a quality education and would do radical things to force the districts to provide them with the tools needed for success.[56] These actions were not anti-Americanist but rather called on the state to follow its own rules and abide by a militant new style of Americanism that allowed for cultural nationalism, civil rights, and upward mobility. After a long and difficult protest and sit-in movement for reinstatement and reform, Sal Castro was returned to the school and the students he fought for.[57] The ELA13 and the reinstatement of Castro did away with the legal fiction of Mexican American 'whiteness' for many activists who increasingly saw themselves as 'brown' in the face of illegal discrimination.[58]

The Chicano Moratorium Movement

Another signal movement that developed in Los Angeles and reflected changes in the nature of the Chicano Movement was the Chicano Moratorium, a protest and march against the war in Vietnam. Led by some of the same organizations involved in the walkouts, the Moratorium was a rejection of long-standing views of Mexican American masculinity and the notion of earned citizenship for minorities. Mexican American organizations such as the American GI Forum (AGIF) argued for civil rights based on the fact that members were mainly comprised of military veterans. Veterans, by putting their lives on the line in military positions, were not merely citizens but had earned a right to be treated fairly. Chicano activists rejected this view—deeply held in the Mexican American community—and argued that the war in Vietnam was disproportionately being fought by the poor and minorities and that Chicanos should reject participation and oppose a war waged against fellow minority people and focus their attention on the dire needs of the Mexican American community in the United States. Chicanos had no need to earn their human rights or citizenship rights—they were due these without having to die in uniform fighting, as the logic went, against other brown low-income people in Asia.[59]

The third Chicano Moratorium (there were several) would mark the high point and nadir of the Chicano Movement and the mainstream reaction to it, and would sadly result in the police killing of leading Mexican American journalist Rubén Salazar, correspondent for the *Los Angeles Times*. Salazar reported on the development of the Chicano Movement from Los Angeles for the *Times*, and his stories also ran as special reports for other papers. As the turbulent 1960s unfolded, Salazar often wrote the most detailed and accurate pieces on the rise of the Chicano Movement from its early days in Texas, California, and Colorado through its participation in the Poor People's Movement and the Chicano Moratorium. While considered by most to be a neutral or moderate-minded reporter, the Federal Bureau of Investigation and the Los Angeles Police Department considered Salazar to be a radical or at the very least sympathetic to the Chicano Movement. Whatever his sympathies, he would not live through the Chicano Moratorium. More than a mere episode that resulted in the death of a gifted journalist, the Chicano Moratorium reflected changes in the Chicano Movement itself.[60]

The first Chicano Moratorium, which involved many of the same activists involved in the 1968 student walkouts, was held on December 20, 1969, in East Los Angeles and was followed by a second in February 1970. Chicano activists were increasingly concerned with the high rate of Mexican American deaths in Vietnam, and this issue became a central reason for Chicano opposition to the Vietnam War, with some even labeling the high number of Chicano deaths a 'genocide.'[61] The Brown Berets were prominently represented at the 1969 event, which 70 of the group's members attended in their uniforms—'berets, army jackets, and dark pants for the men, brown skirts for the women.'[62] These Moratorium demonstrations made the case that 'Chicanos have served in the United States in World War II, the Korean War, and in Vietnam and have given their blood for this country' and went on that they now 'merely' requested that they 'be given the same rights that every American supposedly has.'[63] The second Chicano Moratorium helped build momentum and was much larger than the first and involved activists from across the Southwest and California.[64]

The third Chicano Moratorium took place on August 29, 1970, and was the largest of the three, as the demonstration filled the streets of East Los Angeles with antiwar protesters. The Moratorium began as marchers moved down Whittier Boulevard to Laguna Park, three miles away. At Laguna Park demonstrators were greeted with refreshments, and were able to relax after the march before the rally took place at the park. Rosalio Munoz, the Chicano Moratorium Committee chairperson, spoke at the event and outlined the reasons for organizing against the war. A University of California, Los Angeles student who had garnered some media attention due to his position as a class president, his strong views about Chicano politics, and his nonviolent protest ethics, spoke not only of the antiwar movement but also of the increasingly important issue of police brutality.[65] Soon after these remarks, the police entered the park with clubs swinging and under a veil of tear gas. The police claimed that they were pacifying an unruly mob, but to many observers it appeared that the police were attacking the peaceful crowd. Munoz remembered, 'I saw a sweep of sheriffs moving in and the people panicking,' and went on to claim that 'the sheriffs gave no notification, nothing' before attacking the crowd with clubs and gas.[66] Some of the protesters under attack decided to fight back while others fled the scene. The disturbance spread throughout East Los Angeles and was dubbed 'a riot' by the national press. The Chicano Moratorium, which had hoped to focus attention on the deaths of Mexican Americans in Vietnam, press for an end to that conflict, and convince the community that an antiwar stance was the correct one, ended with a riot, the arrest of Rodolfo 'Corky' Gonzales on weapons charges, and the sad news that Rubén Salazar had died of injuries resulting from a tear gas shell that was shot into a crowded bar.[67] Moreover, the 'riots' led to intensified policing by the Los Angeles Sheriff's Department and a 'stop and frisk' policy that many saw as racially motivated.[68]

Munoz soon after called for a fourth Moratorium, but this time the topic had shifted from the antiwar effort to a focus on police brutality. The event held on January 31, 1971, was peaceful, yet after the dispersal of the crowd another police riot occurred, leaving one person dead.[69] The riot was followed by a march to Sacramento which began on Cinco de Mayo (May 5), 1971, and ended with the marchers greeted by riot police at the capital.[70] While the Moratorium Committee was focused on nonviolence, an end to discriminatory draft policies, and what might be termed racial profiling and police brutality, the police response demonstrated the degree to which local authorities reacted with force disproportionate to the threat posed by Chicano efforts to exercise their rights to assembly and free speech. From the school walkouts through the end of the Chicano Moratorium Committee's activities, the Chicano Movement in Los Angeles and California more broadly was militant, yet the demands were calls for reform in the face of schools that failed to teach, police that failed to protect community members, and a draft system that sent Chicanos off to die in a war against another brown people halfway around the world.

The War on Poverty in East Los Angeles

Community members and community leaders dedicated to reform reacted to the Moratorium disturbances by refocusing efforts on community betterment. One such organization was the East Los Angeles Labor Community Action Committee (ELALCAC) founded in February 1968, which soon became The East Los Angeles Community Union (TELACU). TELACU, with support from the UAW and labor activists within the Chicano community, emerged as a strong force for community activism after the disturbances of August 1970. After several failed attempts in 1970 and 1971, TELACU eventually found a focus in redevelopment of dilapidated housing and a program of community renewal (which, while dependent on government funding, did bring renovated and new housing and opportunity to East Los Angeles) and led the movement to incorporate East Los Angeles as a city. Through these efforts to improve conditions in the community, TELACU, an organization that reflected Chicano demands for community control—run by a Chicano Movement-influenced staff—navigated the changing waters of government funding to improve the lives of East Los Angeles residents. These efforts were not without critics, and TELACU's long history has been politically turbulent, but as the Chicano Movement ebbed in Los Angeles, others committed to community action continued those efforts with roots in the War on Poverty even after the demise of the OEO.[71]

The Urban Chicano in San Antonio

San Antonio, the largest Mexican American population center in the United States for nearly a century, in the 1960s maintained its role as the center of political development for Chicanos. Religious organizations, most importantly the Catholic Church, as well as *barrio* and university youth created the infrastructure for poverty reform, social organization, and militant politics. While Anglos and priests tended to serve as administrators for Church-developed organizations, these organizations included the community at most levels of planning and consultation due to the large and politically active Mexican American establishment in San Antonio. For the young men and women who helped establish the Mexican American Youth Organization (MAYO) and the Brown Berets in San Antonio, the politics of cultural nationalism committed them to community control of all aspects of *barrio* betterment. Chicanos—in this case Tejanos—had to build pride in their cultural and civic accomplishments, and it was up to members of the community to fix the problems they faced. Both radical and reformist impulses altered the landscape of San Antonio's *barrios* in the era of the Chicano Movement.

The War on Poverty in San Antonio

Religious leaders and community leaders came together in 1965 after the creation of the OEO to establish the San Antonio Neighborhood Youth Organization (SANYO), which would become the most effective and influential War on Poverty organization in Texas. SANYO, a Neighborhood Youth Corps affiliate, was the brainchild of local Polish American priest Father John Yanta (who later became a bishop) and committed Mexican American community leaders. SANYO used the Catholic parishes of San Antonio's historic West Side *barrio* to organize this heavily Catholic community and attract the input and participation of everyday people. This strategy, which organized people on their streets and used the Catholic Church to bring them together in a familiar setting, worked to make SANYO a strong and successful organization. Mexican American men and women worked at every level of the organizational structure—except for management—and populated the various advisory boards and served as youth counselors at the neighborhood centers. *Barrio* youth benefitted through employment opportunities focused on community beautification and betterment, and many of these same student workers later served as tutors and trainers for the next wave of Youth Corps workers. In this way, the organization focused on the group and the individual, as it brought young Chicanos into the execution of the program and made them stakeholders in its success.[72]

SANYO had powerful friends in Texas. Archbishop Robert E. Lucey with the personal support of Lyndon Johnson, who counted the Archbishop among his personal friends, helped ensure funding for SANYO programs. As other OEO organizations struggled in Texas, SANYO had large grants to support its programs from its founding. It was a well-organized agency, and while it was headed by Father Yanta, SANYO brought Mexican Americans into the organization as stakeholders. SANYO, because of its many neighborhood centers and clear links to parish communities, also became a potent force for political change in San Antonio as the organization, which benefitted from connections to establishment politicians and officials, challenged the status quo in San Antonio according to the demands and wishes of the various community advisory groups and program participants. Through its Neighborhood Councils, SANYO became a potent political force in San Antonio politics—committed to 'maximum feasible participation' in nearly every sense—even as it continued to be led by an Anglo priest. Several former SANYO employees and participants played a role in the making of the Chicano Movement in San Antonio, even as many, though they may not have said as much to Father Yanta, were increasingly disillusioned by his unwillingness to create opportunities for Chicano leadership and advancement within the group.[73]

The Mexican American Youth Organization (MAYO)

By 1967 a group of Mexican American college students at Saint Mary's University came together to establish the Mexican American Youth Organization (MAYO), which was one of the central forces in the Chicano Movement and later political developments of both a radical and reformist bent for decades to come. José Ángel Gutiérrez, Willie Velásquez, Mario Compean, Ignacio Perez, and Juan Patlán—all students—came from different backgrounds and reflected the rich mix of culture and class within Tejano life. Influenced by the rise of farm labor activism in South Texas and California, as well as intellectual movements in anti-colonial theory, Black Power, and the work of Saul Alinsky, the group adopted both radical and reformist rhetoric from its founding. These college students visited the older leaders of Mexican American radical life, such as Corky Gonzales and Reies López Tijerina of New Mexico, and Black Power leaders, as well as reformist labor activist Cesar Chavez.[74] The young college students considered the various ideologies, personalities, and strategies of older Mexican American activists, relevant literature, and analogous Black Power contemporaries before defining their own movement and setting out on their own path. Unlike Gonzales, Tijerina, or Chavez, the leaders of MAYO were 'baby boomers' and reflected the youthful exuberance of radical politics in the 1960s.[75]

While given to dramatic demonstrations and media spectacles meant to bring attention to the dissatisfaction of Chicano youth and the problems of the *barrio*, MAYO was, like SANYO, a focused and well-organized group dedicated to organizing and improving life for those within the Mexican American community. Within a year of its founding MAYO established the Mexican American Neighborhood Community Organization (MANCO), the Committee for Barrio Betterment (CBB), the Mexican American Unity Council (MAUC), La Universidad de los Barrios (LUB), and the Texas Institute for Educational Development (TIED), which became funding vehicles for federal antipoverty grants in urban areas and health care development in rural areas—a reflection of MAYO's roots in both the West Side of San Antonio and the farm-ranch towns of South Texas as well as the well-educated background of many of its founders.[76]

Regardless of its declared radicalism, MAYO relied on OEO funds and the War on Poverty infrastructure for much of its funding, and several founders were past OEO agency employees or political operatives for established Mexican American politicians. Mario Compean worked as a recruiter for Volunteers in Service to America (VISTA) and José Ángel Gutiérrez was a SANYO youth counselor, positions that enabled them to gain useful organizing and administrative experience through the OEO. Willie Velásquez had served as an operative for San Antonio politicians, including Henry B. Gonzalez, before helping to found MAYO. MAYO saw the War on Poverty as the foundation that provided its community and political organizers with salaries, and enabled it to bring in *barrio* youth as VISTA volunteers through the Minority Mobilization Program (MMP), which sought to train local youth to become VISTA volunteers. Recognizing that VISTA tended to bring middle-class Anglos into low-income minority areas, MMP was devised as a vehicle for poor youth to become part of the solution to the problems faced by *barrio* residents. In this way MAYO through its various institutions utilized the funding mechanisms and programs of the War on Poverty to bring about radical change in San Antonio and South Texas.[77]

LUB became a central training ground for male Chicanos, many of whom had roots in West Side gangs, and for a time became a central force in the reduction of intraethnic conflict and violence in San Antonio. Understanding that college-educated Chicanos had many opportunities inside and outside the Chicano Movement, the LUB sought to educate gang members and at-risk teens about the long history of Mexican American life in North America, provide them with practical organizing skills, and train them as leaders of their own communities. By accepting at-risk Chicano youths' backgrounds, giving them the space and freedom to explore the meaning of their existence, and helping them to channel their energies to positive social change in the *barrio*, the LUB became a radical challenge to the status quo.[78] The police and moderate Mexican American politicians spied on the LUB and its members who, through their connections to MAYO, were also involved as grassroots activists in the CBB effort to organize West Side residents politically. When the group seemed likely to bring in young radical voters, Congressman Henry B. Gonzalez perhaps saw a threat to his power base in San Antonio and began a sustained attack (described by the *Washington Post* as a 'Family fight') on MAYO and the LUB and the small number of supportive Mexican American politicians. Radicals and moderates within the Mexican American community in San Antonio and nationwide were choosing sides.[79]

'Kill the Gringo'

Into this tense political environment in 1969, MAYO leader José Ángel Gutiérrez, by employing the language of the Chicano Movement and the Black Power Movement, brought the full weight of establishment Texas down on the organization. Throughout the life of MAYO, Gutiérrez made statements that some took as violent threats against whites, yet more often than not he was speaking metaphorically about a racist 'gringo' worldview in Texas that needed to be changed in order for Texans to live in harmony. In a famous episode in 1969, it was reported that he threatened to 'Kill the Gringo,' which was a mischaracterization of his statements yet set off a firestorm in Texas and threatened the federal and Ford Foundation support for MAYO and its various organizations—something Congressman Gonzalez had hoped to bring about for some time.[80] By the end of 1969, MAYO's financial base had been completely undermined by the loss of federal funds. The 'Kill the Gringo' rhetoric, which Gutiérrez increasingly emphasized during a march in Del Rio, Texas, and other differences of opinion would lead active MAYO members such as founder Willie Velásquez to strike out on a more moderate path and later establish the Southwest Voter Registration Education Project (SVREP), while other MAYO founders went the direction of third-party politics and founded El Partido de La Raza Unida (RUP), and others channeled their energies into the Texas branch of the Brown Berets.[81]

Meanwhile, SANYO, the mainstream OEO-funded organization on the West Side led by Father Yanta, faced challenges to the priest's leadership in the name of Chicano community control. Yanta fired several 'militant Chicano types' for conspiring, according to a local news story, to bring about the resignation of all non-Chicano employees of SANYO. By the mid-1970s, Father Yanta and SANYO succumbed to pressure for Mexican American leadership, but the end of the OEO and new policies prohibiting federally funded community groups from political organizing meant that the end of Anglo leadership and the rise of Chicano leadership dovetailed with the demise of the Neighborhood Councils as a potent political force.[82]

The Brown Berets in San Antonio

The MAYO activists who had built the LUB—now without funding to support their programs—attempted to shift to a vocational training model. Even with these difficulties the LUB became the foundation for the Brown Berets in Texas. Influenced by the development of the Brown Berets in California, the former MAYO members, gang members, VISTA volunteers, artists, and veterans who formed the San Antonio chapter tended to be more working class than those MAYO members who went on to lead the RUP. The former gang members who played a large role in building the Brown Berets used the networks of gang life and gang reconciliation to build the group. Many of the founders were Vietnam combat veterans attracted to the military style and discipline of the Berets. The masculine, Chicano nationalist, paramilitary-style group appealed to veterans and those with experience in the gangs of San Antonio. The signature brown berets, fatigues, combat boots, and ceremonial weapons often seen in public display conveyed a sense of power and order and linked Chicanos to the Black Power Movement and the pride aesthetic of Chicano nationalism. The group also found adherents in many of the small farm and ranch cities of South Texas where the RUP was organizing politically. From a base in San Antonio the Brown Berets continued many of the educational and self-awakening efforts of MAYO and the Chicano Movement for working-class Mexican Americans, as the organization spread throughout the *barrios*, disrupting gang patterns as they called for Chicano unity.[83]

The Berets dedicated themselves to *barrio* peace, betterment, and safety and quickly won the respect of many community members. By persuading gang members to abandon the micro-spatial focus of most gang territorial world-views in favor of unity and peace the Brown Berets ushered in a period of neighborhood peace in San Antonio. Brown Berets helped people by assisting *barrio* residents with applications for government benefits and other civic educational programs. For members, the discussion of ideas and Chicano nationalism made them part of a rich network of community education that was less about status and degree attainment and more about personal knowledge and growth. The Berets also provided the *barrio* with community patrols. These patrols were meant to keep the streets safe by limiting gang violence and also by monitoring policing, so that the San Antonio Police Department was aware that the Berets were eyes on the street and Chicanos willing to defend themselves and their rights. Thus, the Brown Berets transformed at-risk youth, returning veterans, and non-college-bound Chicanos into *barrio* educators, informal social workers, and protectors.[84]

Women also found a home in the Brown Berets, but theirs was a struggle to be recognized and respected as equals. The Berets opened membership to women in 1972 with the first member, 'Louisa,' stating her reasons for joining as wanting to do more than 'just going around bullshitting and preparing leaflets and all that like a secretary.'[85] Many of the initial female members joined the Berets as a result of family or relationship connections to the male members, but they created their own organization within the larger group. They screened and selected female members and expanded the meaning of Beret *carnalismo* (brotherhood) to include women. As was true for women in many radical organizations of the 1970s, the Chicana berets reported later that they faced harassment from men outside the group and from some new members, as they fought for human rights rather than gendered rights.[86]

San Antonio, like other large cities that saw the development of Chicano Movement organizations, also witnessed a rise-and-fall trajectory from the late 1960s to the early 1970s, as radicalism was replaced by institutional development on the one hand, and a decline of radicalism in the mid 1970s. The Brown Berets were a short-lived organization, which suffered from both its success and stereotypes about its working-class, poor, and former gang members, as well as opposition from middle-class Chicanos in the movement. Facing criticism from outside and from within the Mexican American community, the San Antonio Brown Berets had weakened by 1973, as had many chapters across the United States, yet continued on into the middle 1970s. Several of the organizations that grew out of the

War on Poverty and MAYO organizational efforts in San Antonio continued to thrive and expand, including MAUC and MANCO, which survived the turbulent early 1970s to become important institutions. The Chicano Movement in San Antonio had several key accomplishments. It broke the monopoly in local politics held by the Anglo business and Mexican American political elite and opened city politics to grassroots activism and a much more diverse political framework. It also developed a group of Mexican American activists from working-class and middle-class backgrounds who continued to participate in community activities long after the collapse of radical Chicano nationalism in the city. The Brown Berets, in perhaps the group's most important effort, provided a pathway out of gang life for many low-income Chicanos often neglected or marginalized by the mainstream. With all the different acronyms and short-lived organizations, the lasting impact of the movement in San Antonio was a complete realignment and expansion of political life in one of the oldest and largest Mexican American urban population areas in the nation.

Chicanos and Puerto Ricans in Milwaukee

So much of the scholarship of the Chicano Movement is focused on the epicenters of Mexican American life and culture in Los Angeles and San Antonio, yet many key moments in the movement took place across the Mexican American diaspora.[87] In places such as Saginaw, Michigan, Saint Paul, Minnesota, and Milwaukee, Wisconsin, important movements developed in tandem with the national movement. By considering events in Milwaukee, Wisconsin, we can see how the movement developed along parallel lines and how the multiethnic, multiracial cities of the Midwest may provide insight into the politics of the era outside the vast Mexican American metropolises of Texas and California. As was true in Texas and California, the War on Poverty and the Farm Workers Movement served as the foundation for Chicano activism in Milwaukee, Wisconsin, a medium-sized city some 90 miles north of Chicago. In many ways, the movement in Wisconsin mirrored developments in California, Denver, and Texas and encompassed elements found in these movement centers. Milwaukee had many similarities to Chicago—large numbers of Mexican-ancestry immigrants, Tejanos, and Puerto Ricans. In some ways it was a microcosm of that Midwestern metropolis, with one important difference: Milwaukee was also linked to the development of an independent farm labor organization, Obreros Unidos (OU), which both worked with and came into conflict with the United Farm Workers union based in California.[88] Thus, the Wisconsin movement linked several strains of the Chicano Movement in a place where the African American civil rights movement, in Milwaukee, was one of the strongest and most sustained in the urban north. Milwaukee serves as a useful case study of the movement outside the Southwest in a space that linked key elements of the movement: urban politics, farm labor organizing, and pan-Latino activism.[89]

Pan-Latino Activism

The War on Poverty and social reform efforts in Milwaukee involved both Puerto Ricans and Mexican Americans. Catholic priests together with members of the long-established Mexican immigrant and more recent Tejano migrant communities established the Spanish Center with assistance from the Milwaukee archdiocese. The Spanish Center offered a variety of programs, including daycare, education, a credit union, and housing services, and became one of the largest service providers on the city's South Side. Puerto Ricans also established a variety of organizations, most prominently 'The Spot,' which became the United Community Center, established by a Puerto Rican minister. These centers engaged in outreach to the youth of both communities and provided meeting spaces and recreation spaces that became central to the development of 'Latin' or 'Spanish-Speaking' activism in Milwaukee. Because Milwaukee, like Chicago, was a Midwestern city, it took in migrants from the two dominant Latino streams and reflected pan-Latino activism from the beginning even as Tejanos became the dominant leadership group among activists.[90]

The South Side of Milwaukee had been home to several waves of immigrants and had a long history of settlement house and religious migrant assistance. With dozens of churches serving German, Polish, Ukrainian, and Russian immigrants, among others, the neighborhood known for its 'Polish flats' continued to be the point of entry for new migrants, as Latinos came to dominate the neighborhood. While churches often remained ethnic in focus, the neighborhood experienced white flight as European migrants abandoned the inner city for suburbs. The pace was slower than that seen on the German and Jewish North Side of Milwaukee, where African American migration from the American South and Chicago led to rapid white flight across the area. While Latinos faced discrimination from their mainly European American neighbors, the churches and religious leaders of the South Side were able to adapt migrant service strategies to the needs of new migrants in a city long accustomed to immigrant and migrant culture and life. This meant that the creation of social space in Milwaukee was often cooperative, even though tensions arose as an outgrowth of desires among Latinos for community control.[91]

The War on Poverty in Milwaukee was organized at the county level with leadership from the mayor's office and local political officials. Much as in other cities, there was limited participation from the minority and low-income communities being served. Gripped by an active school desegregation effort among African Americans and whites, defined by sit-ins and street demonstrations, many of these same activists began the call for control of the Social Development Commission (SDC), the countywide OEO agency serving Milwaukee. United Migrant Opportunity Services, Inc. (UMOS), based in the Milwaukee suburb of Waukesha, sought to meet the needs of all of the migrant farm workers in the entire state and thus escaped the city or county oversight and control issues so common to OEO agencies in major cities.[92] In 1968, UMOS moved its offices to Milwaukee's Latino *barrio*, but while the agency employed many Tejanos and Mexican Americans, it did not have any among its management ranks. Later in that same year, employees and the newly created Latin American Union for Civil Rights (LAUCR) joined together to protest discrimination at the agency. This became the foundation for the Brown Berets in Wisconsin, which held sit-ins and protests at the SDC and UMOS in Milwaukee as it successfully pushed for community control. African Americans also protested the lack of 'maximum feasible participation' (a goal of the War on Poverty) at the SDC and won concessions from the county poverty agency. In a city with an active African American civil rights movement and with the development of the OU farm labor union in the state, the Wisconsin Chicano Movement by the late 1960s had given rise to two movement newspapers edited by community leaders who had participated in activism in Texas. The Chicano Movement also had the active involvement of Puerto Rican activists with roots in Chicago's Near Northwest Side *barrio*, which led to the founding of organizations that reflected this diversity. This creative mélange of movement forces meant that the Chicano Movement in Milwaukee blended several key streams of Mexican American and pan-Latino politics thousands of miles from Los Angeles or San Antonio, or San Juan, Puerto Rico, for that matter.[93]

Milwaukee had an active civil rights movement among African Americans, Chicanos, and Puerto Ricans, and while the state and local government were not necessarily inclined toward support, activists did not face the forceful opposition that confronted Chicago activists who sought to participate in social-movement activities. The history of the War on Poverty and the rise of Latino political activism in Chicago prominently featured the anti-activist tendencies of Richard J. Daley's administration and his dominant political machine which managed many neighborhood programs, and the police department and its significant role in meeting protest and militant groups with violence. One leading historian of the War on Poverty labeled the model in Chicago 'minimum feasible participation,' a play on the concept of 'maximum feasible participation' enshrined in the War on Poverty's founding legal document, the Economic Opportunity Act of 1964.[94] The site of the police execution of Black Panther Party leader Fred Hampton and the violent police riot during the 1968 Democratic national convention stand as testaments to the history of community action repression in the Windy City. When activism occurred in Chicago, it did so on the margins of that city's famous machine political infrastructure, yet it bore results later on.

Without a machine and with a recent history of electing Socialist mayors, Milwaukee, while it did not greet activism with open arms and had a police department that also used questionable tactics, tended to cede control of community organizations in response to protest—and in fact activism flourished in the city. Within this milieu, local Chicanos and Puerto Ricans established LAUCR, dedicated to reform in education and politics and an end to police brutality. LAUCR became the primary recruiting ground for the Milwaukee Brown Berets, which had members of both Mexican American and Puerto Rican backgrounds. (The Young Lords Organization [YLO] in Chicago also had a mixed group of Puerto Ricans, and Mexican Americans in leadership ranks.) The Brown Berets in Milwaukee were really an outgrowth of LAUCR, a pan-Latino organization that outlived the Brown Beret moniker. In 1968 LAUCR pressed for control of all War on Poverty organizations on Milwaukee's South Side and succeeded in placing Latinos at the helm of almost all of them. Working together with African American civil rights activists, LAUCR protested against prominent Milwaukee employer Allen-Bradley as it sought to bring about an integrated workforce at the mostly lily-white company. Slowly Allen-Bradley relented, and LAUCR and other groups continued to pressure the union and the company to increase diversity. Also in 1968, members of LAUCR and War on Poverty employees from the Latino and African American community, together with Milwaukee's Black Commandos (a Black Panther-inspired group), travelled to Washington DC to participate in the Poor People's Campaign, where the Latinos camped, unlike Corky Gonzales and other Latino leaders, together with the African American contingent in the tent city dubbed 'Resurrection City.' The Chicano Movement in Milwaukee, which gave rise to militant protest, university and business take-overs, and cooperative protests with African Americans and Puerto Ricans, developed as an interracial movement. Although tensions sometimes arose between African Americans and Latinos and, within the Latino community, between Puerto Ricans and Mexican Americans (and also Tejanos), the politics of ethnicity were such that groups worked together more than they worked against each other in an environment that, while not ideal, lacked the forceful anti-movement actions of Chicago's mayor. Thus they created in the Midwest a movement that linked the Chicano Movement to a variety of bases of operation and influences.[95] The Milwaukee case is just one example of the many various locations that developed sustained Chicano Movement activities and organizations among the Mexican American diaspora in places such as the Midwest, the Great Plains, and the Pacific Northwest and that fostered an interracial and pan-Latino environment whenever possible.

La Raza Unida Party in Texas

Several founding members of San Antonio-based MAYO began to think outside the 'Mexican American' framework and, like those who established Brown Berets organizations in Los Angeles and elsewhere, sought a group that would emphasize Chicano nationalism and political power within the US electoral framework. These MAYO activists, led by José Ángel Gutiérrez and Mario Compean, felt that South Texas, because of its Mexican American majority in several counties, was the perfect test case for Gutiérrez's master's thesis argument: that electoral democracy for South Texas's Mexican ancestry majority offered a revolutionary challenge to the status quo. Seeking to implement this program, dubbed the 'Winter Garden' project after Gutiérrez's home region of Southwest Texas, several MAYO founders and activists led by Gutiérrez left San Antonio for the farm and ranching town of Crystal City, Texas, where over 80 percent of the population was of Mexican ancestry. Other MAYO activists, prominently Willie Velásquez, were in disagreement with the third-party model, and eventually chose to break with MAYO over the creation of the RUP as a third party. The breakup of MAYO, which did not happen immediately yet resulted from the establishment of the RUP, was the end result of the division between the RUP group and the more traditional group within MAYO.[96]

Crystal City Texas Redux

In moving activists to Crystal City, the RUP focused first on the schools. By working with activist teens following the walkouts in East Los Angeles, the RUP had in the walkouts a template for action. Young activists from the Mexican American-majority high school—some of whom were migratory farm workers whose families travelled to California and knew of the walkouts and the rise of Cesar Chavez's United Farm Workers and related unions in South Texas and Wisconsin—had an understanding of both the discrimination faced by Chicanos and strategies to confront oppression. After a series of brainstorming sessions with José Ángel Gutiérrez and his wife Luz Gutiérrez, high school student activists led by Severita Lara began the process of mobilizing students and the community. They made contact with the students who were already perturbed by a couple of issues, including a ban on speaking Spanish on school grounds and the anti-democratic management of school honors and participation on the cheerleader squad. Young women and men came together in the name of democratic participation and supported efforts to challenge the school over issues of language, curriculum, Chicano history, and discrimination against Mexican American women who wanted to participate in cheerleading—an important activity for young people (then and now). This pent-up activist potential was released by several tactics. Gutiérrez had the students air their grievances and then brainstorm solutions and possible protest avenues. The East Los Angeles walkouts provided a template for the 1969 walkouts in Crystal City (and other places in the Southwest and Midwest). Severita Lara had traveled to Gilroy, California, where she spent time with migrant workers and California Chicanos, who told her about the East Los Angeles walkouts of 1968. On this trip she and her sister were confused by the fact that many California Chicanos did not speak Spanish at all and spoke English exclusively, yet were committed to Chicano liberation. Using the knowledge she had acquired about the Los Angeles walkouts, on her return Lara implemented a similar plan. Students first circulated petitions requesting changes and, when these requests were denied, asked parents to demand change. When these demands were rejected as well and parents were ill treated, the students led a walkout with community support. Calling for 'Brown Power' and making reference to the 'Huelga,' young people walked out of Crystal City high school, an event that soon led to a boycott across the entire school district.[97]

The Crystal City walkouts were followed by community organizing and the establishment of the RUP as a local, statewide, and national political party between 1970 and 1972. The RUP, learning from the lessons of past efforts in Crystal City to bring Mexican Americans into the public sphere through elective office, moved from school boycotts to school board elections and from school board elections to city, county, and statewide elections. By 1972, the RUP, led by former MAYO founders Gutiérrez and Compean, had established strongholds in Zavala County, LaSalle, Dimmit, and other counties in South Texas. In the development of the RUP the activists utilized a polarization model to divide the community and define the issues that mattered to the Mexican American majority. An Anglo minority had controlled the educational, political, and economic system locally and limited the life chances of Mexican Americans. While many Anglo Americans disputed the claims of the RUP, the data told a story of economic, educational, and social exclusion. This model was common to Mexican Americans across South Texas and other places in the Southwest and California, and polarization was a strong organizing tool for local Mexican Americans who had personal stories and experiences of exclusion and discrimination. Treated like an inferior and foreign minority group and often considered little more than a labor input in the production of agricultural products, Mexican Americans, through what might today be termed 'town hall' meetings at which Spanish was the dominant language, began to define the nature of exclusion in South Texas and propose solutions. All of this resonated with the rhetoric of Americanism and democracy, yet locally these ideals were not followed by the Anglo American majority. The result was massive 'white flight' from Crystal City after the victory of the RUP, as Anglos rejected majority rule and open democratic principals in action.

Raza Unida as Third Party

In 1971–1972, against opposition from Gutiérrez, the RUP committed itself to the development of a statewide and national party. MAYO founders Compean and Gutiérrez, who had brought the party to Crystal City, had a difference of opinion regarding the next step for the RUP. Gutiérrez felt the party should build on its strengths in South Texas and not make the jump to statewide and national party status. Compean pressed for a statewide party, and soon enough activists in Colorado, California, Michigan, and elsewhere were establishing affiliate groups. By this point, moderates like Willie Velásquez had split completely with the group.

In 1972 the RUP organized a national convention and ran candidates for Governor and other posts in Texas. The September 1972 RUP Convention in El Paso brought together all the various communities committed to third-party Chicano political power. Participants came from across the nation, from California, Colorado, and the Southwest as well as the Great Lakes and the Pacific Northwest. Women and men debated and argued about the issues facing the Chicano Movement and possible solutions to the many problems facing Chicanos as a people. The cultural nationalism and educational components of the national meeting were positive benefits, and the 1972 meeting allowed Chicanos to see themselves as a national minority group, as activists from Wisconsin and Michigan met with fellow militants from California and Texas, and women collaborated and brought the issues that motivated them into the debate. This coming together was a major step forward for activist development, and the meeting also brought Reies López Tijerina and Rodolfo 'Corky' Gonzales (both older than many activists at the meeting) together with Gutiérrez, a younger and then rising star in Chicano Movement circles. (Cesar Chavez, also older than many of the activists at the convention, did not attend.) The conference led to a disagreement between Gonzales and Gutiérrez over the leadership and mission of the party. Gutiérrez won the vote and Gonzales, who apparently never accepted this verdict, withdrew to Denver. While Gonzales continued as a national activist in many ways, the loss to Gutiérrez over the mission and meaning of the RUP was the end of his leadership role outside of Denver, and he increasingly rejected participation with other activists.[98]

The RUP, having decided to run candidates statewide in Texas, had to find candidates to place on the ballot in many counties and for statewide posts in November 1972. After soliciting established Mexican American leaders, the RUP selected Ramsey Muniz, a 29-year-old lawyer and Waco Model Cities Program administrator. A former Baylor University football star and a charismatic speaker, Muniz was a strong candidate and won 6 percent of the vote—enough to get the attention of Democrats and, some would argue, President Richard Nixon, who would be accused of assisting the RUP in Crystal City to take votes away from Democrats in the future. In a close election, the RUP could swing an election away from the one-party dominance of the Democratic Party in Texas (later this dominant one-party status shifted to the Republican Party). Yet, the failure to recruit mainstream Mexican Americans and win elections statewide or bring liberal democrats, women, and the majority of Mexican American community to the party was evident. The RUP embraced Chicano nationalism in Texas and defined the Chicano Movement in that state yet failed outside of South Texas. Gutiérrez was right that the party was not viable as a statewide or national experiment in 1972, and he was also right in thinking that taking 6 percent of the vote in statewide elections would win the attention of both major parties, who might then bargain with the RUP.[99] This practical politics was rejected by some who dreamed of the RUP as a key component in a separatist and irredentist fantasy. After the party's demise, Mexican American organizations lobbied and bargained, just as Gutiérrez had envisioned and as MAYO founder Willie Velásquez had argued was the only path forward.

Conclusion: The Chicano Movement and Community Control

This chapter has considered the development of the community control phase of the Chicano Movement in different places across the Southwest and Midwest, in rural and urban areas alike. The interplay between the Chicano Movement's most radical strains and the War on Poverty programs is a needed corrective. In rethinking the Chicano Movement, we see that the radicalism of the Brown Berets and the various community programs sought not literal revolution but rather access to education, upward mobility, and recognition for Mexican American people's place in North American history. These activists, who often simultaneously and intermittently worked in community and War on Poverty programs, also sought an end to policing models that often led to the deaths of Mexican Americans at the hands of police—often over minor conflicts—and tried to bring the concept of self-defense and self-protection to the streets in the *barrios* of Denver, Los Angeles, San Antonio, and Milwaukee, among other places. Rather than anti-Americanism, this was a new, more militant form of Mexican Americanism and an expression of Chicano understandings of what exactly 'maximum feasible participation' meant. This was an Americanism defined by the self-making of Chicano nationalism focused on the protection and development of the *barrio* and its residents. While many young Chicanos flirted with irredentism and rebellion, this was a Chicano-style Americanism that rejected the outmoded view of early twentieth-century assimilation in favor of a hybrid form of social acculturation that allowed for the maintenance of culture, language, and social practices among minorities, while also demanding a place in the architecture of upward mobility, safety, and community well-being. Chicanos were embracing their own worldview as they sought to perfect and remake the United States.

Notes

1 See Introduction, note 31 for definitions.
2 See Introduction, note 28.
3 Often Reies López Tijerina is given a central role in the Chicano Movement due to his efforts as the leader of the *Alianza Federal de las Mercedes*—the Federal Alliance of Land Grants (also translated as the Federal Alliance of Free City States) in New Mexico, a group that sought the return of federal lands to the Spanish and Mexican colonial settlers in an area that also had a long legacy of Native American resistance to these colonial forces, and those that came afterward. In this reconsideration Tijerina is considered

marginally. For information on Tijerina see Rudy V. Busto, *King Tiger: The Religious Vision of Reies López Tijerina* (Albuquerque: University of New Mexico Press, 2005); Lesley Poling-Kempes, *Valley of Shining Stone: The Story of Abiquiu* (Tucson: University of Arizona Press, 1997); David Maciel and Erlinda Gonzales-Berry, *The Contested Homeland: A Chicano History of New Mexico* (Albuquerque: University of New Mexico Press, 2000).

4 On the ideology and history of Chicano Movement thought and community control activism, see Armando B. Rendón, *Chicano Manifesto: The History and Aspirations of the Second Largest Minority in America* (New York: Macmillan, 1971); Ignacio M. García, *Chicanismo: The Forging of a Militant Ethos among Mexican Americans* (Tucson: University of Arizona Press, 1997). For case studies, see Armando Navarro, *The Cristal* [sic] *Experiment: A Chicano Struggle for Community Control* (Madison: University of Wisconsin Press, 1998); John R. Chávez, *Eastside Landmark: A History of the East Los Angeles Community Union, 1968–1993* (Stanford: Stanford University Press, 1998).

5 On the grassroots implications and impacts of the War on Poverty, see Annelise Orleck and Lisa Gayle Hazirjian, eds., *The War on Poverty: A New Grassroots History, 1964–1980* (Athens: University of Georgia Press, 2011).

6 On the possibilities and problems of interracial reform during the War on Poverty, see Robert Bauman, *Race and the War on Poverty: From Watts to East L.A.* (Norman: University of Oklahoma Press, 2008).

7 Christine Marin, 'Rodolfo "Corky" Gonzales: The Mexican American Movement Spokesman, 1966–1972,' *Journal of the West* 14, no. 4 (1975): 107–8.

8 Marin, 'Rodolfo "Corky" Gonzales,' 108–9.

9 Tom I. Romero II, 'Wearing the Red, White, and Blue Trunks of Aztlán: Rodolfo "Corky" Gonzales and the Convergence of American and Chicano Nationalism,' *Aztlán* 29, no. 1 (2004): 99–101.

10 See Ernesto B. Vigil, *The Crusade for Justice: Chicano Militancy and the Government's War on Dissent* (Madison: University of Wisconsin Press, 1999), 18–21.

11 Quoted in Jack Gaskie, 'Gonzales Views His Poverty Role,' *Rocky Mountain News*, September 25, 1965; see also Vigil, *Crusade*, 21–2.

12 Romero, 'Wearing the Red, White, and Blue Trunks of Aztlán,' 102–4; Marin, 'Rodolfo "Corky" Gonzales,' 108–9.

13 Quoted in Vigil, *Crusade*, 27.

14 Armando Navarro, *Mexicano Political Experience in Occupied Aztlán: Struggles and Change* (Walnut Creek: Alta Mira Press, 2005), 364. Navarro here refers to Gonzales as having a 'charismatic *jefe* (boss) or *caudillo* (political-military leader or dictator)' style.

15 John L. Espinoza, 'Corky Speaks on Spectrum of Movement,' *El Diario De La Gente* (Boulder: United Mexican American Students, Chicano Studies, 1972).

16 See Rodolfo Gonzales, *I Am Joaquín / Yo Soy Joaquín; an Epic Poem. With a Chronology of People and Events in Mexican and Mexican American History* (Toronto: Bantam Books, 1972). Gonzales had self-published the poem in 1967, and many copies survive from this edition.

17 For the diversity, competition, and evolution of Gonzales as a clear leader at the Poor People's Campaign, see Gordon Mantler, *Power to the Poor: Black-Brown Coalition and the Fight for Economic Justice, 1960–1974* (Chapel Hill: University of North Carolina Press, 2013); Faith Berry, 'The Anger and Problems and Sickness of the Poor of the Whole Nation,' *New York Times*, July 7, 1968, SM5; Bert Mann, 'Wiggins Confers with Militant Mexican Americans in Washington,' *Los Angeles Times*, June 17, 1968, C8;

Stuart Auerbach and Paul Valentine, 'Marchers Blocked at Justice Department,' *Washington Post*, June 4, 1968, A1; Paul Valentine, 'Civil Rights Leaders Set up "Poor Peoples Embassy",' *Washington Post*, September 7, 1968, B2. Among other things, while at the Poor People's Campaign, Gonzales led protests in defense of the East LA 13 (those arrested for allegedly heading the 'conspiracy' to organize the walkouts covered later in this chapter).

18 Homer Bigarts, 'A New Mexican-American Militancy,' *New York Times*, April 20, 1969, 1.

19 Rubén Salazar, 'Chicanos Hold 5-State Event in Colorado,' *Los Angeles Times*, March 30, 1969, 8. In his report, Salazar highlighted 'Ethnic nationalism' specifically as the 'unofficial theme' of the meeting, yet when it came to women he only mentioned that those in attendance wore 'miniskirts and Mexican serapes.'

20 Rubén Salazar, 'Mexican-Americans to Hold Youth Conference,' *Los Angeles Times*, March 23, 1969, B3, and 'Militants Denounce Traditional Stands at Chicano Parley,' *Los Angeles Times*, March 31, 1969, 3.

21 Rubén Salazar, 'Anglo "Integration" Rejected by Chicanos,' *Los Angeles Times*, April 7, 1969, C4.

22 Mirta Vidal, 'New Voice of La Raza: Chicanas Speak Out,' in *Chicana Feminist Thought: The Basic Historical Writings*, ed. Alma M. García (New York: Routledge, 1997), 22–3.

23 Rubén Salazar, 'Chicano Must Be Nationalist to Last in U.S.,' *Los Angeles Times*, April 18, 1969, SF1; 'Clash in Denver,' *Chicago Tribune*, March 21, 1969, 6; Lawrence May, 'Emergence of Militancy Seen for Chicanos,' *Los Angeles Times*, August 25, 1969, A24; Robert Kistler, 'Police Reports over Militant's Arrest Differ,' *Los Angeles Times*, August 31, 1970, 3; Anthony Ripley, 'Chicanos Seeking a National Role,' *New York Times*, November 29, 1971, 33; 'Denver Man Killed, 6 Wounded in Gunfight at Chicano Building,' *New York Times*, March 18, 1973, 46. For an impassioned history of the Crusade and Gonzales by one of the organizations leaders see, Vigil, *Crusade*. For years Vigil was Gonzales's lieutenant and this is evident in his well-written history. For the tensions between Gonzales and José Ángel Gutiérrez at and after the National La Raza Unida Party Conference in 1972, see Ignacio M. Garciá, *United We Win: The Rise and Fall of La Raza Unida Party* (Tucson: University of Arizona Press, 1989).

24 The Watts Riots or Rebellion of 1965 occurred in August of 1965 and led to millions of dollars of damage as buildings were looted and burned following an arrest and scuffle between police and an African American family, which some considered another example of police brutality. Martin Luther King, Jr. visited Los Angeles soon after the riots and claimed that the rebellion's causes were not racial but a reaction to the social isolation, poverty, and environmental problems faced by the inner-city poor. For a good summary of the events see, Martin Luther King, Jr. Encyclopedia, Entry: Watts Rebellion (Los Angeles, 1965) retrieved from: http:// mlk-kpp01.stanford.edu/index.php/encyclopedia/encyclopedia/enc_watts_ rebellion_los_angeles_1965/.

25 Jack Jones, 'Watts Riot Shows Need for Responsible Adults,' *Los Angeles Times*, March 20, 1966, B.

26 Gladwin Hill, 'Los Angeles Rioting Is Checked,' *New York Times*, August 16, 1965, 1; William S. White, 'After Los Angeles,' *Washington Post*, August 25, 1965, A19.

27 See Mary C. Waters, Reed Ueda, and Helen B. Marrow, eds., *The New Americans: A Guide to Immigration since 1965* (Cambridge: Harvard University Press, 2007), 511. On the large and often unacknowledged migration of Tejanos to California after

World War II, see James N. Gregory, *The Southern Diaspora: How the Great Migrations of Black and White Southerners Transformed America* (Chapel Hill: University of North Carolina Press, 2005), 35.

28 On Los Angeles' Mexican American community generally, see Ricardo Romo, *East Los Angeles: History of a Barrio* (Austin: University of Texas Press, 1983); George Sánchez, *Becoming Mexican American: Ethnicity, Culture, and Identity in Chicano Los Angeles, 1900–1945* (New York: Oxford University Press, 1995); William Deverell, *Whitewashed Adobe: The Rise of Los Angeles and the Remaking of Its Mexican Past* (Berkeley: University of California Press, 2004).

29 On the prospects and problems of African American/Mexican American cooperation and conflict in Los Angeles, see Robert Bauman, 'The Neighborhood Adult Participation Project: Black-Brown Strife in the War on Poverty in Los Angeles,' in *The Struggle in Black and Brown: African American and Mexican American Relations during the Civil Rights Era*, ed. Brian D. Behnken (Lincoln: University of Nebraska Press, 2012), 104–24.

30 Jack Jones, 'Efforts to Divide and Control Poverty Project Stir Dispute,' *Los Angeles Times*, November 8, 1966, A1; Art Berman, 'Latin-American Quits Antipoverty Job in Row,' *Los Angeles Times,* September 16, 1966, 32; Ken Fanucchi, 'Latins Demand Poverty Probe,' *Los Angeles Times,* October 3, 1966.

31 Irene Tovar quoted in Bauman, 'The Neighborhood Adult Participation Project,' 104.

32 'La Raza Interviews Mrs. Cardenas,' *La Raza, Yearbook* (Los Angeles), September, 1968, 10–11.

33 Quoted in Jennifer G. Correa, 'The Targeting of the East Los Angeles Brown Berets by a Racial Patriarchal Capitalist State: Merging Intersectionality and Social Movement Research,' *Critical Sociology* 37, no. 1 (2001): 83–101, at 89–90.

34 Edward J. Escobar, 'The Dialectics of Repression: The Los Angeles Police Department and the Chicano Movement, 1968–1971,' *Journal of American History* 79, no. 4 (March 1993): 1483–514, 1486–7; Ian F. Haney-López, 'Protest, Repression, and Race: Legal Violence and the Chicano Movement,' *University of Pennsylvania Law Review* 150 (2001): 205–44, 215; Ernesto Chávez, '¡Mi Raza Primero!' (My People First!): Nationalism, Identity, and Insurgency in the Chicano Movement in Los Angeles, 1966–1978* (Berkeley: University of California Press, 2002), 207–9; Rubén Salazar, 'Brown Berets Hail "La Raza" and Scorn the Establishment,' *Los Angeles Times,* June 16, 1969, 3.

35 'Time of Studies & Statistics Over!' *La Raza*, December 25, 1967, 3.

36 For an interesting exploration of the founding of the coffee house, initial problems with the Los Angeles Police Department, and founding of the Brown Berets, see Rona M. Fields, 'Interviews with Brown Berets, Part 1,' June 17, 2013, retrieved from: www.youtube.com/watch?v=Q3wupE4eatU.

37 'Sheriffs Harass Brown Berets,' *La Raza, Yearbook* (Los Angeles), September, 1968, 29.

38 See Carlos Muñoz, *Youth, Identity, Power: The Chicano Movement, Revised and Expanded Edition* (New York: Verso Press, 2007), 79–82. Sal Castro was a Korean War veteran and proponent of the ideology of Mexican Americanism as were others of his age group at the time; yet he had grown clearly more militant in the face of continued opposition to Mexican American advancement in the high school where he worked and the community in which he lived.

39 See Carlos Muñoz, 'The Politics of Protest and Chicano Liberation: A Case Study of Repression and Cooptation,' *Aztlán* 5, no. 1–2 (Spring–Fall, 1974): 119–41;

Dolores D. Bernal, 'Grassroots Leadership Reconceptualized: Chicana Oral Histories and the 1968 East Los Angeles School Blowouts,' *Frontiers* 19, no. 2 (1998): 116–19.

40 Ray Rogers, 'Unique School Problems Linked to Latins Here,' *Los Angeles Times,* June 9, 1967, 13; Jack Jones, 'Education of Latin-Americans in L.A. Area Called Inadequate,' *Los Angeles Times,* May 1, 1968, SG1; 'Teachers and Parents,' *La Raza, Yearbook* (Los Angeles), September, 1968, 14.

41 See 'Who Are the Brown Berets,' *Chicano Student News* (Los Angeles), March 15, 1968, 6. For a personal view of the changing influences in East Los Angeles at this time, see Julian Nava, *Julian Nava: My Mexican-American Journey* (Houston: Arte Público Press, 2002), 94–6.

42 Jack McCurdy, 'Student Disorders Erupt at 4 High Schools,' *Los Angeles Times,* March 7, 1968, 3.

43 'Blow Out,' *La Raza, Yearbook* (Los Angeles), September 1968, 16; 'Student Demands,' *Chicano Student News* (Los Angeles), n.d., 1968; 'Walkout,' *Chicano Student News* (Los Angeles), February 1969, 1–2.

44 On the walkouts, subsequent court cases, and continued activism of Sal Castro, see Mario T. García and Sal Castro, *Blowout! Sal Castro and the Chicano Struggle for Educational Justice* (Chapel Hill: University of North Carolina Press, 2011).

45 Jack McCurdy, '1,000 Walk Out in School Boycott,' *Los Angeles Times,* March 9, 1968, 2.

46 Quoted as written and underlined in 'Outside Agitators,' *Chicano Student News* (Los Angeles), March 15, 1968, 3.

47 See Vigil, *Crusade,* 135–8.

48 Jack McCurdy, 'Latins Urge Reinstatement of Teacher Who Led Walkout,' *Los Angeles Times,* August 30, 1968, B.

49 Jack McCurdy, 'East Side Still Plagued with Hangover from School Boycott,' *Los Angeles Times,* September 15, 1968, eb, and 'Lincoln High Pickets Protest Absence of Indicted Teacher,' *Los Angeles Times,* September 17, 1968, 3.

50 Raul Ruiz, 'Sal Castro,' *Chicano Student News* (Los Angeles), April 25, 1968, 2.

51 Ron Einstoss, 'DA's Office Hits Back at Criticism in Sal Castro Case,' *Los Angeles Times,* October 2, 1968, 3. See also Haney-López, 'Protest, Repression, and Race,' 230–5; more generally, see Ian F. Haney-López, *Racism on Trial: The Chicano Fight for Justice* (Cambridge: The Belknap Press of Harvard University Press, 2003).

52 Dial Torgerson, 'Start of a Revolution?' *Los Angeles Times,* March 17, 1968, B1.

53 Sal Castro remarks, 'Hispanic Experience Panel,' Los Angeles Times Festival of Books, University of Southern California, April 30, 2011. Retrieved from: www.c-spanvideo. org/program/HispanicEx; and Sal Castro remarks, 'A Discussion of Mario T. García and Sal Castro Blowout!' Western History Association, annual meeting, Oakland, California, October 15, 2011. Castro discussed the goals of the movement; the focus, for him, on opportunities for students to go to college; and African American and Chicano cooperation.

54 See Correa, 'The Targeting of the East Los Angeles Brown Berets,' 91.

55 See Sergio Elizondo, 'La Voz Del Barrio: Chicano Liberation,' *El Chicano* (Colton), May 28, 1971, 3.

56 'Freemont Demands' and 'Chicano Students Blow Out!' *La Hormiga* (Oakland), October 7, 1968, 2; Raul Ruiz, 'One Year Ago,' *Chicano Student Movement* (Los Angeles), March 1969, 1; 'Parents Unite to Oppose Closing of Westside Schools,' *El Chicano* (Colton), May 21, 1971.

57 Jack McCurdy, 'Student-Parent Sit-in Continuing on Weekend,' *Los Angeles Times*, September 28, 1968, 2, and 'Castro Restored to Teaching Job,' *Los Angeles Times*, October 4, 1968, 1.

58 While no reasons were given, 40 Lincoln High School teachers requested transfer out of the school after Castro was reinstated. Other Mexican American and Anglo parents protested the requested transfers, making the argument that Castro did not represent the majority of parents and asking the teachers to remain. The community was deeply divided over the issue of protest, tactics, and strategy, yet quality education was the goal for all. See Jack McCurdy, '40 Teachers Ask for Transfers after Reinstatement of Castro,' *Los Angeles Times*, October 8, 1968, 1; 'Pickets Urge Teachers to Remain at Lincoln,' *Los Angeles Times*, October 23, 1968, 1.

59 See Lorena Oropeza, *¡Raza Sí! ¡Guerra No! Chicano Protest and Patriotism during the Viet Nam War* (Berkeley: University of California Press, 2005).

60 Rubén Salazar Mallén and Mario T. García, *Border Correspondent: Selected Writings, 1955–1970* (Berkeley: University of California Press, 1995), 1–5.

61 See 'Chicano Vietnam,' *La Raza* (Los Angeles), November 1969; 'Chicano Moratorium,' *La Raza* (Los Angeles), December 10, 1969; 'Chicanos 20% of Viet dead,' *Adelante* (Riverside, California), October 14, 1969; 'Chicanos' Plans for Big Antiwar Rally Here Told,' *Los Angeles Times*, March 29, 1970, B.

62 Oropeza, *¡Raza Sí!*, 135.

63 'Chicano Moratorium,' *Sal Si Puedes* (Santa Barbara, California), January 1970.

64 Forben Lozada and Mariana Hernandez, 'The Chicano Moratorium—How It Developed,' *The Militant*, September 4, 1970.

65 Oropeza, *¡Raza Sí!*, 160.

66 Quoted in Robert A. Wright, 'East Los Angeles Calm after Riot,' *New York Times*, August 31, 1970, 30.

67 See Juan Gómez-Quiñones, *Chicano Politics: Reality and Promise, 1940–1990* (Albuquerque: University of New Mexico Press, 1990), 126–8; Doug Shuit and John Sheibe, 'Rioting Spreads to Wilmington,' *Los Angeles Times*, August 31, 1970, 1; 'L.A. Police Seal off Chicano Riot Area,' *Washington Post*, August 31, 1970, A4; Kistler, 'Police Reports over Militant's Arrest Conflict,' 3.

68 'Chicanos Hit Sheriff Searches in East L.A.,' *Los Angeles Times*, September 5, 1970, A10.

69 'Won't Change Plan for Jan. 31 March, Chicano Leader Says,' *Los Angeles Times*, January 12, 1971, 3; 'Mexican-Americans Stage Demonstration in Calif.,' *Atlanta Daily World*, January 14, 1971, 5; Paul Houston and Ted Thackrey Jr., '1 Slain, 24 Hurt in Violence after Chicanos' Rally,' *Los Angeles Times*, February 1, 1971, 1.

70 Frank Del Olmo, 'Special Preparations to Police Chicano Marches Being Made,' *Los Angeles Times*, January 27, 1971, A3; 'Chicano Group Plans Walk to Sacramento,' *Los Angeles Times*, May 5, 1971, C7A; Jack Jones, 'Chicanos 3-Month March to Capital Reaches Salton Sea,' *Los Angeles Times*, May 13, 1971, B1; 'Chicanos Plan Rally, Service for War Dead,' *Los Angeles Times*, June 17, 1971.

71 On TELACU, see Chávez, *Eastside Landmark*, 77–106. Some certainly felt that as grant funding became more important and the terrain of financial support shifted, the organization became less committed to its radical origins, yet it survives today, providing useful services to a community that is still primarily Chicano and Mexican and low income.

72 William S. Clayson, *Freedom Is Not Enough: The War on Poverty and the Civil Rights Movement in Texas* (Austin: University of Texas Press, 2010), 67–75.

73 Clayson, *Freedom Is Not Enough*, 110–11.

74 Juan Sepúlveda, *The Life and Times of Willie Velásquez: Su Voto Es Su Voz* (Houston: Arte Público Press, 2003), 49–55.

75 On the militancy of the era, and national coverage of Gutiérrez alongside Gonzales and other Chicano Movement leaders, see Bigarts, 'A New Mexican-American Militancy,' *New York Times*, April 20, 1969, 1; David Montejano, *Quixote's Soldiers: A Local History of the Chicano Movement, 1966–1981* (Austin: University of Texas Press, 2010), 59–62.

76 For a well-researched study of the way MAYO utilized the War on Poverty to fund a variety of community-based organizations and build a cadre of activists, see Montejano, *Quixote's Soldiers*. On MAYO generally, see Armando Navarro, *Mexican American Youth Organization: Avant-Garde of the Chicano Movement in Texas* (Austin: University of Texas Press, 1995).

77 Montejano, *Quixote's Soldiers*, 60–7. On the foundation the War on Poverty provided to the Chicano Movement in Texas, see Clayson, *Freedom Is Not Enough*, 108–10.

78 Montejano, *Quixote's Soldiers*, 117–43.

79 William Greider, 'A Family Fight Embitters Chicanos,' *Washington Post*, May 25, 1969, B1.

80 José Ángel Gutiérrez's remarks are identified as 'scholarly' and 'calm' and quoted at length in 'A Challenge to Build a New Society,' *New York Times*, April 20, 1969, 55. On the Ford Foundation pull-out, see Laurence Stern and Richard Harwood, 'Ford Foundation: Its Works Spark a Backlash,' *Washington Post*, November 2, 1969, A1.

81 Bert Wise, 'Mexican-American Militancy Rises,' *Washington Post*, April 1, 1969, A1; Richard Avena, 'One Last Vote for Willie Velasquez,' *Los Angeles Times*, June 18, 1988, A8.

82 Clayson, *Freedom Is Not Enough*, 111–13, 143–4.

83 For the best study to date on the Brown Berets in Texas, see Montejano, *Quixote's Soldiers*, 126–43, 176–90.

84 For an insightful reflection on the Brown Berets see, generally, David Montejano, *Sancho's Journal: Exploring the Political Edge with the Brown Berets* (Austin: University of Texas Press, 2012).

85 Interview quoted in Montejano, *Quixote's Soldiers*, 174.

86 Montejano, *Quixote's Soldiers*, 174–6, 186.

87 Mexican Americans lived and worked across the labor networks of North America. It is this vast network of large cities, and small towns linked by kith and kin networks that I refer to when I speak of the Mexican American 'diaspora.' Mexican Americans in places like Oregon, Minnesota, and Michigan are part of social networks with origins in California, Texas, and for more recent immigrants the small towns and large cities of Mexico.

88 For more on the farm workers see Chapter 1.

89 On Milwaukee's many social movements in the 1960s, see Mark Edward Braun, *Social Change and the Empowerment of the Poor: Poverty Representation in Milwaukee's Community Action Programs, 1964–1972* (Lanham: Lexington Books, 2001); Jack Dougherty, *More Than One Struggle: The Evolution of Black School Reform in Milwaukee* (Chapel Hill: University of North Carolina Press, 2004); Avelardo Valdez, 'Selective Determinants in Maintaining Social Movement Organizations: Three Case Studies from the Chicano Community,' in *Latinos and the Political System*, ed. F. Chris Garcia (Notre Dame: University of Notre Dame Press, 1988), 236–54.

90 See Joseph A. Rodriguez, 'Latinos at UWM: A History of the Spanish-Speaking Outreach Institute and the Roberto Hernandez Center' (unpublished paper, 2005), retrieved from: https://pantherfile.uwm.edu/joerod/www/ssoi.html.

91 See John Gurda, 'The Latin Community on Milwaukee's Near South Side' (Milwaukee: Milwaukee Urban Observatory, University of Wisconsin-Milwaukee, 1976).

92 City- and county-based OEO agencies had to contend with the control of city- and county-elected officials, yet state-level agencies, such as UMOS, faced oversight from the governor, and in Wisconsin this enabled them much more freedom from political control by local elected officials.

93 See Marc S. Rodriguez, 'Defining the Space of Participation in a Northern City: Tejanos and the War on Poverty in Milwaukee,' in *The War on Poverty: A New Grassroots History, 1964–1980*, ed. Annelise Orkeck and Lisa Gayle Hazirjian (Athens: University of Georgia Press, 2011), 110–30.

94 See J.D. Greenstone and Paul E. Peterson, *Race and Authority in Urban Politics: Community Participation and the War on Poverty* (Chicago: University of Chicago Press, 1976), 19–24.

95 On activism in Texas and Wisconsin, see Marc S. Rodriguez, *The Tejano Diaspora: Mexican Americanism and Ethnic Politics in Texas and Wisconsin* (Chapel Hill: University of North Carolina Press, 2011); Avelardo Valdez, 'Selective Determinants,' 241–2.

96 See José Á. Gutiérrez, *The Making of a Chicano Militant: Lessons from Cristal* [sic] (Madison: University of Wisconsin Press, 1998), 177–92; Jason Mellard, *Progressive Country: How the 1970s Transformed the Texan in Popular Culture* (Austin: University of Texas Press, 2013), 106–8. Willie Velásquez, a MAYO founder and a former lieutenant of San Antonio Congressman Henry B. Gonzalez, decided that voter education and voter registration within the system was the most productive path forward for Chicanos. He founded the Southwest Voter Registration Education Project (SVREP) in 1974 to work exclusively on this project.

97 For an account of the walkouts based on hours of interviews with Severita Lara and other student activists, see José Á. Gutiérrez, *We Won't Back Down: Severita Lara's Rise from Student Leader to Mayor* (Houston: Piñata Books, 2005).

98 García, *United We Win*, 114–15; Rodriguez, *Tejano Diaspora*, 145–9.

99 Armando Navarro, *La Raza Unida Party: A Chicano Challenge to the U.S. Two-Party Dictatorship* (Philadelphia: Temple University Press, 2000), 41–58; Jack Bass and Walter DeVries, *The Transformation of Southern Politics: Social Change and Political Consequences since 1945* (Athens: University of Georgia Press, 1995), 329–31.

3

YOUTH AND THE CAMPUS

Chicano Students and Chicano Education

Introduction

The push for Chicano Studies and Chicano student inclusion on university campuses began in California at a historic meeting in Santa Barbara yet was a percolating movement nationwide among Chicano youth activists. While it is true that the meeting at Santa Barbara was the genesis for much of the thinking that would guide the Chicano Studies component of the Chicano Movement, the trend toward university activism was taking place nationwide and grew out of the same desire among Mexican American college students for a place within the campus—a move deeply influenced by the push for Black Studies on many college campuses across the United States. *El Plan de Santa Bárbara* (PDSB) was both a radical statement and a call for reforms within the university, meant to open it to Chicano students and connect the university to the community.[1] This sense that Chicano Studies needed to engage in action research and pedagogy for both the advancement of the individual and the community was a driving force in the national movement for Chicano Studies departments and, depending on the region, Latino or Latin American Studies departments that would include the histories of Puerto Rican and other US Latino groups.[2] The student activists used protests, sit-ins, and campus mobilization to press for the expansion of the curriculum, and often did so in partnership with other minority and New Left student groups.[3]

This chapter shifts our focus to college campuses to demonstrate the transfer of activism between community and campus. As Chicano high school students across the nation walked out, protesting an educational system that failed to account for their needs, many of these students continued their activism on college campuses. At colleges and universities in California, Texas, and elsewhere, Chicano students established organizations and demanded that universities create Chicano Studies departments and open admissions to minority and non-traditional students at even the most prestigious universities. They also called for the hiring and retention of Chicano and Chicana faculty with students playing a role in hiring decisions. This push for affirmative action for Chicano students, faculty, and the establishment of Chicano Studies programs and departments was part of a larger effort to democratize and open the university in the 1960s. For Chicano activists, these efforts meant to establish mini-Aztláns (homelands) on college campuses and provide greater opportunities for an increasingly self-aware racial minority's college-bound and college-educated elite.

This chapter examines the rise of Chicano student activism as part of the larger effort to institutionalize the movement on college campuses. First, it explores the founding of the student organization Movimiento Estudiantial Chicano de Aztlán (MEChA) in 1968 out of older established Mexican American student groups in California. MEChA and MEChA-affiliated groups led the push for Chicano student representation, affirmative action, and Chicano faculty recruitment and retention efforts in the Golden State. Second, the chapter considers the development of the PDSB's role in providing a template for Chicano Studies programs, campus–*barrio* relations, and Chicano recruitment campus wide. Third, the chapter explores Chicano activism in California, Texas, Washington, Indiana, and Wisconsin to consider the similarities and differences in the efforts to institutionalize Chicano Studies and retention (lowering dropout rates among Chicano students). The chapter also explores the creation and development of stand-alone Chicano colleges and the link between student activism and community organizations in Arizona, and it concludes with a consideration of Chicano Studies as a campus-based discipline.

Movimiento Estudiantil Chicano de Aztlán (MEChA) Takes Shape

As Mexican American college students in California gained experience in the educational protest movement locally and the Chicano Movement nationally, they sought to establish new student organizations committed to the evolving principles of the movement. Within this context members of the United Mexican American Students (UMAS) and others met at the University of California, Santa Barbara, in April of 1969 to establish a student organization committed to the principles of the Chicano Movement. This meeting in the seaside campus town of Santa Barbara led to the production of a detailed action plan for the creation of a new student organization with a commitment to community work and to the institutionalization of Chicano Studies within the university curriculum. Although UMAS was essentially a California and West Coast organization, it sought to bring together all Chicano student organizations into a loose confederation.

The organization they founded, MEChA, embraced Chicano nationalism, the concept of Aztlán as homeland, a commitment to educational advancement for Mexican American students, and the creation of campus-based homelands within the system of colleges and universities in California. While radical in tone and rhetoric, the student movement represented a vanguard of talented upwardly mobile Mexican Americans from communities where very few graduated from high school. These college students represented the educational elite of their communities, and they were aware of this reality. Their conversion of self-identity from 'Mexican American' to 'Chicano' reflected their youth and their militant fervor and played a large role in their construction of a Chicano Studies and Chicano student outlook.

From Mexican American to Chicano

MEChA took the big leap of rebranding itself and doing away with the UMAS moniker for political reasons. After interactions at the National Youth and Liberation Conference organized by Rodolfo 'Corky' Gonzales, UMAS members returned to California intent on putting that meeting's manifesto, *El Plan Espiritual de Aztlán*, into effect. These college students sought to engage in nation-building as they embraced the process of becoming Chicanos. The small group that participated in this first Denver meeting was a mix of acculturated college students, street youth, and older leaders like Gonzales. This unique mix of street and academia would define the Chicano Movement's aesthetic and style for much of its life. *El Plan Espiritual* reflected this in its effort to create space for the acculturated Mexican American to discover and refashion him or herself as a Chicano. Thus, aware of the space between the upwardly mobile acculturated Mexican Americans of California and the street youth of Denver, *El Plan Espiritual* created a space for both to reaffirm shared ties of community and work together for a new society. There were limitations of course. The plan neglected the role of women, as was true in many New Left and minority rights movements of the era. In Denver, organizers rejected women's calls for space within the movement in favor of unity. This move allowed sexism to continue even as women became increasingly active as leaders and participants. *El Plan Espiritual* and its goals would define the movement and its commitment to throw off the identification with a Mexican American 'hyphenated' self and substitute for it a new self as Chicanos and Chicanas.[4]

For Mexican Americans in the process of becoming Chicano, establishing the organization as MEChA was an important way to link to the mythic past and make a statement in the present. For its founders this was not to be a student group like others; it was a 'Movimiento' and part of the movement for Chicano rights taking place on and off campus, yet it was also a campus group focused on issues of student life. It was important to the founders and later members that MEChA was a 'Chicano' group. There was something different about being a self-identified Chicano. The term itself was a declaration of pride, a rejection of assimilation and moderate politics and an embrace of cultural nationalism in America—and on the campuses where MEChA sought to establish Aztláns. The members of MEChA 'committed themselves to return to the *barrios*, colonias, or campos and struggle against the forces that oppress our gente.'[5] The embrace of the concept of Aztlán made a direct connection to the indigenous ancestry shared by the majority of Chicanos in the United States. By claiming indigenous status, they were tying themselves to a long native history of which, as Chicanos, they were a part.

El Plan De Santa Bárbara (PDSB): A Chicano Plan for Higher Education

Those who gathered in Santa Barbara in the spring of 1969 saw their work as representing a conscious break with the past. The 'Manifesto' portion of the 155-page document spelled out the basic concepts that would drive Chicano student activism. This work was, for the founding activists, part of a *renacimiento* (renaissance) and creation story for Chicanos in higher education. A 'new consciousness' had bred in the students and academics present a desire to 'move forward toward our destiny as a people,' 'tempered by the lessons of the American past.' The document goes further in making its case—much as 'Yo Soy Joaquín' did—for a subaltern male worldview by arguing that Chicanismo is a reflection of and a reaction to the 'racist structure of society' and that a growing ethnic solidarity will pave the way for a 'new cultural identity for our people.'[6]

Affirmative Action and Cultural Nationalism

While steeped in cultural nationalism, the PDSB continued a quasi-acculturationist stance in relation to the institutions of American higher education. The student activists and faculty mentors gathered at Santa Barbara did not see their project as acculturationist (the PDSB has often been considered anti-assimilationist). Nevertheless, context is important: they held their meeting at a bucolic oceanfront University of California campus dedicated to research, rather than a teaching college, a community college, or a *barrio* church meeting room. This tension may account for the degree to which the PDSB tied individual upward mobility to a commitment to serve the people of the *barrio*. In this view, a university education was not a means of escape for Chicano students, but rather a binding commitment on the part of MEChA members to *barrio* uplift. This 'strategic use of education' permeates the document.[7] Creating a Chicano space on campus was central to this hybrid pedagogy of action education, scholarship, and community participation in the academic universe. To this end, the plan called for:

1. admission and recruitment of Chicano students, faculty, administrators, and staff;
2. a curriculum program and an academic major relevant to the Chicano cultural and historical experience;

3. support and tutorial programs;
4. research programs;
5. publications programs;
6. community cultural and social action centers.[8]

These demands can be broken down into three parts—affirmative action, program and scholarly development, and community action—which paralleled several federal legislative efforts emanating from the Economic Opportunity Act of 1964, Higher Education Act of 1965, and Higher Education Amendments of 1968, and foreshadowed the Higher Education Amendments of 1972. In the mid to late 1960s there was growing concern with creating opportunity for low-income, first-generation, and minority college students, and as a result the federal government in incremental fashion addressed the problem in response to community demands and a growing sense that pathways to college and technical college education were needed for low-income and minority students nationwide.[9] The creation of Chicano Studies departments and support for faculty recruitment, research, and publication support fit within the Chicano worldview as key to the success of programs for affirmative action in education.

What is striking about the PDSB is that it focuses on institutionalization while rejecting the traditional notion of university hierarchy. In many ways, it reads like a plan for a department. Yet at each step, the plan reminds the reader, and perhaps the Chicano student and graduate student population writing it, that the writers are radical and seek to build departments that link the community to the university and create space for a voice for their people. However, they remind themselves throughout their effort that they are no longer 'Mexican American,' and that they are now 'Chicanos' intent on becoming a people and utilizing the university—itself an acculturationist institution—for the liberation of a people. The PDSB acknowledges the potential for activism among the Chicano educational elite but also the very real issue of alienation.[10]

College Students and the *Barrio*

One primary focus of the PDSB is maintaining a commitment to linking the campus to the *barrio*. Thus, MEChA sought to establish a 'feeling of familia' among fellow 'Chicano brothers' within the group to develop a level of 'loyalty and support' that can be 'relied upon when a crisis faces the group or community.'[11] The PDSB's authors considered 'being in the *Barrio* as often as possible' the best way to avoid alienation on campus and felt it the 'best educational device' for Chicano students.[12] The authors also directly addressed the possibility of tensions arising between *barrio* residents and college students seeking to help the less fortunate. In order to avoid creating a sense of 'mistrust and even envy' among *barrio* residents, the MEChA students were instructed to prove themselves to residents, and that if it was 'merely a cathartic experience to work among the unfortunate in the *Barrio*' they should 'stay out!'[13] MEChA established a set of guidelines for *barrio* participation that focused on monitoring 'social and governmental agencies' and the police department to ensure responsiveness to the *barrio*. MEChA was also to help *barrio* residents with consumer protection issues, promote higher education in the schools, serve as the mouthpiece for the Movement, and expose discrimination. MEChA students were to work with *barrio* organizations and consider such work 'an honor' and 'a right.'[14] MEChA saw its engagement with the community as more than what might be termed service learning but, rather, playing a part in the long struggle for Chicano liberation.

A Model for Chicano Studies Programs

The PDSB lays out the basis for the creation of departments, programs, research institutes, and a curriculum that is strikingly similar to standard departmental models—although the topic is Chicanos. The authors of the plan were 'in-between' in many ways, as individuals and as a 'people.' The tension and contradictions between a plan for upward mobility and one focused on revolution are apparent. These Chicano college students may have seemed sophomoric in many ways when it came to statements about revolution, but they understood the very real problems faced by the majority of Mexican American students who lacked the basic study skills for college success. The PDSB expressed a fear of alienation among the students and faculty recruited to academic posts and reveals a fixation on the faculty maintaining a commitment to Chicano nationalism rather than mere individual advancement. The authors consider the university as a powerful social and economic institution that can help to produce Chicano leaders, intellectuals, and the space for students to do the work MEChA hopes to accomplish. This Chicano nation required research to develop the 'historical consciousness which Chicanos must possess in order successfully to struggle as a people toward a new vision of Aztlán.'[15] The education of Chicanos was central to the Movement's goals. The university had the potential for the development of a 'new Chicano political sector' as a vanguard for political activity in the *barrio*. There is an acknowledgement that this Chicano student cohort was an elite group because their education, training, and skill set 'far exceeds that of almost all other Chicanos.'[16]

Giving Back

The PDSB also detailed a practical model for the retention of disadvantaged Chicano students. Committed to increasing opportunity for disadvantaged Mexican Americans, the authors expressed a deep understanding of the problems minority students faced when it came to university admission and retention. Emphasized explicitly is the notion of a specific effort to provide Chicano students with student services to overcome common skill deficits. The plan focused on the creation of orientation, training, and tutoring programs in the areas of English composition, study skills, and many of the things that Chicanos' substandard high schools failed to provide them. The PDSB understood that low-income students often attended substandard high schools that, while they may have given graduates diplomas, certainly did not train them for college, or even community college attendance. In many ways, this is one of the most radical components of the document, even with the various programs for minority recruitment and retention available or under consideration at this time. Certainly the plan echoes federal and state Educational Opportunity Programs (EOPs) of the era, and foreshadows many Affirmative Action programs developed in the 1970s such as the 'Philadelphia Plan' established by the Nixon Administration, but the understanding of the issue is an original one rooted in a real understanding of the difficulties faced by Chicano students.[17]

MEChA was a cultural nationalist organization. With the motto 'Por La Raza Todo … Fuera De La Raza Nada' (within the people, everything; outside of it, nothing) new members who joined the student organization linked cultural nationalism and MEChA directly.[18] The language of the documents and reports at the time of MEChA's founding express a desire among participants to both learn of their own history and culture and express them within the new Chicano culture they are making. While the language of the documents incorporates irredentist and separatist language (claims to the US Southwest as a Chicano homeland), much of the plan of action identified at Santa Barbara is focused on participation within the system and using this exposure to a university education to benefit the community.[19]

One central element is the Chicano student's role in his or her own community. MEChA students, who demanded that Chicanos embrace an ethic of community service, rejected the connection between university education and selfish upward mobility. College and university education should serve the Mexican American community and the *barrio*. This notion of the *barrio* as a homeland challenged the narrative of upward mobility and the 'American Dream.' While some of this may seem naive today, the worry was that educated Chicanos (much like educated African Americans and white ethnics) tended to leave the neighborhoods they grew up in as soon as they could. This economic and intellectual flight injured the *barrio* community by depriving it of the best and brightest. Yet, these were university students and they demanded professionalization. They sought to establish a curriculum, a major, and areas of Chicano expertise within the academy: an institution that focused on career and topically based majors. One wonders how many of these Chicanos followed the plan outlined at Santa Barbara and how many engaged in individual economic mobility and maintained a Chicano outlook. California, after all, was an open society compared to South Texas, and Mexican Americans experienced high rates of geographic and intergenerational economic mobility as well as high rates of intermarriage with non-Chicanos.

Despite the many contradictory social realities in California at the end of the 1960s, the ethic of community service and community maintenance were central to the MEChA plan. *El Plan de Santa Bárbara* became the template for MEChA and for Chicano Studies programs, centers, and institutes nationwide.[20]

Practical Radicalism

A review of MEChA's publications in the period after its founding reveals a complex relationship with the issues of the era. While cultural nationalism, service, and affirmative action remain important topics in these publications, the anti-middle class/mobility rhetoric is mainly hyperbolic, whereas in the main, authors are quite attentive to gender and cultural issues. There are few attacks on the Mexican American community for failing to adopt a Chicano outlook. Also scarce are calls for the 'Mestizo Nation' outlined by radicals.[21] Most organizations focused on student issues and practical community service. Articles discussed the place of Chicanos within the university and demonstrated a real commitment to serving the Chicano communities near campus as volunteers.[22] MEChA publications provide many examples of real soul-searching on the part of young Chicanos and Chicanas on university campuses and philosophical considerations of Chicano identity. Thus MEChA publications offer glimpses into the tensions between the American Dream and Chicanos' view of themselves as a minority bicultural student population resisting assimilation yet seeking educational advancement and professional development. MEChA newsletters also explored the problems of educational preparation for Chicanos, with an eye to higher rates of college and university matriculation.[23] One interesting issue explored in some California MEChA publications dealing with women in the MEChA community is the amount of space dedicated to the perceived problem of intermarriage with Anglos, with one report noting, '40% of all Chicano marriages in Los Angeles county were intermarriages' and worrying that such marriages led to the weakening of the culture.[24] There is also ample critique of machismo and macho attitudes among Chicano men within the group.[25] The Chicano college students and graduate students who helped shape the PDSB were attending university for many reasons, but despite the radical rhetoric of the document many MEChA activists from this period became legal, academic, and political leaders—often the goals of the upwardly mobile—and embraced a Chicano version of the American Dream that was tied to community service and the provision of opportunities for others to follow in their footsteps.[26]

California and the Movement for Chicano Studies

The PDSB set out an agenda for Chicano Studies and specific curricular demands that served as a template for Chicano Studies programs across the Golden State even as activists softened some of the more radical rhetoric in later efforts. From San Diego to the megalopolis of Los Angeles and north to the Bay Area, students and Chicano faculty mobilized for Chicano Studies on campus. The push for Chicano or Raza Studies programs and departments had already begun by the late 1960s and some, such as San Fernando Valley State College (now California State University, Northridge), were set to begin teaching in September 1969. Others in attendance at the meeting at the University of California, Santa Barbara, would become important mentors training a generation of Chicano graduate students in California. Thus, the documents prepared at the PDSB meeting did in fact constitute a template that with some revision would become concrete proposals later. Juan Gómez-Quiñones of UCLA and Jesus Chavarria of UCSB were, according to one historian, the 'major personas' who had links to most of the graduate students present. For some leaders it appeared that the PDSB was in fact a very real template for program development.[27]

The colleges and universities where MEChA and Chicano activist academics planned to develop Chicano Studies programs varied in size and academic setting. They included UCLA, UCSB, and UC-Berkeley, the flagship of the University of California's research university system, as well as the then state colleges (now State University System) and urban community colleges. The task of creating a program required the input of committed current faculty and students, and this core group was available at many of the colleges and universities in California. While Chicano enrollments were low, there was often a commitment from the small number of faculty and graduate students to make Chicano Studies a reality. A central issue in the development of Chicano Studies at campuses nationwide was the lack of trained Chicano faculty that could meet the standards of promotion and tenure at research and teaching universities. In the late 1960s and early 1970s, universities hired Chicano graduate students as specialists, instructors, and directors even though they had not completed their doctoral studies. While many of those hired would complete doctoral dissertations and prepare themselves to meet the burden of publication and tenure, some never did so. From the start Chicano Studies, as well as Black Studies and Third World or Ethnic Studies more generally, suffered from an impression that the staff and faculty did not have traditional academic backgrounds and that these programs were outreach or service oriented and not valid academic programs.[28]

Bay Area Activism

In the Bay Area, San Francisco State College (SFSC) students took the lead in the push for Ethnic Studies and Chicano Studies in Northern California. In 1968, students at SFSC had established the Third World Liberation Front (TWLF) to push for the admission of more minority students and the creation of a Third World College to house a Raza Studies Department, among other minority-group-focused departments. In 1960, the state of California established a master plan that set percentage quotas for admission based on one's place in the high school graduating class, which negatively affected minority student admissions. The TWLF protested this restrictive policy and pressed for a Third World College. In the TWLF, Chicanos joined Filipinos, African Americans, and others in the effort to push for an open admissions policy and create what might today be termed Ethnic Studies. The students engaged in a strike movement that trained many of them in the production of posters, leaflets, mass meetings, sit-ins, and other demonstrations of massive resistance that led to many arrests. The strike succeeded in bringing about better minority recruitment and admissions policies and the 1969 creation of an Ethnic Studies Department that housed Black and Raza Studies.[29] This strike wave spread to the campus of the University of California, Berkeley, where similar protests took place, giving rise to the development of an interracial interethnic movement for Ethnic Studies at California's flagship state university. This was a dynamic time to be in the Bay Area, and students might have spent more time working on the UFW grape strike, the Third World strike, and activism than in the classroom.[30]

At the University of California, Berkeley, where activist students emulated their peers at SFSC, a Third World strike began in 1969 with many of the same goals. The Berkeley TWLF protests began in January 1969 and demanded the creation of a Third World college, the recruitment of Third World faculty and students (minorities), and close ties to minority communities. The activists settled for an Ethnic Studies department. Ethnic Studies was, however, a successful effort at UC Berkeley, and the department expanded and flourished compared to most program efforts. MEChA students felt that vigilance was required and were aware of the constant need to 'wake up and renew the revolutionary goals which founded the Ethnic Studies department' and 'serve students, faculty, and the community.'[31] At Stanford, there were fewer Chicano students, yet the Mexican American group on campus became a MEChA organization in 1969 and began the push for a Chicano-themed dormitory, a research library, and a fellowship program to recruit faculty. It would take longer for Stanford to institutionalize Chicano student services and a Chicano Studies program, but Stanford hosted many important MEChA events and its students and graduates became leaders in the field of Chicano education, history, and other related disciplines.[32]

Southern California Activism

In Southern California, a similar pattern emerged, with community and state colleges as well as the research units of the UC system developing programs and departments after student protest. At UCLA Chicano Studies emerged out of nontraditional models in the period between 1968 and 1973, with Chicano Studies functioning as a research center and home to *Aztlán*, the leading journal of Chicano Studies, and the National Association of Chicano Social Scientists (later to become the National Association for Chicana and Chicano Studies), in part due to the influence of Juan Gómez-Quiñones and his graduate students in history. It would take nearly two decades for a campus whose students and faculty had been central to the call for Chicano Studies to establish a department.[33] At California State University, Los Angeles, another center of student activism, the university established Chicano Studies as a service unit led by graduate students and nontraditional academics. This model, which became quite common, met some of the goals of MEChA by creating a space for the recruitment and retention of Chicano students, but it delayed the incorporation of Chicano faculty into the traditional academic ranks. At San Diego State, the post-PDSB movement and MEChA involvement led to quasi-departmental status and a mixed model that answered the call of the PDSB by offering a curriculum, courses taught by many temporary faculty members (some of whom would go on to become leaders in the field), student participation, and community-based programs; yet management remained in the hands of graduate student administrators well into the 1970s.[34] UC-San Diego followed a model similar to the Third World demands in the Bay Area. Students in the organization that became MEChA and the Black Student Union (BSU) worked together to create Lumumba-Zapata College to replace the proposed Third College at UCSD. The idea of naming it for Congolese independence leader Patrice Lumumba and Mexican revolutionary Emiliano Zapata expressed a commitment to liberation and to cooperation between African American and Mexican American students at this seaside UC campus. The curriculum was radically different from others, featuring training in revolutionary praxis, and the goals of student recruitment were to reflect a need for greater acceptance of African American and Mexican American students.[35] Opened in 1970, Third College (Lumumba-Zapata College) floundered before it was stripped of its radical commitments. Third World Studies became a program along with Chicano Studies and African American Studies as minor fields in the general college system.[36]

Other colleges and universities in California underwent MEChA-led protest movements that followed the PDSB call for a greater Chicano campus presence. At Fresno State College Chicanos demanded Raza Studies as part of an Ethnic Studies Department. These efforts followed protest demands from students for a Raza Studies program to teach Chicano history and culture, work as a space for organization, and encourage ethnic pride.[37] These demands were echoed at Loyola Marymount in Los Angeles, where the university president spoke openly of a commitment to minority recruitment and diversity, yet MEChA students still demanded expansion of efforts to recruit and retain Chicano students and faculty at this leading Catholic university. Despite the creation of a Chicano Studies department and a Chicano leadership grant program, MEChA feared that these programs needed more academic permanency.[38]

As California colleges and universities became the leading centers for Chicano Studies in the nation, producing an entire generation of scholars at UCLA (and later Stanford) and many more undergraduate minors and majors, the partial institutionalization of Chicano Studies in the Golden State became a model for the nation. While those who met at Santa Barbara in 1969 to draft the PDSB played leading roles in the development of a discipline, they mainly did so within the confines of traditional departments and academic disciplines, except for the small number trained in Ethnic Studies departments offering doctoral degrees. On the student services and outreach front, schools increasingly responded to the demands of students for greater recruitment and retention efforts for Mexican American students and the creation of often short-lived community-based units. Overall, it was, perhaps, the vast population of relatively acculturated Mexican Americans and the middle class within this community that led to the demographic expansion of Mexican American students across disciplines and in the graduate programs from San Diego to the Bay Area. California's large acculturated Mexican American population, perhaps central to the continued expansion of Chicano Studies, still awaits its historian.

Texas and the Movement for Chicano Studies

Texas was the second-largest population center for Mexican Americans in the late 1960s, and perhaps the state with the longest and largest settled population of Spanish speakers, Chicano Studies, or Mexican American Studies as it continued to be called, followed a pattern of institutional development similar to that of California's. At the University of Texas, Austin (UT), student protests and faculty demands led to the university establishment of a center for Mexican American studies. Austin was, like Berkeley, California, and Madison, Wisconsin, a center of New Left, the antiwar movement, and student protest, and Texas was by 1969 the center of a Mexican American activist movement led by the Mexican American Youth Organization (MAYO) and later La Raza Unida Party (RUP). At UT, students organized together with the support of key faculty member Américo Paredes and a cadre of graduate students that included José Limón. Student protestors, graduate students, and key faculty worked together to create and implement a model for Mexican American studies (Chicano self-identification never really gained traction in Texas), which resulted in the founding of the Center for Mexican American Studies at UT-Austin in 1970. It is worth mentioning the cross-pollination between California and Texas, as a generation of academics trained during this early period of disciplinary development often spent time as postdoctoral scholars, instructors, and later faculty members at Texas and California institutions, where they learned from more established scholars such as Paredes, the author of seminal works on Tejano resistance, history, and folklore.[39] At the University of Texas, El Paso, students organized and worked with faculty to develop a curriculum for Mexican American studies in 1970 and, after failed negotiations and a sit-in at the administration building in 1971, they won. The sit-in and takeover that followed forced the university to respond and led to the creation of a Chicano Studies program under the direction of an instructor and later a department. Student protests would continue at UTEP as MEChA pressured the university to provide more courses and stability in the department for much of the 1970s.[40] At Our Lady of the Lake College (OLL), MEChA students protested discrimination at this Catholic college due to its lack of significant Chicano faculty and trustee positions, despite the facts that OLL had a student body that was over 60 percent Chicano and that the administration had made promises to diversify the campus in 1971.[41] In the spring of 1973, Chicano, African American, and Anglo OLL students prepared a list of demands for greater diversity, student services, and closer ties to San Antonio's Chicano community. Students and community activists picketed the administration building with support from La Raza Unida Party gubernatorial candidate Ramsey Muniz.[42] OLL faculty voted for the dismissal of the campus's only Chicano dean, and nuns allegedly threatened reporters asking for information about the racial climate on campus.[43] Similar protest movements led to the creation of Mexican American and Chicano Studies programs across the Lone Star State, most of which faced the same struggles for legitimacy and funding and confronted the tensions of a program of study that sought academic acceptance, a role for student participation, and a commitment to community action.

Wisconsin, Washington State, and the Movement for Chicano Studies

The University of Wisconsin, Madison (UW), was a central space for the development of the New Left and antiwar movements of the 1960s. The university at both its Madison and Milwaukee campuses was also home to active movements for Chicano and Latin American Studies programs, led by Mexican American and Puerto Rican activists. While UW had an active place in the history of the 1960s, the effort for Chicano Studies at UW followed the movement for Chicano and Latino studies at the University of Wisconsin, Milwaukee (UWM), which began in 1969 and led to dramatic sit-ins led by Tejano labor leaders, students, and the local Brown Berets. At UWM, members of local activist organizations, the Brown Berets, and the Latin American Union for Civil Rights (LAUCR) established the Latin American Education Committee (CELA) to push for greater opportunities and a Latino Studies curriculum at UWM. Rooted in the Mexican American and Puerto Rican communities of Milwaukee, the effort brought together activists from a variety of US Latino communities into an organization that, while it adopted the Latin American name, focused on Latino student recruitment, retention, hiring, and the development of a Latino Studies program. In the summer of

1970, UWM's small Chicano and Latino student group, led by community-based activists (many of whom were also students), staged a series of protests at the UWM campus. Protesters attempted to register for classes speaking only Spanish and eventually staged massive sit-ins at the chancellor's office, a post held by historian and proponent of the urban university model Martin Klotsche. Between August and October of 1970, CELA students camped out on the campus and occupied the chancellor's office where campus police arrested several. To end the sit-in and bring peace to a campus now occupied by protesters, Chancellor Klotsche proposed the establishment of a Spanish-Speaking Outreach Institute (SSOI) on campus and a satellite center in the heart of the city's *barrio*. Thus, through protracted negotiation with the chancellor and drawing on academic, student, and community synergy, the CETA activists won. But what did they win? They won a community-based center that did not survive the 1970s, and they won a student-oriented outreach institute that played a role in the EOP and the recruitment and retention of Latino students from the Mexican American and Puerto Rican communities. However, UWM would fail to establish a Chicano/Latino Studies program or recruit many Chicano or Puerto Rican faculty, even as the Latino student population grew.[44]

At the UW campus, student activists began calls for a Chicano Studies department in 1970, also echoing the PDSB's call for the hiring of faculty, the recruitment of students, and a community-connected program. Advocates for Chicano Studies faced strong opposition from the flagship campus at Madison, which rejected the concept of Chicano Studies outright. The effort to establish a Chicano Studies department continued, with Chicano activists seeking to include the creation of the department in the funding for the University of Wisconsin system at the state budget level. This led to the inclusion of a Chicano Studies department in the budget, but Chicano Studies soon devolved into a service-based unit within an Ethnic Studies program directed by former MAYO and RUP activist Mario Compean and a revolving group of young Chicano academics who often served as lecturers.[45] At the much smaller University of Wisconsin, Whitewater, where the history of activism was much more muted, Chicano Studies courses were taught across a wide variety of departments, with one scholar claiming that Whitewater had the 'broadest range of Chicano Studies course offerings in the region' in the 1980s.[46]

Washington State was part of the vast system of migratory labor for Texas-based farm workers due to large agricultural areas in Eastern Washington centered at Yakima and the Tri-Cities region. This meant that Washington had among its population both the descendants of settled Mexican contract workers (Braceros) and settled farm workers from Texas and California. This reality placed the advocates for Chicano Studies in Washington within an active milieu of influences that tied the Pacific Northwest movement to California, Texas, and the other locations to which farm workers traveled for work—giving them many traditions to build on. Students at the University of Washington began to push for greater diversity, led by the Black Student Union (BSU). In ways similar to the cooperative activist model at UCSD where African Americans and Mexican Americans worked together, the BSU spearheaded the call for greater African American and Mexican American student recruitment and retention at the University of Washington in Seattle (UWS). Students and former migrants in Eastern Washington gained experience through exposure to the work of the California-based United Farm Workers Organizing Committee (UFWOC) in the state and established the United Farm Workers Cooperative (UFWC). Already home to a United Mexican American Students (UMAS) chapter, UWS's Chicano Students adopted the MEChA moniker in 1969. MEChA and the Brown Berets soon had recruits both at UWS and at the smaller colleges and universities in Eastern Washington, holding conferences and pushing for the development of Chicano Studies and the hiring of Chicano faculty statewide. Adopting an approach that accepted both the community and campus aspects of MEChA's founding documents, students led sit-ins to establish a community center, El Centro de La Raza, in an abandoned school district building in 1973. Between 1972 and 1974 MEChA led a series of meetings and later, throughout the 1970s, a series of sit-ins at administrative offices at the UWS campus to press for the hiring of Chicano faculty and the expansion of affirmative action. It would take decades before UWS established an Ethnic Studies program, and the university would always face student protest over the lack of affirmative action.[47]

The Washington and Wisconsin cases were similar in that the universities, whether flagship or regional campus, often rejected the idea of an academic department or program in favor of outreach models for student recruitment. Rather than accepting the idea of Chicano Studies or Latino Studies, these campuses tended to react to student protests demanding the establishment of a curriculum and the creation of departments and programs with support for greater Chicano student recruitment and retention as well as greater efforts toward community outreach. This reaction on the part of these two prominent state universities accepted the need for greater campus diversity, yet sidestepped the need for curricular change and the development of a faculty committed to the study of Chicanos or Latinos. This strategy of answering the multi-issue protests of students with student centers and recruitment efforts was echoed at nearby campuses, including the University of Illinois, the University of Michigan, and to a lesser degree the University of Minnesota, where protests in the 1970s often yielded recruitment programs and the hiring of Chicano and Latino admissions and Educational Opportunity Program (EOP) staff but seldom led to the creation of stable programs or departments or faculty until the Ethnic Studies protests of the 1990s forced the issue.[48]

Julian Samora and Notre Dame

At the University of Notre Dame in Indiana, student protests and the committed activism of Julian Samora led to the development of one of the few doctorate-granting programs in Mexican American Studies in the United States. Julian Samora was born and raised in Southern Colorado, where he confronted racism on a daily basis and experienced the sting of discrimination throughout his educational career. This personal connection led to his sustained interest in Mexican American sociological research. Educated in the Midwest, Samora was always attentive to the long history of Mexican Americans in the Midwest and the Great Plains. Samora worked at Michigan State University before taking a post at the University of Notre Dame in 1959.[49] Samora and a small cadre of Chicano scholars formed the Southwest Council of La Raza (SCLR) in 1968 to serve as an advocacy group for Mexican Americans, which later evolved into the National Council of La Raza (NCLR).[50] In spring 1970 students from Michigan State and Notre Dame, as well as Brown Berets from Milwaukee and activists from Chicago and Detroit, attended the Midwest Conference of La Raza at Notre Dame. This event, which brought Ernesto Galarza, Jorge Bustamante, and Julian Samora together with members of La Raza Unida Party from Texas and students, served as a spark to activism in the Great Lakes and became a recruiting event for young scholars, including Bustamante, who sought to study with Samora.[51] MEChA pressed Notre Dame, a Catholic university that had educated children of immigrants for generations, to expand opportunity for Chicanos as part of its commitment to Catholic values.

During the conference, students formulated demands to broaden opportunities for Chicanos at Notre Dame. Led by Gilberto Cárdenas, a graduate student who had participated in the push for Chicano Studies at California State College, Los Angeles, students demanded that Notre Dame admit more Chicano students, create support programs for them, establish links between the campus and local Mexican American communities, and recruit Chicano faculty. Father Hesburgh, who prided himself on his participation in African American civil rights activities and was fond of an often circulated photograph showing him in locked arms with Martin Luther King, Jr. in Chicago, responded that he was not in disagreement but that the university had no funds for such a program. Cárdenas reminded Hesburgh of his recent comment that the 'status of the nation's six million Mexican-Americans is even worse than that of the twenty million blacks in the country' and wondered why Hesburgh, then serving as chairman of the US Civil Rights Commission, committed 90 percent of minority fellowships to African Americans (largely Protestant) and so little to Mexican Americans, the largest minority constituency among Catholics.[52]

In 1971, MEChA members continued their campaign to compel Notre Dame to treat the largest Spanish-speaking Catholic minority community in the United

States with dignity and answer the demands of the previous year. They called for increased admission of Mexican American students, greater training in the history of Mexican Americans, and support for students while attending college. MEChA also demanded a Chicano dormitory or off-campus Chicano house as well as a Chicano counselor, and claimed that the university's statement that it could do nothing to boost Chicano admission was false.[53] In 1971, MEChA put on a student-organized festival of La Raza Art, which included participation of leading Chicano artists from Chicago. The university did not support the event and in fact upset the students and invited artists with what MEChA considered discriminatory treatment. The art festival and the poor treatment by Notre Dame led some to wonder if Notre Dame was 'solely an "Irish-Catholic" institution' open only to the rich.[54] The protest movements at Notre Dame yielded little in the way of reform, yet Notre Dame published many of the seminal texts in Chicano Studies under the direction of Julian Samora, and the Mexican American Studies graduate program funded by the Ford Foundation trained a generation of Chicano scholars until Notre Dame dismantled the program in 1985 following Samora's retirement.[55] Despite its mixed record, the University of Notre Dame through its press and the efforts of Samora led to the publication of many important texts in the field of Chicano Studies.

The Chicano University Model

Activists in Texas who saw the university and college systems of the United States as committed to the preservation of the status quo met and decided to create Chicano universities and colleges in the 1970s in an effort to build a new model of higher education. In the first national MAYO conference in December 1969, MAYO activists, in addition to creating La Raza Unida Party (RUP), called for the establishment of Mexican American Studies. Several MAYO activists established Jacinto Treviño College in Mercedes, Texas, soon after the conference 'to develop a Chicano with conscience and skills, [to give] the *barrios* a global view, [and] to provide positive answers to racism, exploitation, and oppression' with support from Antioch College, based in Yellow Springs, Ohio.[56] Several board members and staffers soon left Jacinto Treviño College to establish the Juárez-Lincoln Center in Fort Worth in 1971, which relocated to Austin in 1972. Between 1972 and 1975 the school maintained offices at St. Edward's University, eventually moving into its own space and developing a separate relationship with Antioch and the establishment as a university offering bachelor's and master's degree programs. The school focused on bicultural and bilingual educational topics and supported connections to farm worker programs. In a 'university without walls,' students developed their own programs of study in consultation with Juárez-Lincoln University and Antioch faculty. Both Juárez-Lincoln University and Jacinto Treviño College were defunct by the late 1970s.[57]

A Native American and Chicano University

In California and Oregon, the same impulse led to the establishment of Chicano colleges and universities. In a merger of indigenous and Chicano activism, Native American protesters took control of abandoned US Army buildings in Yolo County, California, to establish Deganwidah Quetzalcoatl University (DQU) in 1971 to honor Deganwidah, the leader of the Iroquois Confederacy, and Aztec deity Quetzalcoatl. Part of the Native American college movement, this occupation led to the transfer of the land to the DQU and the establishment of a university with Native American orientation that also included Chicano Studies. The DQU functioned through the twenty-first century before losing accreditation in 2005.[58] A faltering Catholic women's college in Mount Angel, Oregon, lost accreditation in 1973 and became the site for Colegio Cesar Chavez (Cesar Chavez College) when two Mount Angel College employees suggested its reorganization as a Chicano-serving institution. The college functioned for a while as a university without walls and emphasized bilingual and bicultural training, before reverting to the Catholic Church in the 1980s.[59] For the most part the Chicano university model collapsed within a few years with only two examples of continued operation, yet by the twenty-first century Hispanic-Serving Institutions (HSIs) had expanded from the Southwest, Texas, and California to the Pacific Northwest, the East Coast, and the Midwest, as the number of colleges and universities serving at least 25 percent 'Hispanic' students grew annually.[60]

Taking It to the Community: Chicanos por La Causa in Arizona

In Arizona the student movement, while also seeking to establish Chicano Studies at Arizona colleges and universities, provides an example of a moderate form of Chicano civic action that linked campus and community in unique ways. At both the University of Arizona and Arizona State University, students established Mexican American organizations whose members, together with activists from the United Farm Workers Organizing Committee (UFWOC) in Arizona and *barrio* residents, established Chicanos por La Causa (CPLC), which linked labor, university, and community activists in South Phoenix. The Mexican American Student Organization (MASO) at Arizona State University and the Mexican American Student Association (MASA) at the University of Arizona grew because of individual students' links with the Chicano Movement and the farm labor movement based in California. MASO students in particular were involved in labor disputes, claims against university vendors accused of discrimination by workers, and the California grape boycott. Despite the practical radicalism of MASO, one leader said, 'I just couldn't relate completely to his [a founding member's] notion that Ho Chi Minh was a figure that we should emulate.'[61] By 1970, MASO had become a MEChA organization; it led the student push for Chicano Studies that highlighted ethnic pride, the 'reappropriation of Spanish,' and increasingly embraced the nationalist rhetoric of MEChA.[62] The MASO students who helped establish the CPLC created one of the longest-lasting community-based organizations in the Southwest focused on providing community programming and assistance. MEChA at Arizona State held further protests for Chicano faculty and student recruitment, led the drive to end employment discrimination, and continued the decades-long effort to establish Chicano Studies on the campus. At the University of Arizona, the MASA group split over the issue of radicalism. The more nationalist students formed the Chicano Liberation Committee (CLC) to press for Chicano Studies and Chicano recruitment and retention. They also built connections to the Chicano *barrio* in Tucson with the establishment of Chicano House, which played a significant role in Chicano activism as the home for El Rio Coalition (ERC). The coalition helped establish community centers, parks, and other resources for *barrio* residents and became a springboard for La Raza Unida Party in Arizona. CLC and successor organizations would press the issue of Chicano Studies at the flagship campus in Arizona for years to come.[63] The Arizona case reveals the ways in which Chicano student activism linked campus and community during a period of radicalism and yet yielded reformist results on the two largest campuses in Arizona and in the *barrios* of Tucson and Phoenix.

Conclusion: The Chicano Studies Model in a Latino World

The experiences of the Chicanos who led the push for a voice and space on campuses throughout the Southwest and Midwest were quite similar across regions. These young people represented an educated elite within a mainly working-class ethnic community in the United States. In a world shaped by the antiwar movement, Black Power, the women's liberation movement, and the New Left and Free Speech movements on American campuses, Chicano students borrowed tactics and ideological tropes from these parallel efforts as they mixed revolutionary ideology, Mexican folklore, and binational history to create a Chicano identity within the context of a movement dedicated to the opening of the American university. The demands for Third World, Ethnic, and Chicano Studies were part of a larger effort meant to provide opportunities to poor, minority, and first-generation students in the late 1960s and remedy the worst aspects of educational discrimination and exclusion in the United States. As the barriers to entry broke down for a small vanguard of minority students, these students in turn created organizations such as MEChA and related groups to press for greater inclusion of Chicanos on campuses across the nation. The advocacy for Chicano students on campus yielded real results, as the number of students from minority and disadvantaged backgrounds grew each decade following the push for change on college campuses in the late 1960s.

The movement for Chicano Studies and Chicano affirmative action on college campuses had mixed results. While it bore fruit in terms of the slow process of increasing admission and graduation rates for Chicano students nationwide and helped to increase campus diversity, the effort to establish Chicano Studies as an academic discipline faltered in many places. Chicano students attended more colleges, universities, technical schools, and professional programs across the country by the end of the twentieth century, but the percentages of minority students remained cause for serious concern in Texas, California, and other states with sizeable Chicano populations. Nevertheless, universities created support, admissions, and advising programs to assist Spanish-speaking and Latino students from New York to California and points in-between because of the activism of the Chicano movement's demands for bicultural programs and culturally sensitive staff on campus. While faculties diversified and California, Texas, and other states witnessed the advancement of many Mexican Americans to high positions as tenured faculty, deans, and presidents, the issue of graduate education for Chicanos and other minorities remained a concern, especially in the so-called STEM fields (Science, Technology, Engineering, and Mathematics) where women and minorities are still underrepresented compared to Education and the Humanities, where they have made significant inroads.

Chicano Studies departments have not fared well. While several departments, major programs, institutes, and research centers exist, universities have often incorporated these into Latin American, Ethnic Studies, and American Studies departments and programs, which may weaken their US Latino content and focus. This model has several strong graduate training examples, such as the American Studies programs at Yale and the Ethnic Studies Department at UC Berkeley, but many other programs struggle to survive in an increasingly efficiency- and profit-focused environment on many campuses. Chicano Studies programs were a major goal of the PDSB, and there are still few programs or departments nationwide. Yet, the number of graduate students and academics writing dissertations and books in fields that might be broadly termed 'Chicano' studies has grown over time, with much of this work completed in the traditional disciplines at prestigious colleges and universities. Therefore, while dedicated Chicano Studies programs and departments are few, Latino Studies is a growing field with stronger institutional representation each year, and the number of specialists has grown significantly in traditional departments. Scholars find a place within the National Association of Chicana and Chicano Studies (NACCS) as well as the mainstream professional associations, which have seen several Chicanos and Chicanas elected to presidential and other leadership positions within the dominant professional associations by the first decade of the twenty-first century. Chicano Studies as a field within traditional disciplines (rather than as a department-based program) is thriving in an academic world that increasingly looks to work that considers race, class, sexuality, and transnationalism as markers of rigor and quality. In this light, the push for Chicano Studies and Affirmative Action policies has succeeded in doing many of the things the framers of the PDSB sought to do even without the institutionalization of Chicano Studies departments at most universities.

Notes

1 For a narrative discussion of these events see Juan Gómez-Quiñones and Irene Vásquez, *Making Aztlán: Ideology and Culture of the Chicana and Chicano Movement, 1966–1977* (Albuquerque: University of New Mexico Press, 2014), 168-78.

2 By 'action research,' I refer to research 'leading to action' that is tied to specific improvement projects for the people of the Chicano community. See Kurt Lewin, 'Action Research and Minority Problems,' *Journal of Social Issues* 2, no. 4 (November 1946).

3 See Lee Bebout, *Mythohistorical Interventions: The Chicano Movement and Its Legacies* (Minneapolis: University of Minnesota Press, 2011), 62-8.

4 See Carlos Muñoz, *Youth, Identity, Power: The Chicano Movement* (New York: Verso Press, 1989), 78-81; Alicia Schmidt Camacho, *Migrant Imaginaries: Latino Cultural Politics in the U.S.–Mexico Borderlands* (New York: New York University Press, 2008), 166-76.

5 Quote taken from Movimiento Estudiantil Chicano de Aztlán, 'About Us,' retrieved from: www.nationalmecha.org/about.html.

6 All quotes from the Chicano Coordinating Council on Higher Education, *El Plan De Santa Bárbara: A Chicano Plan for Higher Education* (Santa Barbara: La Causa Publications, 1970), 9.

7 *El Plan De Santa Bárbara*, 9.

8 *El Plan De Santa Bárbara*, 10.

9 J. Herman Blake, 'Guest Editor's Comments: The Full Circle: TRIO Programs, Higher Education, and the American Future—Toward a New Vision of Democracy,' *Journal of Negro Education* 67, no. 4 (Autumn, 1998): 329–32. While focused on issues related to African American success and the Trio Program, the Autumn 1998 volume of the *Journal of Negro Education* is dedicated fully to the TRIP Programs and the articles section was titled 'The Full Circle: TRIO Programs, Higher Education, and the American Future.' See also Tara J. Yosso, Laurence Parker, Daniel G. Solórzano, and Marvin Lynn, 'From Jim Crow to Affirmative Action and Back Again: A Critical Race Discussion of Racialized Rationales and Access to Higher Education,' *Review of Research in Education* 28 (2004): 1–25.

10 See Bebout, *Mythohistorical Interventions*, 62-8.

11 Quoted in *El Plan De Santa Bárbara*, 55.

12 Quoted in *El Plan De Santa Bárbara*, 56.

13 Exclamation point in original. Quoted in *El Plan De Santa Bárbara*, 61.

14 Quoted in *El Plan De Santa Bárbara*, 61.

15 Quoted in *El Plan De Santa Bárbara*, 78.

16 Quoted in *El Plan De Santa Bárbara*, 79.

17 *El Plan De Santa Bárbara*, 79.

18 'El Plan Espiritual de Aztlán,' *Chicano Resource Journal & Service Handbook*, University of California, Berkeley (1972).

19 See *El Plan De Santa Bárbara*; Manuel G. Gonzales, *Mexicanos: A History of Mexicans in the United States* (Bloomington: Indiana University Press, 2009), 213-14.

20 See Javier Rangel, 'The Educational Legacy of El Plan de Santa Barbara: An Interview with Reynaldo Macias,' *Journal Of Latinos & Education* 6, no. 2 (April, 2007): 191-9.

21 Carlos Muñoz, 'UC Irvine Philosophy,' *El Mestizo* 1, no. 1, May, 1971 (Irvine).

22 Teresa Montoya, 'Sellouts and Bandits,' *Es Tiempo!* June 1972 (Los Altos Hills); 'MECHA Meeting,' *MECHA Newsletter* 1, no. 1, 1972 (Stanford).

23 Rudy Torres, 'Bi-Culturalism: Its Effect on the Personality of the Mexican American,' *Es Tiempo!* June 1972 (Los Altos Hills); 'Education and Culturally Different Children,' *El Griton*, June 1972 (Porterville); Rudy Torres, 'Teacher Expectations in the Chicano Classroom,' *Es Tiempo!* 2, no. 2, August 1972 (Los Altos Hills).

24 Quoted in Velia Hancock, 'Viva La Chicana,' *El Mestizo* 1, no. 3., 1971 (Irvine); E. Garcia, 'Flower of Aztlan: The Chicana,' *Es Tiempo!* 2, no. 2, August 1972 (Los Altos Hills). For intermarriage data, see Edward Murguía, *Chicano Intermarriage: A Theoretical and Empirical Study* (San Antonio: Trinity University Press, 1982).

25 Richard Espinoza, 'Machismo,' *Es Tiempo!* 2, no. 2, August 1972 (Los Altos Hills).

26 For one of the few studies to consider the role of the Chicano movement, upward mobility, and the large post-Movement middle class in California and elsewhere see Tamis H. Renteria, *Chicano Professionals: Culture, Conflict, and Identity* (New York: Garland Publishers, 1998).

27 Rodolfo Acuña, *The Making of Chicana/o Studies: In the Trenches of Academe* (New Brunswick: Rutgers University Press, 2011), 59–60.

28 See generally Acuña, *Making of Chicana/o Studies*.

29 David Yamane, *Student Movements for Multiculturalism: Challenging the Curricular Color Line in Higher Education* (Baltimore: Johns Hopkins University Press, 2001), 13–14.

30 Carlos F. Jackson, *Chicana and Chicano Art: Protestarte* (Tucson: University of Arizona Press, 2009), 65–6; 'On Mecha/UC Berkeley,' *Chispas* 2, no. 3, August 1974 (Berkeley).

31 Oscar Treviño Jr., 'Students,' *Chispas* 2, no. 3, August 1974 (Berkeley).

32 Phone conversation, Antonia Castañeda, September 10, 2012; Tamis H. Renteria, *Chicano Professionals: Culture, Conflict, and Identity* (New York: Garland Publishing, 1998), xviii–xxii; 'MECHA Meeting.'

33 Dean A. Harris, ed., *Multiculturalism from the Margins: Non-Dominant Voices on Difference and Diversity* (Westport: Bergin & Garvey, 1995), 95–8. On the 1990s activism that led to the creation of a department, see Acuña, *Making of Chicana/o Studies*, 179–89.

34 Acuña, *Making of Chicana/o Studies*, 80–8.

35 See George Mariscal, *Brown-Eyed Children of the Sun: Lessons from the Chicano Movement, 1965–1975* (Albuquerque: University of New Mexico Press, 2005), 210–46.

36 Sylvia Tiersten, 'What's in a Name? The Long Saga of Third College,' *At USCD* 7, no. 2 (May 2010), retrieved from: http://ucsdmag.ucsd.edu/magazine/vol7no2/features/feat4.htm.

37 'FSC Kills La Raza Studies,' *Raices*, September 16, 1970 (Fresno).

38 John Halcon, 'A New Direction for MECHA,' *Vida*, October 1973 (Los Angeles); Fr. Donald P. Merrifield, 'Chicanos and the Rest of Us at Loyola Marymount,' *Vida*, February 1974 (Los Angeles); Armando Dubon, 'The Inside Word,' *Vida*, December 1974 (Los Angeles).

39 Acuña, *Making of Chicana/o Studies*, 55–6; José E. Limón, *Américo Paredes: Culture and Critique* (Austin: University of Texas Press, 2012), 118–21; Maggie Rivas-Rodriguez, *35 Years: The Center for Mexican American Studies, the University of Texas at Austin* (Austin: Center for Mexican American Studies, 2005).

40 Acuña, *Making of Chicana/o Studies*, 89–92.

41 Irma Navarro, 'MECHA Students at OLL Plan Active Campaign,' *Chicano Times*, November 1972 (San Antonio), 6.

42 'OLL Labeled Racist and Discriminatory,' *Chicano Times*, March–April 1973 (San Antonio).

43 'OLL Faculty Members Blare Racism,' *Chicano Times*, May–June 1973 (San Antonio).

44 Joseph A. Rodriguez, 'Latinos at UWM: A History of the Spanish-Speaking Outreach Institute and the Roberto Hernandez Center' (Milwaukee: University of Wisconsin, 2005). Retrieved from: https://pantherfile.uwm.edu/joerod/www/ssoi.html.

45 See Dennis N. Valdés, *Barrios Norteños: St. Paul and Midwestern Mexican Communities in the Twentieth Century* (Austin: University of Texas Press, 2000), 206–8.

46 Valdés, *Barrios Norteños*, 206.

47 For the history of the Chicano Movement and Farm Workers and Chicano Students Movements in Washington, see 'Chicano/a Movement in Washington State History Project,' Pacific Northwest Labor and Civil Rights Projects, University of Washington, Digital Collection, retrieved from: https://depts.washington.edu/civilr/mecha_intro.htm.

48 See, generally, Valdés, *Barrios Norteños*.

49 Robert Thomas Jr., 'Julian Samora, 75, a Pioneering Sociologist,' *New York Times*, February 6, 1996.

50 Michael Anft, 'Giving a Voice to Hispanics,' *Chronicle of Philanthropy*, January 20, 2005.

51 See Jorge Bustamante, 'Julian Samora: Mentor,' in Alberto L. Pulido, A.B. Driscoll, and Carmen Samora, eds., *Moving beyond Borders: Julian Samora and the Establishment of Latino Studies* (Urbana: University of Illinois Press, 2009).

52 Dave Lammers, 'Chicanos Blast Hesburgh Policy,' *The Observer*, April 23, 1970, 1 (Notre Dame); 'Form Midwest Council of "La Raza",' *Latin Times*, April 24, 1970 (East Chicago).

53 Jim McDermott, 'MECHA Seeks Aid, Chicano Counselor,' *The Observer*, February 22, 1971 (Notre Dame).

54 Quoted in 'Was It Discrimination at Notre Dame?' *Latin Times*, May 28, 1971 (East Chicago).

55 See 'Timeline,' Julian Samora Legacy Project, retrieved from: http://samoralegacymedia.org/?page_id=1052.

56 See Aurelio M. Montemayor, 'Colegio Jacinto Treviño,' Handbook of Texas Online, June 12, 2010, retrieved from: www.tshaonline.org/handbook/online/articles/kbc51; 'El Colegio Holds Seminar,' *MAYO Newsletter*, January 29, 1971 (San Antonio); Colegio Jacinto Treviño was named after the hero of a border ballad who fought off and evaded the Texas Rangers. For this and other border ballads in cultural context see Américo Paredes, '*With His Pistol in His Hand': A Border Ballad and Its Hero* (Austin: University of Texas Press, 1986).

57 See María-Cristina García, 'Juárez-Lincoln University,' Handbook of Texas Online, June 15, 2010, retrieved from: http://www.tshaonline.org/handbook/online/articles/kcj03.

58 Donald Fixico, *The American Indian Mind in a Linear World: American Indian Studies and Traditional Knowledge* (New York: Routledge, 2003), 148; D-Q University History, National Park Service, November 17, 2004, retrieved from: http://www.cr.nps.gov/history/online_books/5views/5views1h18.htm.

59 See Glenn A. May, *Sonny Montes and Mexican American Activism in Oregon* (Corvallis: Oregon State University Press, 2011).

60 On HSI status, see Christiane R. Herber-Valdez, 'Understanding a Hispanic-Serving Institution beyond the Federal Definition: A Qualitative Analysis of Mexican American Student Perceptions and Experiences,' PhD thesis, University of Texas at El Paso, 2008.

61 Quoted in Erik Meeks, *Border Citizens: The Making of Indians, Mexicans, and Anglos in Arizona* (Austin: University of Texas Press, 2007), 193.

62 Quoted in Meeks, *Border Citizens*, 199.

63 Meeks, *Border Citizens*, 190–210; John R. Chávez, *Eastside Landmark: A History of the East Los Angeles Community Union, 1968–1993* (Stanford: Stanford University Press, 1998), 152–6; Armando Navarro, *La Raza Unida Party: A Chicano Challenge to the U.S. Two-Party Dictatorship* (Philadelphia: Temple University Press, 2000), 205–9.

4

NEWS AND THE MOVEMENT

Newspapers and Ideas in the Chicano Movement

Introduction

This chapter will examine the role of print media by considering the development of alternative newspapers as an outgrowth and defining component of the Chicano Movement. In much the same way that local militants sought control of the schools, the creation of cooperatives and credit unions, a political voice, and alternatives to gang life and an end to police brutality, the variety of activist centers of the Chicano Movement also engaged in the production of cultural, political, and informational media through the creation of a movement-driven press. The newspapers established were often the work of a small cadre of committed activists who reported on local news, politics, education, and culture, and reprinted national items from national Chicano leaders, journalists, and eventually the Chicano Press Association (CPA). The Chicano newspapers established in the 1960s and 1970s included weekly, quarterly, and other publications that served a variety of Chicano communities large and small. Some were neighborhood or campus papers that covered the minute details of local Chicano politics, while others highlighted poetry, art, the farm workers movement, politics, or the academic issues of the modern university. The chapter begins with an exploration of ethnic newspapers in America, the Mexican American press, and the underground and counterculture press as antecedents. The chapter then details the main development of the Chicano newspaper movement, the founding of the CPA, and the role the press played in building a movement culture, exploring and defining Chicano identity, as well as revealing and giving voice to Chicana women's issues. In many ways, the Chicano press was the primary educational and propaganda vehicle for the Chicano Movement nationwide.

Scholars have long considered the print media central to the production of 'imagined communities' among groups and nations. The Chicano newspapers of the 1960s and 1970s sought both to imagine a new community and establish a distinct Chicano nation. The press defined what it meant to be a Chicano. They did so by exploring the history of Mexican Americans and the civilization of the Aztecs, imperial Spain, and revolutionary Mexico as well as the history of Mexican-ancestry working-class life in the Southwest. Some of the papers also considered the links between Chicano nationalism and that of Puerto Rican independence activists. Much as the Black Power press did, Chicano essayists reported on the rise of anti-colonial movements in Africa, Vietnam, and Cuba and drew connections between these Third World movements and their own efforts in the United States. Placing their own movement within this global revolutionary context linked Chicanos to an international imaginary that took them out of the *barrio* while also legitimizing the *barrio* as cultural center and homeland analogous to the new nations then seeking independence. Chicano newspapers also explored masculinity in primitive and creative ways as they wrestled with the meaning of manliness in an era of expanding women's liberation. Chicano authors sought to define machismo and male pride as they connected themselves to the martial history of the Aztecs and Mexico, while Chicanas often established their own organizations and newspapers to redefine their place as women and imagine the Chicano movement as a non-patriarchal freedom struggle. The press linked Chicanos from the global and transnational cities of Los Angeles and San Antonio, the urban centers at Denver and Chicago, with those living in the Great Plains, the Great Lakes region, and the Pacific Northwest. The news service and informal reprinting and information sharing linked core and periphery as they sought to create a national Chicano community through the press.[1]

Ethnic Newspapers in America

Most Americans have immigrant origins, and the ethnic newspapers established by migrants and settlers have played a large role in advocating for the rights of non-English speakers, exiles, refugee radicals, and new US citizens alike. These papers often embraced homeland/country of origin-specific nationalism in reaction to imperialism in Europe, Latin America, and elsewhere. In other cases, ethnic newspapers became an opposition mouthpiece from the United States in the national politics of various homelands. Often short-lived and driven by the charisma of an editor or publisher, the ethnic newspaper kept immigrants appraised of events back home, supported national liberation or independence movements, and reported on the basic issues faced by settler neighborhoods, detailing the provision of services and the 'how to' of adjustment to life in so-called ethnic slums in the United States.[2] Following World War I-era attacks on leftist, Socialist, and Communist immigrant radicals, some ethnic newspapers embraced Americanism as they instructed readers on civic duty, naturalization, and voting and called on ethnics to support candidates for office from within their kinship communities.[3] Despite the hyphenated-Americanist worldview of some papers, ethnic papers continued to reflect the vast diversity of ethnic and language communities, as many continued to publish in native languages, emphasize transnational links to a variety of homelands, and engage in lobbying on various issues of importance to the ethnic or national group served by the newspaper.[4] Many of these papers were small, undercapitalized, and short-lived, yet all reflected a hybridity and commitment to an ethnic view, though many became increasingly 'hyphenated' in outlook (they emphasized their patriotism and Americanism) as the twentieth century progressed and the post-1945 Cold War set in and stifled dissent.

The Mexican American Press

Like other American ethnics, Mexican Americans have been producing newspapers and print media since the nineteenth century, and if one includes heritage publications from the Spanish and Mexican period in the Southwest, much longer. In the late nineteenth and early twentieth centuries the Mexican immigrant community, like their European immigrant counterparts, published newspapers in the language of their country of origin, Spanish, which were often linked to nationalist movements in Mexico. Expatriates in San Antonio, California, and other locations in the Southwestern United States produced a media culture that looked to Mexico yet also often detailed local events and politics, with many speaking forcefully in defense of the rights of Mexican immigrants in the United States. Newspapers were also produced in major cities of the Mexican immigrant experience with sporadic publication in many Midwestern railroad cities with concentrations of Mexican workers or where a Mexican consulate fostered a print culture.[5] By mid-century some newspapers, such as the *LULAC News*, had adopted a US-citizenship-oriented cultural outlook defined by a 'Mexican American' worldview, even as they pushed for political, educational, cultural, and civil rights and an end to discrimination against Mexican Americans.[6] Other publications, sometimes supported by Mexican consulates, maintained a commitment to a Mexican identity, the maintenance of Mexican citizenship, and the celebration of Mexican holidays.[7] Mexican American newspapers before the 1960s in general reflected the great diversity of the Mexican-ancestry community as both a domestic ethnic group and a transnational one.

Most importantly for the development of Chicano newspapers was *Regeneración*, published and edited by the exiled Flores-Magón brothers in the United States after 1900, which became a model for papers of the 1960s. Written in Spanish (and later in an English edition), *Regeneración*, published by Jesús Flores-Magón and edited by Ricardo Flores-Magón, was linked to the Junta Organizadora del Partido Liberal Mexicano (a Mexican political party) and railed against the dictatorship of Porfirio Díaz in Mexico. *Regeneración* featured essays by Ricardo that served as templates for reform in postrevolutionary Mexico. The paper was quite influential and moved with the brothers as they criss-crossed the US–Mexican border during times of conflict. *Regeneración* had its biggest US impact during its publication in Los Angeles after 1907, when Ricardo Flores-Magón shifted from liberal to anarchist politics in his writings, developed relationships with prominent US-based radicals, and turned his attention from Mexican revolutionary discourse to US politics, racism, labor unionization and other issues facing Mexican immigrants. This move to US topics drew criticism from Anglo elites in Los Angeles and from the US government. Due to his increasing radicalism, participation in border skirmishes, and revolutionary writings, Ricardo Flores-Magón was arrested and charged under the Espionage Act of 1917 for sedition and sentenced to 20 years in prison in 1918 for allegedly attempting to foment revolution in the United States. He would die in Leavenworth Penitentiary, Kansas, in 1922 and be celebrated as a Mexican national hero. Mexico requested that his remains be repatriated, a request that was not honored until 1945 when he was returned to Mexico and interred at the Rotonda de las Personas Ilustres in Mexico City alongside some of Mexico's most important revolutionaries, artists, writers, and scientists. Flores-Magón's radicalism, active transnationalism, and commitment to revolution—and to taking up arms if need be—made him a hero to many young Chicanos in the 1960s, and the newspaper he produced with his brother became a template for the Chicano publications of the era.[8]

Underground Newspapers and the 1960s

The underground press or alternative press defined and detailed the counterculture of the 1960s. To understand the Chicano Press Movement, one must put it in the context of the underground press movement of the same era. With new and cheap typesetting and printing technology and the mimeograph machine (an early relative of the photocopier), starting a paper was within reach of high school students and members of the counterculture. As one observer put it, '[f]or $200, almost anyone could start a paper, and almost anyone did—this flooded the hip media scene until the local underground paper became as institutionalized as the head shop.'[9] The underground press was part of the massive social dislocation known as the counterculture and often served as a missionary for leftist politics, rock and roll, antiwar ideology, the recreational use of drugs, and open sexual relationships.

The underground press in the late 1960s established a network for the sharing of news nationwide. The Underground Press Syndicate (UPS) was established with 125 members in 1967 and covered national events in the counterculture, enabling smaller papers to run stories of national significance. The papers varied in quality, longevity, and message, with some of the urban newspapers covering politics and calling for revolution, as others detailed the various excesses of the local music and drug scenes, and yet others tended toward academic and philosophical discourse. Often underground papers were short-lived experiments in journalism, printed as editors struggled to pay rent, purchase paper, and find people to distribute and sell the papers. Many turned to music venues, night clubs, record shops, head shops, and adult personals for advertising revenues. The comparatively few underground papers that lasted often had to compromise their message over time as advertising became important and the counterculture became part of mass culture.

The underground press often nurtured the development of new papers, and some supported minority papers to the extent of sharing printing facilities. Some of the larger newspapers of the era, founders of the UPS, included *Los Angeles Free Press*, the *Berkeley Barb*, the *East Village Other*, and Detroit's *Fifth Estate*. These founding counterculture papers were soon joined by others, including Austin's *The Rag*, Iowa City's *Middle Earth*, Chicago's *Seed*, San Francisco's *Oracle*, Milwaukee's *Kaleidoscope*, and by the editors and writers of the Liberation News Service (LNS), which supplanted the UPS as a more focused compiler and distributer of news. These papers and their staffs often grew out of the various student and campus newspapers, some of which were participants in the campus free speech movement and played a role in the operation of the United States Students Press Association (USSPA). With over 125 alternative newspapers publishing, as well as many more student papers put out by high school and college journalists, the countercultural press had a national impact and even printed in the Deep South. The underground press was targeted by the FBI and by local officials whose corruption was often exposed and who lobbied record companies to halt the purchase of advertising or used local obscenity statutes to close the newspapers owing to their coverage of the sexual liberation of the era. It was reported that the FBI actually established some underground newspapers itself as fronts to lure in unsuspecting radicals and countercultural types.[10]

The underground press set the tone and format for radical journalism in the 1960s and shaped the development of the Chicano press in real ways. In the pages of many underground newspapers, the police were referred to as 'pigs' and often considered little more than occupation forces in the counterculture and minority neighborhoods of major cities. The countercultural press covered developments in Black Power, Chicano Power, and the American Indian Movement, and most were strongly against the war in Vietnam. The discussion of the war as an expression of imperialism linked the US underground press to antiwar activists nationwide. While often fixated on the United States, the underground press was also aware of the changes going on globally as anti-colonialism, anti-police brutality, and the suppression of free speech in the West were covered within the context of a global youth movement which included both the Third World and domestic minorities. While often primitive in terms of printing technology, the underground press paid significant attention to covering art and often incorporated art and poetry throughout the paper. The cover design was meant to grab the attention of people who might be walking past a salesperson on the street and highlighted the artistic spirit of the counterculture. The underground press often included shocking covers akin to poster art or collage-format use of photos, graphics, and intricate mastheads to grab attention. This style became standard for countercultural publications nationwide.[11] In many ways, the Chicano press and the Black Power press were outgrowths of the broader movement culture of the 1960s and grew in tandem with the underground press movement. The Chicano and Black Power presses were perhaps more inclined than the rest of the underground press to cover specific cases of police brutality in detail as examples of the historical tensions between the police and minority people. The youth focus was also evident. The Chicano press often adopted the underground press cover style, incorporating photographic collage, line drawing, and poster art motifs in the covers of newspapers which, like their underground counterparts, were often sold on street corners and benefitted from a cover that captured the attention of passersby and made them readers. Most importantly the Chicano press, like the underground and Black Power presses, presented a counter-narrative to the mainstream media.[12]

The Rise of the Chicano Press

The growth of the United Farm Workers Organizing Committee (UFWOC) in California led to the establishment of a Mexican American newspaper that set the tone for the Chicano press era to come. In the mid 1960s groups such as the UFWOC in California and Texas and Obreros Unidos (OU) in Wisconsin were publishing newspapers and newsletters that pressed for local participation in the grape boycott and farm labor organizing efforts. These labor newspapers were meant to educate workers on the issues facing the unions and inform them of their rights under labor, housing, education, and health law, as well as provide a connection to the services provided by the union or other supportive groups. The newspapers also shared information on farm labor organizing in other places across the nation, with the California paper reporting mainly on the grape boycott and the Wisconsin and Texas union-affiliated papers and newsletters seeking support both for California's grape boycott and for local organizing drives. *El Malcriado* (the ill-mannered or the brat), established in Delano by Dolores Huerta and Cesar Chavez in 1964, became a forum for news about farm workers, a vehicle for political organizing, and a venue for artistic expressions of Mexican American working-class culture and life filtered through the struggle to establish the farm workers' union in California. In Wisconsin, where migrants established *La Voz Mexicana* as a seasonal publication in 1964, the newspaper became a farm labor publication by 1966, reporting on the UFWOC effort in California and the OU union drive in Wisconsin, as well as informing seasonal migrants about their rights and local services and providing news clips from hometowns in Texas. Radical commitment to the labor cause and the focus on providing accurate information about health, safety, and civil rights to Mexican American farm workers were both definitive aspects of what became Chicano journalism. Education and public service news were central to the Mexican American labor press, as well as the youth-driven Chicano press. Labor movement papers educated Mexican-ancestry workers as to the ideology, praxis, and activities of the movement, as they also provided a key public service by reporting in a direct and clear way on the law, educational opportunities, health services, and other important news to local working-class communities.[13]

Building a Movement Culture in Print

As is true of any nation-building endeavor, those seeking to build a national consciousness must be clear about who exactly comprises the nation and which space or territory belongs to the nation. In the Mexican American route to becoming Chicano, the Chicano Movement and the Chicano press did the work of imagining a Chicano community in which activists and *barrios* could claim a position as the inheritors of Aztlán in the American Southwest.[14] Almost from the start, this nationalist project was full of contradictions. In *El Plan Espiritual de Aztlán* one sees the contradictions clearly. Chicanos are a 'new people' who are proud of a 'historical heritage' and reject the 'brutal "gringo" invasion of our territories' yet also embrace the imperial role as 'civilizers' of land held by independent Native American tribes before going on to reclaim the Southwest as the land of their 'forefathers,' claiming it as 'Aztlán' (mythical homeland of the Aztecs) as part of a 'Bronze Continent.'[15] In Aztlán, mythic in orientation and makeup, the sharp edges of Spanish colonialism and Mexican colonialism among the Native peoples of the Southwest are softened by the 'civilizing' aspect of the 'Mestizo Nation' brought north by the ancestors of the Chicanos.[16] For Mexican American youth in the 1960s, living between Mexican and American cultures, this hybridity itself is fluid and perhaps required a softening of the jagged edges of history. There were many questions to be sure. As Chicano movement leaders sought to claim the mythic space of a new nation for the Chicano people, they confronted the very contradictions of a people who lived between two national histories and across several indigenous histories. The Chicano press sought to explore the meaning, potential, and limits of the Chicano imaginary as they built a nation for an in-between people in North American national histories.[17]

Much of the project of the Chicano Movement was focused on the process of building a sense of self as Chicanos rather than as Mexican Americans. Mexican-ancestry people in the US Southwest were a product of the vast process of imperialism, colonialism, war, and migration in North America, and as such they were a bicultural and often bilingual people, reflecting the great diversity of a borderland and a migrant community. To understand the Chicano position within and between the two largest population centers in North America was part of the Chicano intellectual project. The bicultural reality of Mexican American life was a topic that drew quite a bit of attention in the Chicano Movement print media. In a common examination, Chicanos had to confront the 'demands of two cultures' and 'comply with the requirements of both cultures,' a process that writers reasoned may have left Chicanos 'without an identity.'[18] Mexican Americans were torn between an Americanist imaginary that highlighted liberty and individualism, and a Mexicanist and largely Catholic imaginary that placed the focus on family and community. These essentialized tensions impacted understandings about gender, politics, and culture in ways that some believed compelled Mexican Americans to choose or face the confusion of living between both imagined communities. Chicano journalists criticized the educational, political, and social system in the United States for failing to create a truly pluralistic society that would adequately accommodate the 'culturally different,' and they set out to create their own Chicano nation.[19]

The first component of Chicano nationalism was the reimagining of Aztlán as a homeland. To establish a sense of nationhood, Chicano writers and activists renamed the US Southwest 'Aztlán' after the mythical homeland of the Aztecs, thus claiming this territory. The renaming of the US Southwest as Aztlán gave Chicanos a territory that was theirs and neither Mexican or American but important to both national histories. The creation stories of modern Mexico and of current-day Mexico City, as represented on the Mexican flag's image of the golden eagle on a prickly pear cactus killing a serpent, are tied together with the myth of Aztlán and the founding of Tenochtitlan (Mexico City). By claiming the American Southwest as Aztlán, Chicanos were placing themselves at the heart of the indigenous Mexican creation myth and claiming an Aztec inheritance. Rather than a peripheral people between two nations, Chicanos were the essentialized heart of the Mexican people and the rightful heirs to Aztlán. Chicano newspapers printed images of Aztlán that encircled the US states of Texas, New Mexico, Colorado, Arizona, and California, claiming this space and setting this new nation apart from both the US and Mexico. For Chicanos at the time, Aztlán was 'the new Chicano nation' born out of the Chicano Youth Liberation Conference of 1969, and it consisted of those 'Chicanos who live in the five southwestern states and other parts of the U.S. where Chicanos live.'[20] Chicano newspapers reminded readers that they should 'be a living part of Aztlán and of her thought' and of 'that divine energy which is called for by the sun for the liberation, the self-determination, and destiny of Aztlán and her Raza de Bronce' (bronze race).[21] With this reinterpretation of the Aztlán myth, Chicano writers and activists gave their people an identifiable homeland.

For some activists and authors Aztlán was meant to be a new nation, yet for others Aztlán served as an apt metaphor for the establishment of Chicano community control in Mexican American neighborhoods and population centers. Irredentist rhetoric (calls for armed rebellion), similar to that of Rodolfo 'Corky' Gonzales, was quite common in Chicano newspapers, as writers claimed that 'La Raza de Bronce' required independence to win 'total liberation from oppression, exploitation, and racism.' Yet this rhetoric is often tempered by calls for a role within the US economic, educational, and political system, defined by 'revolutionary acts' to build a 'revolutionary culture' via an 'independent local, regional, and national political party' able to make decisions about land use, taxes, criminal justice, and 'the utilization of our bodies for war.' Quite often the language of those seeking to create Aztlán contained both separatist and accommodationist rhetoric when calling on Chicanos to embrace nationalism.[22]

The second component of Chicano nationalism was to remake Mexican Americans as 'Chicanos.' Chicano newspapers explained the project on the part of 'Raza Nueva to declare itself a nation' as an effort to 'bring attention to the fact that the Spanish Indian Mestizo Culture has been totally ignored and discouraged by the gringo establishment,' alongside reports of Latin American revolutionary and independence movements in Puerto Rico, Cuba, and Uruguay.[23] The conquest of Mexico by the United States during the 1845–1848 war and ceding of the Southwestern states by Mexico are seen as part of a wrongful conquest led by 'gringos.' Despite being 'invaded' and 'oppressed,' Chicanos were now able to claim status as a people, with a territory and a history.[24]

Every Mexican American had the potential to become Chicano within the context of the movement. As the Chicano press developed, Chicanos rejected the term 'Mexican American' as a product of the Americanization that had had a negative impact on the Mexican-ancestry population in the United States. Compelled to pay taxes, serve in the military, and perform the obligations of citizenship, Mexican Americans were nonetheless refused acceptance in schools, the economy, and the mainstream society. In most publications, some Mexican Americans were criticized for embracing the term—and, presumably, adopting an assimilationist or acculturationist view. By becoming hyphenated Americans, Mexican Americans had become a people who 'exist in a limbo' where they 'are neither accepted or rejected . . . Mexican or American.'[25] As an alternative to living between cultures, Mexican Americans could place themselves at the center of José Vasconcelos's concept of 'La Raza Cósmica' (the cosmic race) with great potential for creativity and perfection.[26] Some, spurred on by post-World War II efforts among Mexican Americans to 'make their sacrifice count,' spoke of La Raza and Chicano interchangeably as a 'blending of a new family of man composed of original inhabitants of the Americas . . . and all immigrants from throughout the earth.'[27] Others argued that La Raza was perhaps the 'most integrated "race" there is,' due to its great diversity and potential to be 'all encompassing.'[28] According to Rubén Salazar, the reporter for the *Los Angeles Times* whose piece on Chicano identity was reprinted in many Chicano newspapers, a Chicano had a 'non-Anglo image of himself,' saw some Mexican Americans as 'brainwashed,' and rejected the notion that he was 'culturally deprived.'[29] Others within the movement pointed out that the whole idea of defining an essentialized Chicano self was a waste of time, since most Chicanos were too busy 'trying to strive for better housing, for better jobs, for a better education, and for unity among Chicano people' rather than ruminating about the 'activities of Columbus five centuries ago.'[30] One critic rejecting the essentializing project argued that Chicanos should not 'become bitter towards all white people' because people of many different backgrounds, including whites, had supported and joined the Chicano struggle for civil rights.[31]

Those who embraced this new Chicano identity also adopted the philosophy of 'Chicanismo' to guide their actions and relations with others. Adherents of Chicanismo claimed status as mestizo (mixed race) people of the Americas. The essence of this identity was indigenous. Chicanos focused on a retelling of the proud history of indigenous peoples in Mexico and the Americas and placing themselves within this historical and mythical space. To be a Chicano was to embrace one's status as a brown person, and in making claims to nationhood and a new identity, one needed also to embrace one's compatriots in the struggle. Part and parcel of the ideology of Chicanismo was an active commitment to *carnalismo* (brotherhood) among activists in the struggle to build and maintain Aztlán. This was not merely about male brotherhood—carnalismo was seen as a practice meant to strengthen the Chicano community by reimagining it as a family of interconnected people committed to work together to build Aztlán after the Spanish and American conquests.[32] Through the Chicano press and newsletters, authors and activists explored and explained the meaning of an individual's place within this new Chicano world and the community-based commitment to Chicanismo as praxis.[33]

In most cases a Chicano was a man. Most publications speak of 'he' when referring to the Chicano, with reference often made to the 'vato loco.' Chicano rhetoric is full of examples that neglect the presence of women in order to focus on male bonding and male pride within the context of American racism. Women were often relegated to a subservient or passive place in history—and within the Chicano community and Chicano Movement itself. Chicano newspapers promoted masculine images and celebrated the militant as male. When women were reported on or praised in poetry, it was usually in a passive feminine guise rather than an active militant space. Women were well aware of the role of patriarchy within traditional Mexican-ancestry communities and, as Chicanismo matured, they increasingly criticized a supposedly radical movement that clung to a traditional gender hagiography.[34]

A striking aspect of many Chicano newspapers is the amount of space dedicated to poetry. Chicano college students, Brown Berets, and others wrote poetry that expressed the mood of the era. Poets spoke of the hardship of discrimination, the durability of culture, and more usual poetic themes such as love, longing, and desire; the majority of poems expressed the sense of awakening among Chicanos and Chicanas during this era. In a typical poem that blended historical memory with a critique of America and of the bloodshed in Vietnam, one poet called out, 'Open your doors, American, and let us in!'[35] In another poem, the author wrote of waking up and coming to terms with the fact that his 'Chicano brothers have/

been stepped on, cheated/' as he explored his understanding of civil rights, land loss in the Southwest, and a desire to 'fight' for these rights.[36] Another poem, after reflecting on Chicano history and mistreatment, called out for a utopian future and demanded that 'my PEOPLE must be free.'[37] Other publications featured poems written by Chicanos and Mexican nationals in Spanish and hybrid mixes of Spanish and English, which also explored the long history of Mexico and Chicano life and pressed for an education that did not merely assimilate but, rather, allowed for the hybridity that defined life for Mexican-ancestry people.[38] Through poetry, college students, writers, and everyday people expressed in print the feelings of movement participants.

Chicana Women's Identity in Chicano Periodicals

As was true in most social movements of the era, women within the Chicano Movement began to expand movement ideology to allow for a critique of gender discrimination within the movement and the broader society. This effort developed across Chicano periodicals and led to the establishment of a variety of women-centered or women-inclusive journals, magazines, and movement publications. The essays tended to offer a feminist vision that expanded the concept of Chicano nationalism to incorporate many aspects of traditional Mexican nationalism while critiquing those elements that posited a rigid and religiously defined space for women in Chicano society and families. By rejecting a traditional Catholic and Mexican patriarchal view of their place in society and the Chicano liberation movement, women challenged their own upbringing and that of their male counterparts, yet did not abandon the Chicano movement. In some ways, during an era of polemical rhetoric from feminists and misogynists within many social movements of the era, Chicana feminists offered a middle ground: they struggled to find a way to maintain commitment to the cause of the Chicano Movement, and their place in it, as they pressed for a broader understanding of liberation among Chicano men.[39]

Through reflective and short analytical essays, Chicanas introduced the readers of Chicano periodicals to women's place within the movement and explained their criticisms of the movement as an effort to reform it from within. The reflective pieces are often written from personal experience as well as theory, blending personal experiences of objectification and harassment with an understanding of feminist theory as the women writers put forward a positive view of the potential for Chicano men to reform. Not all of their essays were sanguine; some expressed fatigue and a real concern that 'machismo,' even if it had been imposed on Chicanos through the imbricated process of Spanish conquest and the long history of oppression in the United States, was still a central part of Chicano masculinity, exemplified by leaders such as Rodolfo 'Corky' Gonzales and many of the young men they met in Chicano campus organizations. Many women felt let down by the 1969 conference organized by Gonzales and expressed this for years after-wards.[40] Analytical essays written by Chicanas in graduate programs argued from history to refute the idea that Mexican-ancestry women were inherently passive, and provided ample evidence of women's important role in Mexican Independence, the Mexican Revolution, and the labor movement in the United States. By recovering alternative visions of Mexican-ancestry womanhood, these authors developed a counter-narrative to simplistic and patriarchal visions of the role of Mexican and Chicana women in making history. These essays also engaged the critiques of male activists who felt that the push for Chicana rights would weaken the movement by declaring their allegiance to Chicano nationalism and the broader goal of liberation for all Chicanos, including women. This line of analysis challenged the misogynists yet was communicated in a tone that, while militant, reminded Chicano men that the freedom struggle in which they were all engaged was expanding to incorporate women's rights, and in some cases welcomed male support.[41]

The exploration of Chicana identity within the broader Chicano movement is exemplified in the writings of women who questioned—as Chicano men had—the structural and cultural nature of their oppression. Elvira Saragoza explored the role of the Chicana in an essay that expressed sadness and confusion over the state of women in the movement. In her essay that asked whether the Chicana was seen as a slave, companion, or copartner, she reminded readers of 'La Adelita,' the revolutionary women soldiers of the Mexican Revolution, as well as the fact that women have 'played a major role in the strikes led by Mexican field workers,' and mentioned the film *Salt of the Earth* which dramatized the mineworkers' strike and portrayed women as heroic figures in working-class families who fought the sexism of their husbands to make the union and the community stronger.[42] In essays and poetry, Chicanas expressed the need to instruct Chicano men about the heroic, active role played by women in Mexican and Chicano history. For instance, the poem 'I am María' (perhaps echoing and challenging 'Yo Soy Joaquín') by Elena Abeyta runs the course of Aztec history and Mexican experience, pointing out that María is both 'the black-shawled woman who lived and loved' and also 'la hija de la Chingada,' and drawing on the long history of tension within the writings of authors such as Octavio Paz and within Mexican culture itself and also challenging this male-centered view of history.[43] These activists called for greater educational opportunity for their gender, an acceptance of partnership between Chicanos and Chicanas, and a complete rejection of the customary cultural attitude that saw females as suited only to 'get married and to have children.'[44] Women throughout the movement and in a variety of forums demanded an end to patriarchy in the Chicano community while maintaining a commitment to Chicano men and the Chicano Movement.

Railing against machismo's corrosive effect, most Chicana women advocated a new model for gender relations within the Chicano community. The exploration of gender relations by Chicana women—even if it was seen as threatening by some men—was not, in the main, a rejection of men in the life of Chicanas but, rather, a desire to make life better for all. As Juana Serros explained, 'Chicanas have common concerns and recognize the need to work together for the betterment of the entire Chicano community.'[45] One activist argued that *carnalas* (sisters) must dedicate their efforts to 'ourselves, then to "La Raza"', as they make the movement their own.[46] While some called for unity, others analyzed the very real problems faced by women in the Chicano and broader community. In one autobiographical piece, Dolores Huerta described her life-long dedication to activism and the gender-based criticism that she had often faced because of it. She refused to let such criticism bother her or to see female activists as in any way 'bad' mothers or 'unwomanly' women; rather, she embraced the notion of the 'communal family.'[47] Yet, tensions over ideology and self-fashioning were clear in some cases: one woman in a letter to the editor felt obliged to insist that 'I ain't no women's libber,' even as she praised the publication for hiring more female journalists and offering more coverage of women's issues within the Chicano community and the general society.[48]

Longer-format publications explored the Chicana woman's struggle for personhood across time. *Encuentro Femenil* was founded in 1973 for women activist writers to make information available to Chicana women and the broader community in an accessible style somewhere between the Chicano newspaper and the scholarly journal. Essays such as 'The Realities of Being a Woman/Chicana' gave concrete examples of Chicana women as the makers of Chicano history and the heads of Chicano families. This essay pointed out in direct language that over '50% of Chicano families have female heads of households over 40 years of age' in places such as Los Angeles where women provided for families and raised children without a male partner.[49] Chicana women wrote in mainstream publications as well. The rise of Chicanas to leadership positions in public life was charted in the *Los Angeles Times* in articles such as 'From Follower to Leader,' which explored the role played by Lupe Anguiano, a former nun and UFW organizer assigned to Michigan's grape boycott, who led many efforts to bring Chicana women into the political sphere nationwide.[50] In this article Anguiano reflected on her initial reluctance to take charge of activist management as a UFW organizer and her evolution by the early 1970s into a Chicana who worked to help other Chicanas to fight against their oppression as women and as minorities. By the early 1970s women's voices were becoming louder and more compelling, and the end of the decade saw more women in leadership positions in the Chicano Movement.[51]

In the Chicano and Chicana press women called for a brand of liberation that encompassed all of La Raza. Women leveled critiques at the exclusion of women from the formal leadership of organizations and created their own organizations as a result. Women also unraveled the knotted relationship of misogyny in limiting the revolutionary potential of the movement as they demanded an end to calls on the part of men and many women that the Chicana feminist question be set aside to allow Chicano nationalism to proceed without revision. The varied threads of restriction on the potential of women within the movement were roundly critiqued, as was the practice of some men within the movement to marginalize the role of feminists by categorizing them as disloyal movement participants. The revolutionary fervor of the Chicano Movement had inspired men and women to analyze their unequal position in American society and to reject exclusion by calling for revolutionary change. This process included the further step of reconsidering and recasting the place of Chicana women within the movement, the community, and the broader society.[52]

As the 1970s progressed, women organized meetings and in some cases ran for elective office or pushed for a greater role in government-funded or agency work focused on the needs of Mexican Americans. Chicanas brought women together to discuss the issues facing them within society and within the movement. In May 1971 Chicana activists met in Houston, Texas, at 'Mujeres Por La Raza,' a conference meant to explore women's issues in the movement. The conference revealed the degree to which Chicanas experienced discrimination in the mainstream and in the Chicano Movement and highlighted divisions among Chicanas when it came to remedies and relationships with Chicano men. Other meetings were held at the state and city level throughout the 1970s, as Chicana and Latina women considered the issues they faced within their own communities and in the wider world of work, family, and society. Older organizations such as the League of Latin American Citizens (LULAC) also increasingly paid attention to women's issues and held meetings to explore these as the decade wore on. From Kansas to Indiana, New Mexico to Texas, women were meeting and discussing their place in Chicano society and the roles they wanted to play moving forward. They wanted greater educational, economic, and political opportunities. As early as 1972, Chicanas writing for *La Luz*, a monthly based in Denver, had developed a pan-Latino framework and leveled a critique against both internal machismo and sexism within the broader society, as they considered the achievements of Puerto Rican and Chicana women and began to use the term 'Hispanic' in reference to the broader community of Latinas.[53] By the end of the 1970s many Chicana women were running successfully for office and moving into positions of power and responsibility, yet there was much more to accomplish both within the Chicano community and outside in the larger society.[54]

Chicano Publishing and Artistic Expression

While some Chicano newspapers sought to explain the Chicano Movement's ideology and history, others concentrated on expressing movement ideology through art and literary production. Certainly, many Chicano newspapers did both and dedicated ample space for poetry, short stories, line drawing, photography, and art or the promotion of arts events. But other publications focused specifically on the development of Chicano literary and artistic culture. The mix of newspapers and journals that provided space for some level of artistic production included many newspapers that became members of the CPA as well many established in the mid 1970s. Several important Chicano and Chicana poets, authors, and artists wrote for newspapers as did many others who may have produced one or two poems and nothing more.

Con Safos: Reflections on Life in the Barrio was a magazine, published 'twice or maybe thrice a year' in Los Angeles that merged the Chicano newspaper model with that of a literary magazine.[55] In the short time it was published it served as a bridge between movement papers and those seeking a more artistic and literary format.[56] The magazine appeared when the editors had 'money to pay the printer' and material that 'says it.' The editors boasted that a year's subscription entitled the subscriber to four issues even if 'IT TAKES A HUNDRED YEARS' to publish them.[57] This honesty reflected the character of underground and Chicano newspaper and magazine publishing during this period to be sure. *Con Safos* featured striking cover art commissioned from Chicano artists and photographers, who often blended themes evident in Mexican and Chicano muralism with the underground press aesthetic of 1960s and early 1970s countercultural motifs.[58] The staff was divided among fiction, social and political, and arts editors. Poetry and essays were featured alongside graphics and the trademark 'C/S' symbol of the magazine throughout.[59] While the poetry reflects the types of concerns held by poets in more traditional Chicano newspapers of the era, the format was clearly meant to follow the literary magazine model, with each edition offering essays, short stories, poems, graphic art or photography. In one edition the editors provided a glossary of common terms in Chicano Spanish such as definitions for 'Chola' (female friend or gang member), 'Pachuco' (old school gang member or cool guy), and 'Rucas' (slang for girlfriend) among many other common phrases used in *barrio* Spanish.[60] *Con Safos* published in serial the work of movement attorney and counterculture activist Oscar Zeta Acosta and in the last few pages of every issue offered readers pieces such as 'Answers to the Barriology Examination #4,' which added a humorous dimension to the important cultural work presented in its issues.[61] *Con Safos* saw itself as an 'aesthetic outgrowth, which is ultimately the soul of a movement' and 'the soul of history' to give voice to Chicanos and the people of the *barrios* of the United States as 'a gesture of defiance' and 'an overt rejection of the cold and indifferent gabacho (Anglo) imposition.'[62]

Other Chicano publications were meant to function more formally as literary journals or academic quarterlies, yet in the early 1970s they also had a Chicano press aesthetic. Such journals included *El Grito: A Journal of Contemporary Mexican-American Thought*, founded in Berkeley in 1967, which ceased publication in 1974, and *Revista Chicano-Requeña* (Chicano Puerto Rican Review) of Gary, Indiana, which began publication in 1973 and continued through the 1980s. They gave

Chicano, Chicana, and Puerto Rican writers and poets, academics and critics the space to develop early works in Chicano and Chicana history, literature, and criticism as well as more general Latino subject matter. These journals published original research on Mexican American life, history, and social problems, as well as creative work and fiction. Though short-lived, they provided many Chicano academics and writers with a forum for their earliest published works. These journals applied scholarly publication standards such as peer review, yet saw their efforts as an outgrowth of movement politics. These journals were not merely committed to producing Chicano and Latino knowledge but to highlighting this artistic and literary work for a broader community.[63] *Revista Chicano-Requeña* evolved into *Americas Review*, which launched the careers of many Latino nonfiction authors and became the foundation for Arte Público Press (see below).

Chicanos also established academic journals and newsletters focused on the production of a Chicano intellectual project within the academic world. Central to this project was the founding of *Aztlán*, which in its earliest editions resembled the Chicano periodicals being printed in *barrios* and in college towns nationwide. Essays explored Chicano history and intellectual development, and the aesthetic of the journal included space dedicated to art, poetry, and some line drawings and graphics reminiscent of Chicano newspapers. The first few years of *Aztlán* show how a successful journal can have its roots in a movement dedicated to bridging the gap between Chicano faculty and graduate students and the Chicano community. *Aztlán* continues today as a premier scholarly journal and has inspired related law review journals with an emphasis on the publication of scholarly research on Mexican Americans, yet true to its movement roots *Aztlán* still publishes poetry and art.[64]

In addition to journals and artistic magazines, Chicanos and their supporters started programs to publish poetry, fiction, and scholarly work. Key among these was *Editorial Quinto Sol*, founded in 1968 in Berkeley, California, the first Chicano publishing house to grow out of the movement. While it began with the publication of the journal *El Grito*, the mission of *Quinto Sol* expanded to encompass the publication of anthologies and new works of fiction by early Chicano authors. *El Grito* published material in regional and hybrid US versions of Spanish that often engaged in code-switching between Spanish and English. The goal was to produce literary work that reflected Chicano culture and the mood of the Chicano Movement. *Quinto Sol* also established the *Premio Quinto Sol* in 1970, a literary award given to the best work of fiction by Chicano authors, to highlight the accomplishments of Mexican-ancestry writers in the United States. Tomás Rivera, author of the novel *. . . Y No Se Lo Tragó La Tierra* (. . . And the Earth Did Not Devour Him), was the first *Premio* recipient and worked thereafter with *Quinto Sol* to promote the work of Chicano authors. Other *Premio* recipients included Rodolfo Anaya, Rolando Hinojosa, and Estela Portillo-Trambley. In 1979, Nicolás

Kanellos established Arte Público Press, which continues this tradition in a pan-Latino way as a publishing house for Chicano, Puerto Rican, and other Latino authors. Several authors who published important works, often their first, in Arte Público include Ana Castillo, Sandra Cisneros, Helena María Viramontes, and Victor Villaseñor.[65] The growing influence of several Chicano scholars prodded some university press, houses to publish Chicano scholarship. Key among these was the University of Notre Dame Press, due to the influence of Julian Samora, who put pressure on the university to publish Chicano-focused scholarship beginning in the 1960s and flowering in the mid 1970s. Bilingual Review/Press, founded in 1974 by poet and professor Gary Keller/El Huitlacoche likewise published many seminal works of Chicano authors and continues to this date.[66] By the 1980s, while few of the original Chicano presses survived, university presses and mainstream publishers increasingly became aware of the market for books by Chicano and Latino authors. Yet it was often those presses with roots in the Chicano movement that kept canonical texts in print. The Chicano press movement and the Chicano publication movement were intimately linked, as Chicano men and women sought to produce their own culture visually and via the printed word much as previous ethnic communities had done.

Conclusion

As was true for young people across the world in the 1960s and 1970s, Chicanos sought to define themselves and create a new community through their publications and writing. The Chicano press movement grew out of the Chicano Movement and expanded in tandem with it. Chicano newspapers shared stories and format and reported on the important events of the day at the national level but also at the local level. A review of newspapers from Kansas City to Chicago, San Antonio to Los Angeles reveals the truly national aspects of the Chicano Movement, which through dozens of publications told the stories of Chicanos in places as different as Wisconsin and New Mexico, San Diego, California, and Lansing, Michigan, yet in such a way that Chicanos could see all these places as part of a Chicano nation. The Chicano press movement also enabled the expansion into new areas of publication, as it provided a forum for dissent within the community and the expression of viewpoints that critiqued the very nature of Chicano identity. Women both within the Chicano press and in their own publications (which flourished in the 1970s) increasingly brought critique and support to the broader project of Chicano nationalism and identity as they presented models that offered a way for participants to be both Chicano nationalist and antisexist simultaneously.[67] The lasting influence of the Chicano press movement lies in the greater acceptance of Latino journalists and fiction authors nationwide, in mainstream English and increasingly bilingual media outlets.

Notes

1 See Benedict Anderson, *Imagined Communities: Reflections on the Origin and Spread of Nationalism* (London: Verso, 1991); Robert H. Wiebe, *Who We Are: A History of Popular Nationalism* (Princeton: Princeton University Press, 2002); Ignacio M. García, *Chicanismo: The Forging of a Militant Ethos among Mexican Americans* (Tucson: University of Arizona Press, 1997).

2 See Gerald Suttles, *The Social Order of the Slum: Ethnicity and Territory in the Inner City* (Chicago: University of Chicago Press, 1970); Victor Greene, *American Immigrant Leaders, 1800–1910: Marginality and Identity* (Baltimore: Johns Hopkins University Press, 1987).

3 See John M. Allswang, *A House for All Peoples: Ethnic Politics in Chicago, 1890–1936* (Lexington: University Press of Kentucky, 1971).

4 See Works Progress Administration, *Chicago Foreign Language Press Survey* (Washington, DC: Works Progress Administration, 1942); this collection has been digitalized by the Newberry Library and is available at: http://flps.newberry.org/.

5 See América Rodriguez, *Making Latino News: Race, Language, Class* (Thousand Oaks: Sage Press, 1999), 16–25.

6 On LULAC and its message, see Craig Kaplowitz, *LULAC: Mexican Americans, and National Policy* (College Station: Texas A&M University Press, 2005).

7 On the role of the consulates in maintaining a Mexican community in the diaspora, see Juan R. García, *Mexicans in the Midwest, 1900–1932* (Tucson: University of Arizona Press, 1996).

8 On Ricardo Flores-Magón and his brother, see Claudio Lomnitz, *The Return of Comrade Ricardo Flores Magón* (New York: Zone Books, 2014); Ward S. Albro, *Always a Rebel: Ricardo Flores Magón and the Mexican Revolution* (Fort Worth: Texas Christian University Press, 1992); W. Dirk Raat, *Revoltosos: Mexico's Rebels in the United States, 1903–1923* (College Station: Texas A&M University Press, 1981).

9 Jesse Kornbluth, 'This Place of Entertainment Has No Fire Exit: The Underground Press and How It Went,' *Antioch Review* 29, no. 1 (Spring, 1969): 91–9, at 95.

10 See John McMillian, *Smoking Typewriters: The Sixties Underground Press and the Rise of Alternative Media in America* (New York: Oxford University Press, 2011), 82–171.

11 See Geoff Kaplan, *Power to the People: The Graphic Design of the Radical Press and the Rise of the Counter-Culture, 1964–1974* (Chicago: University of Chicago Press, 2013).

12 See Randy Ontiveros, *The Spirit of a New People: The Cultural Politics of the Chicano Movement* (New York: New York University Press, 2013), 44–85.

13 See Carlos Guerrero, 'Silent No More: the Voice of a Farm Worker Press, 1964–1975,' PhD thesis, Claremont Graduate University, 2004; Marc S. Rodriguez, *The Tejano Diaspora: Mexican Americanism and Ethnic Politics in Texas and Wisconsin* (Chapel Hill: University of North Carolina Press, 2011), 64–6.

14 For a single publication-focused study, see Francisco Manuel Andrade, 'The History of *La Raza Newspaper and Magazine*, and Its Role in the Chicano Community from 1967 to 1977,' MA thesis, California State University, Fullerton, 1978.

15 Of course the Native American people of the Southwest may dispute this view since the Spanish and Mexican colonials (even though they were of Mestizo and indigenous background) came as frontier settlers and conquerors, and later Mexican immigrants may have had no immediate indigenous or genetic ties to the US Southwest.

16 All quotes from 'El Plan Espiritual de Aztlán,' *Chicano Resource Journal & Service Handbook*, MEChA, University of California Berkeley (Fall, 1972). Most Chicano newspapers of the era reprinted *El Plan* at some point.

17 The classic exploration of in-between people is James R. Barrett and David Roediger, 'Inbetween Peoples: Race, Nationality and the "New Immigrant" Working Class,' *Journal Of American Ethnic History* 16, no. 3 (Spring 1997), 3–45. The Mexican American case is complicated by the hybrid racial status of Mexican-ancestry people—as seen by institutions, Anglos, and the government.

18 'Biculturalism: Its Effect on the Personality of the Mexican-American,' *Es Tiempo!* June 1972 (Los Altos Hills).

19 'Education and Culturally Different Children,' *El Griton*, June 1972 (Porterville).

20 'Aztlán,' *Truchas y Mujer*, November 1972 (San Pedro); 'Chicano Country,' *El Chicano*, April 5, 1970 (San Bernardino).

21 'El Travieso Believes,' *El Travieso*, July, 1969 (Los Angeles).

22 'The Program of El Plan Espiritual De Aztlán,' *Truchas y Mujer*, November 1972 (San Pedro).

23 'El Plan Espiritual De Aztlán' and 'Puerto Rico,' *Venceremos*, January 1971 (Kansas City).

24 See 'I am an Angry Chicano,' *El Griton*, 1973 (Porterville). For a discussion of Chicano identity, see Rafael Pérez-Torres, *Mestizaje: Critical Uses of Race in Chicano Culture* (Minneapolis: University of Minnesota Press, 2006), 215–18.

25 'Mexican-American or Chicano?' *El Chicano*, April 26, 1972 (Colton).

26 José Vasconcelos and Didier T. Jaén, *The Cosmic Race: A Bilingual Edition* (Baltimore: Johns Hopkins University Press, 1997); Luis Miguel Valdez, 'El Machete,' *El Excéntrico*, January 5, 1964 (San José). In fact, Luis Valdez, who would go on to found *El Teatro Campesino* and play a large role in farm worker organizing and Chicano theater, explored Mexican history, immigration, and other elements of Chicano nationalist identity in his column 'El Machete' several years before young activists declared themselves 'Chicanos.'

27 Quoted in 'La Raza en Las Americas,' *El Grito del Norte*, May 19, 1969 (Espanola).

28 Quoted in Joe Lopez, 'La Raza,' *Chicago Defender*, February 2, 1974, 4.

29 Quoted in Rubén Salazar, 'Who Is a Chicano? And What Is It the Chicanos Want?' *Los Angeles Times*, February 6, 1970, B7. This article was reprinted in many Chicano newspapers. Examples include, Rubén Salazar, 'Who Is a Chicano?' *El Chicano*, February 15, 1970 (Colton); Rubén Salazar, 'Chicanismo,' *Caracol*, February 1975 (San Antonio).

30 Quoted in Sophie Salazar, 'A Reply to "Who Is El Chicano?"' *El Chicano*, March 1, 1970 (Colton).

31 Quoted in Salazar, 'A Reply to "Who Is El Chicano?"'

32 Miguel Pendes, 'I am Joaquín/Yo Soy Joaquín,' *El Renacimiento*, September 24, 1973 (Lansing). This essay explores the meaning of Gonzales's poem as it also explores the essence of Chicano identity.

33 Daniel Valdes and Tom Pino, 'Labels Tell You What You Are,' *La Luz* 1, no. 3, 1973 (Denver); García, *Chicanismo*; Michael Soldatenko, *Chicano Studies: The Genesis of a Discipline* (Tucson: University of Arizona Press, 2009), 71–3.

34 For examples in literature and Chicano movement texts see Angie Chabram Denersesian, 'And, Yes . . . the Earth Did Part: On the Splitting of Chicano/a Subjectivity,' in *Building with Our Hands: New Directions in Chicana Studies* ed. Adela de la Torre and Beatriz M. Pesquera (Berkeley: University of California Press, 1993), 34–56.

35 Eloy L. Gonzalez, 'Where Are You, My America?' *El Renacimiento*, June 25, 1973 (Lansing).

36 Andres Valdez, 'They Will Know,' *El Chicano*, August 23, 1969 (Colton).

37 Ernesto Vigil, 'A Poem of Dedication,' *El Chicano*, August 23, 1969 (Colton).

38 Cesilia Guajardo, 'De origen . . .' *El Sueño*, Supplement to *El Hispano*, December 14, 1971 (Sacramento).

39 See generally Alma M. García, *Chicana Feminist Thought: The Basic Historical Writings* (New York: Routledge, 1997).

40 Anna Nieto-Gomez, 'Chicana Identify,' and Nancy Nieto, 'Macho Attitudes,' *Hijas de Cuauhtémoc*, April/May, 1971 (Long Beach).

41 See the various path-breaking Chicana essays featured in movement periodicals and mainstream magazines in Garcia, *Chicana Feminist Thought*, 17–39.

42 Quoted in Elvira Saragoza, 'Chicana: Slave? Companion? Co-Partner? La Mujer in the Chicano Movement,' *Bronce*, June 1976 (Berkeley), 12–13.

43 Elena Abeyta, 'I am María,' *Bronce*, June 1969 (Berkeley): *Hija de la Chingada* is often a reference to *La Malinche* as both traitor and mother of the Mexican people. For the long and complicated history of *La Malinche*, see Sandra M. Cypess, *La Malinche in Mexican Literature from History to Myth* (Austin: University of Texas Press, 1991).

44 Quoted in Saragoza, 'Chicana: Slave? Companion?' 12–13. See also 'Interview with La Señora Minerva Castillo,' *Hijas de Cuauhtémoc*, April/May 1971 (Long Beach).

45 Juana Serros, 'A La Mujer,' *Nuestra Cosa*, January 1975 (Riverside).

46 Armida (Pee-Wee) Salgado, 'A Letter from Our Editor,' *Carnalas de MAYO*, November 1974 (California Rehabilitation Center, Santa Barbara).

47 Dolores Huerta, 'Dolores Huerta Talks,' *La Voz de Pueblo*, November–December, 1972 (Berkeley).

48 Teresa Reyna, 'I Ain't No Women's Libber,' *La Voz de Pueblo*, November–December, 1972 (Berkeley).

49 'The Realities of Being a Woman/Chicana,' *Encuentro Femenil* 1, no. 1, Spring 1973 (San Fernando).

50 Marlene Cimons, 'From Follower to Leader,' *Los Angeles Times*, February 10, 1972, 11. See also Jorge Mariscal, 'Left Turns in the Chicano Movement, 1965–1975,' *Monthly Review* 54, no. 3 (July 2002): 59–68.

51 For an examination of the interplay between movement participation and intellectual production, see Maylei Blackwell, *¡Chicana Power! Contested Histories of Feminism in the Chicano Movement* (Austin: University of Texas Press, 2011).

52 For an explanation of this process, see García, *Chicana Feminist Thought*, 69–72.

53 Lionila Lopez Saenz, 'Machismo, No! Igualdad, Sí!' *La Luz*, May 1972, 19–21 (Denver).

54 See Consuelo Nieto, 'The Chicana and the Women's Rights Movement,' *LULAC News*, December 1974; 'Chicanas Caucus, Wichita, Kansas,' *El Clarin Chicano*, July 17, 1974 (Chicago); Mike Castro, '2 Women of Mexican Origin Conquer Machismo,' *Los Angeles Times*, September 12, 1974, SF1; Kathy Valadez, 'Women in Politics—Where Does the Chicana Fit in?' *El Chicano*, February 6, 1975 (Colton); 'Vilma Martinez Speaks on Court Decisions and Chicanos,' *El Chicano*, March 20, 1975 (Colton); 'Las Mujeres LULAC Seminar Smashing Success,' *El Clarin Mexico-Americano*, March 29, 1975 (Chicago); 'La Década de la Mujer,' *La Raza Habla*, February 1978 (Las Cruces); Jan Klunder, 'Chicana Council Promises to Resist Male Domination,' *Los Angeles Times*, November 18, 1979, SEA3; Catherine Vasquez, 'Dr. Pantoja Urges Women to Trust One Another, Assume Positions of Leadership,' *LULAC News*, December 1979.

55 *Con safos* is a *barrio* Spanish term represented as c/s or C/S meaning 'with respect.' See José A. Burciaga, *Drink Cultura: Chicanismo* (Santa Barbara: Joshua Odell Editions/ Capra Press, 1992), 6–8.

56 Quoted in editorial section of *Con Safos* no. 7, Winter, 1971 (Los Angeles).

57 All quotes from editorial section of *Con Safos* no. 7, Winter, 1971 (Los Angeles).

58 See *Con Safos* no. 6, Summer, 1970 (Los Angeles).

59 See *Con Safos* 2, no. 5, 1970 (Los Angeles).

60 'Glossary,' *Con Safos* 1, no. 3, March 1969 (Los Angeles).

61 See 'The Autobiography of a Brown Buffalo' and 'Answers to the Barriology Examination #4' in *Con Safos* no. 7, Winter, 1971 (Los Angeles).

62 'Editorial,' *Con Safos* 1, no. 2, Fall, 1968 (Los Angeles).

63 See Octavio Ignacio Romano-V., *Voices: Readings from El Grito, a Journal of Contemporary Mexican American Thought, 1967–1971* (Berkeley: Quinto Sol Publications, 1971). See also Tia Tenopia, 'Latinopia Literature Arte Público Press: Interview with Nicolas Kanellos,' May 1, 2011, retrieved at: http://latinopia.com/latino-literature/ latinopia-literature-arte-publico-press/.

64 Chon A. Noriega, *The Chicano Studies Reader: An Anthology of Aztlán, 1970–2000* (Los Angeles: UCLA Chicano Studies Research Center Publications, 2001), ix–xv.

65 Juan Bruce-Novoa, *RetroSpace: Collected Essays on Chicano Literature* (Houston: Arte Público Press, 1990), 78–80; Katharine Zurek, 'Publishing Profiles: Dr. Nicolas Kanellos of Arte Público Press, Creating a Thriving Latino Literary Community from the Ground Up,' *Independent Publisher*, n.d., retrieved from: www.independentpublisher. com/article.php?page=1687; Dennis López, 'Good-Bye Revolution—Hello Cultural Mystique: Quinto Sol Publications and Chicano Literary Nationalism,' *MELUS* 35, no. 3 (Fall, 2010): 183–210.

66 See Charles Tatum, *Chicano and Chicana Literature: Otra Voz Del Pueblo* (Tucson: University of Arizona Press, 2006), 64–5.

67 For a survey of Latino newspapers see Richard Chabrán and Rafael Chabrán, 'The Spanish-Language and Latino Press of the United States: Newspapers and Periodicals,' in *Handbook of Hispanic Cultures in the United States: Literature and Art*, ed. Alfredo Jiménez, Nicolás Kanellos, and Fabregat C. Esteva (Houston: Arte Público Press, 1994), 360-83.

5

ART AND THE MOVEMENT

Chicano Murals and Community Space

Introduction

The aim of this chapter is to explore and understand the Chicano Movement as it manifested itself in community-based and community-defining mural movements and the broader pan-Latino and interracial public arts movements of the 1960s and 1970s. The Chicano Movement, like other social movements, was as much about claiming political, social, and visual space as it was about making historical claims to peoplehood. Artists in the *barrios* of California, Texas, and across the Mexican American diaspora sought to reshape the visual environment of their neighborhoods to unify people through images that created a shared cultural imaginary and placed the local community within the heroic narrative of Chicano history. The artists of the Chicano Movement represented its nationalist claims through the creation of territorialized community murals, yet the public mural movement was quite often an interracial and pan-Latino affair that linked progressives and minority group artists together in the space-claiming project of urban mural making.

Chicano muralists worked as an ethnically defined artistic community but often labored alongside Anglo, African American, and Puerto Rican artists to produce murals that told Chicano nationalist stories or gave new meaning to racial identity, ethnicity, and class within the context of the urban *barrio*. These muralists helped other minority groups with their mural projects; in many places they created Chicano art collectives or multiracial public mural collectives so that artists could work with and learn from one another. The Chicano Movement's mural movement sought to maintain ethnic neighborhoods in the face of destructive public policy, poverty, and neglect. Through this process Chicano and other muralists not only claimed space within the urban milieu of the modern city but also created an artistic community as they produced murals that essentialized identity to convey the history of Chicanos (and others) and iconic imagery to *barrio* residents. For artists and activists alike, the Chicano mural movement and the Chicano Movement itself were essential to one another and to the nationalist agenda of creating the symbolic homeland of Aztlán wherever Chicanos lived.

While each mural was unique, many shared commonalities and embraced a progressive view of history as they highlighted the long struggles of a minority people over the millennia. The Chicano mural often told the long story of La Raza (the people) as well as the local story of struggle and activism, using essentialized representations of heroes, culturally relevant symbols, and scenes of community mobilization. Scholars of ethnic street art have considered the ways these images explore and expand upon community and ethnic identities among *barrio* residents. Such an engagement with the local audience often also embraces notions of 'strategic essentialism' and 'strategic ethnicity,' which rely on a symbolic 'ethnic' imaginary that borrows from nationalist themes and incorporates specific heroes, visual representation of community struggle and triumph, martyrdom, and strength that resonate with and help mobilize the local ethnic community.[1] Public mural art, while often commissioned by community groups, local government organizations, and individual property owners and undertaken by an individual artist, was usually a cooperative project involving the lead artist, artists' collectives, neighborhood activists, and youth volunteers. Youth participation in the painting process was central, as artists often used the project for instructional purposes with the murals completed by groups of disadvantaged youth. Thus, while many murals documented struggles against oppression, the mural itself was a result of unity; it brought together a diverse group and reflected the positive aspects of the Chicano Movement as local people came together with artists to make the mural a reality.

Mural art, while representing the themes of Chicano nationalism and Third World people's struggles, was also an expression of the politics of self-determination. The artists themselves saw public art as part of the broader struggle for civil rights among Chicanos, Latinos, African Americans, and other oppressed people. In this chapter, we will consider the influence of the Mexican muralists and then explore the diverse and often multi-neighborhood efforts of the pan-Latino public mural movement. We next consider the movement in the city of Chicago, where the mural movement took root in the second-largest urban concentration of Mexican Americans outside of Los Angeles and the second-largest urban concentration of Puerto Ricans outside of New York City and was often pan-Latino and interracial in development and execution. Next, the chapter turns to the public housing murals of East Los Angeles, the West Side of San Antonio, and San Francisco's Mission District. Lastly, shifting to Barrio Logan in San Diego, California, we explore the struggle to establish Chicano Park after the construction of an interstate highway and the Coronado Bay Bridge. These movements all sought to bring the themes of the Chicano and related Latino, minority, and urban civil rights movements into public view through murals that, often in abstract forms and broad brush strokes, celebrated the history and heroes of La Raza and made homeland claims to neighborhood space. The murals of the Chicano Movement were directly influenced by Mexican muralists—perhaps the most important muralist movement of the twentieth century.

Mexican Muralists

The Mexican muralists of the early twentieth century inspired the work of, and provided an ample array of iconographic models for, many of the murals created by Chicano and Latino artists in the 1960s and 1970s. The Mexican muralist movement grew out of the broader Latin American shift toward *indigenismo* in politics and art in the Americas as well as social realism, which depicted the lives of workers as part of the large transformations in society since the conquest. By placing native peoples and workers at the center of history, the muralists made their work overtly political in ways that many in the art world tended to reject. By breaking down the barriers between high culture and working-class life the Mexican muralists challenged artists to reflect their politics in their work, and produce art that spoke not only to other artists, collectors, and critics but also to everyday people as well as those committed to social, even revolutionary, change. Mexico City was at the center of this movement and became the canvas for much of the most important work of the muralist movement.[2]

Public murals in the United States were often modeled after the work of *Los tres grandes* (the three greats) of the Mexican mural movement: Diego Rivera, José Orozco, and David Alfaro Siqueiros who did a residency in Chicago where he trained several Chicano muralists. The typical Chicano mural embraces a social realist style that resembles the classic work of *Los tres grandes*, covers similar Mexican historical themes, yet shifts the focus to the ethnic community of Chicanos within the United States. *Los tres grandes* are widely considered the leaders of the Mexican muralist movement of the mid twentieth century. Philosopher, politician, and noted Mexican nationalist José Vasconcelos, best known for his concept of *La Raza Cósmica* (the cosmic race), which celebrated Mexico as a mestizo (mixed) nation of both European and indigenous ancestry, supported the Mexican mural movement by awarding commissions to *Los tres grandes* within the halls and courtyards of many government buildings. In striking contrast to most public art in government buildings, the often historically themed murals in Mexico City critiqued the Mexican government, capitalism, and the Catholic Church, as they portrayed native peoples and mestizo workers in heroic scenes of resistance. Much as religious art in churches across Mexico and Europe sought to educate an illiterate populace, Mexican historical murals commissioned by post-Revolutionary bureaucrats such as Vasconcelos and completed by the likes of Diego Rivera sought to educate and elevate the masses through art.[3] The work of these muralists became the basic models for the Chicano and other urban mural movements in the United States in the late 1960s and early 1970s.

Space and Community

One central component of the community arts movement was its focus on claiming space within the urban sphere and marking it as community space through the design and local production of murals in a specific neighborhood. This desire for beauty and space took root in American cities that were undergoing rapid transformation through urban renewal programs that often tore down vast tracts of housing and left a scarred landscape of vacant lots in its wake. Urban renewal was supposed to be a good thing. It was created to remove urban blight—dilapidated buildings and crumbling infrastructure—but its impact together with other large-scale public works programs including the Interstate Highway System often was the destruction of urban ethnic and minority communities across the United States.[4] This destruction of the urban environment reflected the transformation of America's inner cities from white and ethnic middle-class and working-class areas to places defined by populations of African Americans, Mexican Americans, Puerto Ricans, and other low-income 'minority groups,' negatively impacted by capital flight and the reduction of public services. Within this changing urban environment, minority communities struggled not only for civil rights but also for the right to shape the environment left behind after the destruction brought by urban renewal and the development of the highway system. As federal policies cut deep scars across the cities to provide arterial roadways that facilitated the flight of the white middle class from American cities, minorities pressed for civil rights and made territorial claims to homelands within the city. Within this context, the community mural movements were efforts to claim space, educate, and agitate as part of the broader social movements for minority group civil rights and self-determination in the *barrios* and inner cities of the United States.[5]

Chicano ethnic nationalism in this case can be viewed as part of a policy of 'strategic essentialism' in both policy goals (claiming space for art) and within the art itself (which often portrayed essentialist ethnic and heroic iconography). In this light, community murals were part of a process of claiming space for communities under siege.[6] In the case of Chicago, the Puerto Rican community had moved within just a few decades from Lincoln Park, to West Town, to Humboldt Park. Likewise, university building forced Mexicans into increasingly dense neighborhoods in Pilsen and the Back of the Yards. In San Diego, Chicano community activists, reacting to the effect on neighborhoods of the construction of highway ramps for the Coronado Bay Bridge, began an occupation of the land underneath and adjoining the ramps to block the development of the site for the California Highway Patrol. In both cases, either before or after the creation of murals, people took to the street in mass protests either to establish mural space or to protect art from destruction. Thus, the historical significance of these community murals lies not only in the presentation of historical material and cultural narrative via the murals themselves, but also in the social movement history of the murals as part of the process of neighborhood claims for spatially grounded control.[7]

Using a variety of tactics, including negotiation, public protest, legal action, and widespread community mobilization, activists brought the lessons learned in other social movements to bear as they made the creation of public and private space for 'public' murals central to their protest agenda. They also made the creation of these murals public educational events in the process. Moreover, these murals often became the focus of continued protest and activism, since they lacked Historical Landmark status or similar cultural/artistic protections. In this cycle of protest, artistic production, and preservation activism, low-income communities battled against and worked with local governments and private property owners, as they sought to mark and maintain control over the spatial territory in which they lived.

For Chicanos the claiming of space, the building of homelands in the face of urban decay, and the politics of the Chicano movement often focused on homeland-making within the urban milieu. The visual territory of the city or the *barrio* took the place of the mythical 'nation' (often named 'Aztlán,' after the mythical homeland of the Aztecs), as the movement sought to build a variety of urban homelands, or Aztláns.[8] In the Puerto Rican case, attacks on efforts to maintain community and create artistic expression in Chicago were linked to Puerto Rican independence efforts, heroes, and martyrs and were experienced as yet another manifestation of American imperialism's negative impact on the Puerto Rican people.[9] In this way, the transformation of the landscape by the state was seen as both an offensive 'attack' on the community and an opportunity for these same people to claim the open spaces created by the wrecking ball and the construction of highways through the heart of vibrant ethnic neighborhoods and remake them as homelands.

Barrio as Homeland

As many aspects of the Chicano Movement focused on the desire to build actual or mythical homelands for the Chicano people, the Chicano arts and mural movement sought to mark out territory through the production of public art. Public art was meant to educate the people and beautify neighborhoods considered blighted. If those outside the *barrios* thought of them as nothing more than low-income neighborhoods plagued by crime, violence, gangs, undocumented immigrants, non-English speakers, and the other telltale signs of poverty, artists and activists living and working in these neighborhoods rejected such appellations and made public art part of the broader movement for better education, social services, and government service in these dense, often walkable, city neighborhoods. While certainly many Chicanos, like other Americans, sought to leave places such as

East Los Angeles, Pilsen, and San Antonio's West Side for suburban districts and suburbs, others aimed to remake the urban *barrio* as a center of strength for the Chicano people. Artist-activists played a role in this effort to reshape the visual environment of the *barrio*.

The Chicano Movement itself fostered artists as participants and activists in the places where it organized. Central organizations such as the Crusade for Justice, La Raza Unida Party, and the United Farm Workers encouraged artistic participation and promoted the work of many artists. Chicano newspapers likewise dedicated ample space to artwork and photography, often alongside literary works. Artists' workshops and galleries opened in Mexican American neighborhoods, with many located in the same buildings that housed community action and community service organizations established by Chicanos. Chicano artists worked together with activists and others committed to community uplift. The fact that space was available for social service offices in former banks, department stores, and government buildings as a result of public policy and white flight allowed for the evolution and refinement of Chicano art and the development of Chicano and Chicana artists both artistically and as part of the broader movement.[10]

In Los Angeles, Chicago, and elsewhere, activists established artists' organizations and collectives to further the development of a Chicano arts movement within the space of the *barrio*. In Los Angeles Frank Romero, Carlos Almaraz, Roberto de la Rocha, and Gilbert Luján established Los Four as an artists' collective which they expanded with Judithe Hernández's membership as Los Four plus One. The collective brought Chicano art to the Anglo public and introduced it to the fine art world through a landmark exhibition at the Los Angeles County Museum of Art.[11] The collective was also committed to public art. The artists painted murals along the highways and in the Ramona Gardens Housing Projects and participated in the *Great Wall of Los Angeles* mural.[12] In 1972 Harry Gamboa Jr., Glugio "Gronk" Nicandro, Willie Herrón, and Patssi Valdez formed the collective Asco ('Asco' in Spanish means revulsion, disgust, urge to vomit) as a Chicano artists' collective in East Los Angeles. The group grew out of the Chicano newspaper *Regeneración*, and members used performance art in their work.[13] In East Chicago, Indiana, José Gamaliel González established the Movimiento Artístico Chicano (MARCH) in 1972. MARCH moved to Chicago in 1975 and expanded to include members and fellow travelers such as Carlos Cortez, Ray Patlan, Mario Castillo, Marguerite Ortega, Salvador Vega, Victor Sorell, Aurelio Diaz, and others who produced public art, poster art, wood cuts, poetry, fiction, and history and played a role in Chicano movement publications such as *Revista Chicano-Riqueña*.[14] Frustrated with the institutional racism he experienced as a student and artist at the University of Notre Dame (Indiana), González intended MARCH to spearhead the individual and collective production and exhibition of Chicano art in the Midwest.[15] In cities across the nation with sizeable Latino populations, Chicano artists established collectives and organized exhibitions at universities, art museums, and community centers as they sought to establish Chicano art in the art world and as a vital part of the *barrio* landscape.

Murals in particular marked out spaces of importance to *barrio* residents, remaking underpasses, walls exposed as a result of demolition, schools riddled with graffiti, and parks that lacked infrastructure into spaces for gathering, reflection, and educational visual experiences. Community groups, artists' collectives, and Chicano activists such as the Brown Berets, La Raza Unida Party, and Chicano newspaper publishers promoted public arts efforts and were increasingly aided by supportive local government agencies and community-focused philanthropic groups. The murals produced portrayed the heroic story of Mexican immigrant workers' contributions to the local economy and culture, incorporated religious iconography such as the Virgin of Guadalupe (the patron saint of the Mexican people), related in abstract form the Aztec and indigenous heritage of the Mexican American people, or merged these themes in a pastiche of narrative, shapes, and color. Whether social realist or abstract in style, the Chicano mural claimed the territory of the *barrio* as it engaged residents in a social epistemological process of discovery and created new landmarks in the territorialized *barrio* as Aztlán/homeland.[16]

Claiming Latino Space in Chicago

Chicago is a city known for its interracial commitment to public art as well as its community murals movement in the African American, Mexican American, and Puerto Rican neighborhoods of the city. While the murals often depict the struggles of distinct communities, many of them were interracial and interethnic collaborative projects. As its many authors and artists have shown, Chicago is a city that does not easily fit delimitation or categorization. Other Midwestern cities where Chicanos settled, including Detroit and Milwaukee, also witnessed mural movements during and after the heyday of the Chicano Movement, yet none rivaled Chicago in diversity, pan-Latino and pan-ethnic cooperation, and sheer numbers. Chicago, as a city of immigrants, where many languages have been spoken in the public sphere since its founding and ethnic groups maintain ties to homelands, was a central location of the Chicano and Latino arts and mural movements.

Chicago's mural movement reflected the changing demographics of the city. Chicanos and Puerto Ricans lived in three distinct areas in the late 1960s and 1970s. The city's far South Side in the shadow of the United States Steel South Works was home to the Mexican immigrants who had poured into Chicago in the early twentieth century to meet the demands of the steel industry.[17] In an area bounded by 78th Street on the north, Interstate 90 on the west, and Lake Michigan and the steel works on the east, Mexican immigrants and their children established churches and became a part of the local fabric of this industrial, multiethnic, and multiracial city.

On the city's Southwest Side, Mexican Americans and immigrants settled in Pilsen near the industrial area around the McCormick Reaper Works in a neighborhood originally settled by Austrians, Bohemians, and Germans and made famous by its ties to the labor struggles of the late nineteenth century, most famously the Haymarket Square Riot of 1886 and other battles between those seeking to establish labor unions and the police, military, and company soldiers.[18] Because of the planned gentrification that began in Lincoln Park, Puerto Ricans settled further west in the 1960s on the Near Northwest Side. ThePuerto Rican *barrio* extended west along Division Street to Humboldt Park. Latinos reinvigorated neighborhoods established by immigrants in wave after wave of migration to Chicago, yet the policies of urban renewal meant that the wrecking ball also tore through these communities as they sought to establish themselves—a process that has been nearly continual for Puerto Ricans on the city's Near Northwest Side.[19]

Chicanos experienced the shifting sands of urban renewal, as the establishment of the University of Illinois campus displaced a longstanding neighborhood. While the struggles of Italians to fight off the land clearance and community destruction in the face of the University of Illinois juggernaut are well documented, the movement of Mexican settlers from the area in and around Hull House into Pilsen and Little Village is less well known.[20] Mexican immigrants, Mexican Americans, and other Near-South-Side Latinos became increasingly concentrated in Pilsen and the Lower West Side neighborhood of Chicago. While Pilsen residents supported the Farm Workers Movement, in many respects Latino politics in Chicago appear muted by comparison to activism in California, Texas, and nearby Wisconsin and Michigan; however, arts activism in Chicago surpassed that of any other Midwestern city.

Into these neighborhoods Latinos came or expanded their presence during the late 1960s and early 1970s. With the onslaught of deindustrialization and the regional transfer of manufacturing work from the Midwest's so-called Rust Belt cities of Chicago, Detroit, Milwaukee, and Cleveland to the Sunbelt cities of the South and to 'Third-World' manufacturing zones (including Mexico and Puerto Rico), Latinos and other minorities increasingly fought for a space in the declining metropolis of nineteenth- and early twentieth-century industrial capitalism.[21] As the buildings around them were torn down or burned down, they sought to make sense out of this new landscape, and artists sought to make the space liveable and even beautiful.

In 1968, artist Mario Castillo created *Metaphysics (Peace)*, a mural considered by most to be the first outdoor mural of the Chicano arts movement in the United States. Painted on the Urban Progress Center, a War on Poverty-funded organization on South Halstead Street and 19th Street in the Pilsen neighborhood, this mural was created one year after William Walker and a group of African American youths, artists, and others painted the *Wall of Respect* on the South Side at 43rd and Langley to honor community heroes and claim public space in their community. Within three years of the completion of *Wall of Respect*, there were 30 public murals, and by 1973 there were 130. This effort to create accessible art where the artist and members of the local neighborhood worked together to create outdoor murals on the sides of buildings exposed as a result of urban renewal and the wrecking ball touched both the African American and Mexican American communities almost simultaneously. Mario Castillo did not work alone on *Metaphysics (Peace)* but rather designed the piece and carried out the painting with a group of art students and community volunteers.[22] In a culminating moment captured on film, Castillo stands with the youth program workers who helped him paint—the group smiling and standing in front of the completed mural. Castillo would be only the first of many Chicano muralists to change the visual landscape of Pilsen and other neighborhoods in Chicago.[23]

Organizations such as the Urban Progress Center, a War on Poverty agency, operated in African American, Mexican American, and Appalachian migrant neighborhoods in Chicago. There was certainly cooperation between activists and organizations in the late 1960s, as minorities and rural white migrants were living in a Chicago that faced economic, structural, and community decline. As the broader community fought for civil rights and a commitment to urban life within the context of 'Machine' politics in Chicago, artists played a role in documenting the struggles of urban living as they sought to beautify cities scarred by the social policies of post–World War II America's 'renewal' programs that often leveled well-built brick buildings and left vast tracts of empty lots in their wake. Mario Castillo's *Metaphysics (Peace)*, now destroyed, was painted in the space between buildings leveled by the wrecking ball and was the opening volley in what became a decades-long commitment to community-based Chicano and Latino public art. Chicanos, Puerto Ricans, and African Americans claimed these walls and painted on them, making them their own even if they were legally owned by others.[24]

Muralists and activists saw Chicano art and the Chicano political movement as one and the same. While the art was part of an effort to improve the surroundings and elevate *barrio* residents, politics were also central to the artist-as-activist model. While Castillo's *Metaphysics (Peace)* was the first Chicano mural, by 1971 other Chicano artists had completed or were working on their own mural projects. Just off 18th Street, the main commercial street of Pilsen, in a former Bohemian settlement house, the Brown Berets established a community organization that became Casa Aztlán. With the assistance of students participating in the War on Poverty Neighborhood Youth Corps program, Ray Patlan painted murals that eventually covered most of the interior and exterior of the building. The Patlan murals depicted the history of Mexico and of Mexican workers

in both farm and industrial work, as well as a portrait of United Farm Workers Organizing Committee (UFWOC) president Cesar Chavez. Patlan's work at
Casa Aztlán eventually incorporated both the internal and external façades of the
building and wrapped it in a retelling of Mexican and Mexican American history
through art. From the exterior, the building paid homage to heroes and—much
like *Metaphysics (Peace)*—incorporated images based on Aztec, Mayan, and other
Amerindian archetypes. These murals marked the visual space of Casa Aztlán as
a virtual 'homeland' for the Chicano community of Pilsen.[25] The Casa Aztlán
murals became a site for community celebration, strategic ethnic storytelling, and
historical representation and critique.

The Casa Aztlán murals incorporate the many signs and symbolic representations of the Chicano Movement and the Chicano arts movement and place
the people of Pilsen and their local struggles for political representation and
jobs for Latinos beside the larger narrative of Mexican American and Chicano
history. By situating the local community alongside Francisco 'Pancho' Villa,
Emiliano Zapata, and the marchers of the United Farm Workers, the visual narrative represented the everyday people of Pilsen and the families and children
served by Casa Aztlán as valued makers of history. Murals were not merely
about representing the long history of Chicanos but also about incorporating Chicano liberation at the local level into the larger story of a people—of
La Raza.[26]

The Chicano arts movement was one part of the broader movement for social
justice in the *barrios* of the United States. This 'mini-Mexican revolution on
the streets,' according to muralist Marcos Raya, was 'one of the ways of changing the status quo,' as 'the movement injected a consciousness of culture into a
working-class neighborhood.'[27] The goal was multifaceted as Chicanos fought for
better living conditions, immigrant rights, housing, and better schools, and created murals 'as a way of showing our anger and confusion—so close to the Loop
[downtown Chicago] and so goddamn fucked up.'[28] For Ray Patlan, likewise, the
murals began as part of the dynamics of change and reform in the American city.
In Pilsen and other low-income communities, the 'idea of being able to change
one's own visual environment' for 'people who have never had any power whatso-
ever' often sparked further activism. As the visual environment altered and murals
became activist accomplishments, other concerns for those living in Pilsen such as
'voting, getting the garbage picked up, calling the city and telling them you need
things' came to the forefront, as participants in making the murals and residents
realized that they could accomplish things and demand accountability from politicians and public service providers.[29] The murals were large public pronounce-
ments that altered the landscape of Pilsen as they became everyday parts of the
urban environment and marked it as Chicano territorial space.

The 1970s became a period of expansion and experimentation in Chicago's
mural movement, as the Latino and African American communities as well as

others, including the Polish American community, commissioned murals or painted murals on their own on the urban canvas of exposed brick walls. In the decades before the widespread reinvestment in cities and the rampant gentrification of low-income areas, Latino and other ethnic communities tried to beautify and claim the urban landscape through public art, while cities tore down 'blighted' buildings exposing ever more brick to the painter's brush. In some ways, the mural movement of the 1960s and 1970s grew in tandem with urban renewal and in opposition to it, filling in the spaces left by the destruction of the built environment, before the murals themselves sometimes faced destruction when the wrecking ball again moved through the neighborhood.[30]

The public mural movement was one part of the dramatic series of events that spread across both Mexican American and Puerto Rican areas of the city. Castillo's *Metaphysics (Peace)* was merely the first spark in a Latino mural movement in the city. In Lincoln Park, where Puerto Ricans faced the onslaught of urban renewal under the 'Chicago 21 Plan,' which ushered in the first wave of gentrification in Chicago, artists painted a mural detailing the history of Puerto Rico and its main independence leaders on the walls of the People's Church at Armitage and Dayton Avenues in Lincoln Park. Soon the building became the national headquarters of the Young Lords, a militant Puerto Rican civil rights organization modeled on the Black Panther Party, even as urban renewal displaced the bulk of the Puerto Rican community from that neighborhood into nearby West Town and Humboldt Park.[31]

The Humboldt Park community was the site of sustained civil rights and artist-led activism in the middle and late 1960s, which continued into the 1970s. The efforts of several waves of artists to alter the visual landscape of the city came into direct conflict with public and private efforts to redevelop sections of the city deemed blighted or considered worthy of private redevelopment. On June 12, 1966, following a routine arrest, 200 Chicago police officers fought what the *Chicago Defender* termed a 'pitched battle' at the corner of Division Street and Damen Avenue against Puerto Rican community residents in an affair that left several dead and caused significant damage.[32] Reverend Martin Luther King, Jr. called for a meeting in Chicago to 'totally free all minority groups,' as it became clear that much of the violence had to do with police firing into the crowd, using night sticks to hit people, and releasing attack dogs.[33] Nearly 10 years later, in 1977, following the June 4 Puerto Rican Parade, a second riot took place and laid waste to sections of Division Street just one mile west of the 1966 riot. Residents and police officers were injured, three people were killed, and several businesses were looted as the riot extended into the next day. Something needed to be done in Humboldt Park, and community leaders knew it.[34]

Following the second riot on Division Street, Humboldt Park residents banded together and united Puerto Ricans, Chicanos, whites, and African Americans to defend murals and the buildings they were painted upon. One such mural, titled *Breaking the Chains*, became the subject of sustained activism in 1978 as residents engaged in street protests and 24-hour vigils to protect the building on which it was painted from demolition by the city.[35] In 1971 the Chicago Mural Group was founded after a group of artists, including Ray Patlan with John Weber at the forefront, sought to coordinate efforts and utilize grant funding agencies in the mural movement. One of the earliest murals painted by John Weber and collaborators, *Breaking the Chains* was itself a victim of the very process it was meant to fight against—wide-scale destruction of the urban landscape via the wrecking ball—despite the fact that it had been funded by the National Endowment for the Arts and the Illinois Art Council. The mural depicted black, brown, and white hands breaking the chains of 'injustice,' 'poverty,' and 'drugs.'[36] In addition to other civil rights motifs typical of the period, ironically it featured a woman hanging out of a window of a burning building to protest the common practice of arson, condemnation, insurance collection, and public demolition of such 'blighted' property. In the 1970s, apparently, buildings were worth more if knocked down than if left standing—to owners, contractors, and city government.

The City of Chicago, to clear what it deemed an unsafe and abandoned building, hired a contractor to tear down the building at 1456 North Rockwell Street which was home to *Breaking the Chains*. In reaction the Chicago Mural Group organized public protests and a legal challenge to the demolition order. In fact, the demolition order helped to unify the inhabitants of Humboldt Park, bringing together Latino organizations to sue for a stay of demolition and a finding of the building as 'structurally sound.' The mural depicted the very process of abandonment, condemnation, and demolition that the building now faced.[37] In this case, a multiracial and multiethnic coalition of artists and activists joined together to stop the destruction of living and visual space—reflecting the potential for cooperation depicted in the mural. A police officer working on the arson taskforce at the time said that 'Mural buildings are never burned' and that 'we should paint murals on every buildings [*sic*] in the city.'[38] The activism of *Breaking the Chains* led to a realization that saving the mural and the building were intimately intertwined efforts in a neighborhood with over 250 vacant lots in a 32-block area.[39]

The mobilization in defense of community art and the preservation of building structures succeeded in saving one of the most militant murals in the neighborhood. *Breaking the Chains*, which still exists, is about the struggles of minority people to cast off oppression in favor of liberty and community. It shows black, white, and brown hands working to free themselves from bondage, accompanied by the symbol for the Latin American Defense Organization (LADO), a group that joined Chicanos, Puerto Ricans, and leftist whites together in the effort to create and defend community in Chicago. The community group that led the mural preservation effort also sought to renovate and rehabilitate the property to provide housing for 14 families and criticized the rapid destruction of city structures rather than renovation. This became a trend in resistance across the city, as communities that increasingly felt boxed in by the wrecking ball and public and private neglect as well as other forms of oppression organized to improve and preserve their neighborhoods.[40] This activism prompted the *Chicago Tribune* to investigate further the mural movement in the city, resulting in an article that celebrated the murals of Chicago for creating a 'museum of the streets' for residents. The *Tribune* noted that several of the murals that embodied the greater meaning of the public mural movement had been demolished within a few years of completion. The article also linked the mural movements of Latinos, African Americans, and white artists to *Los tres grandes* of the Mexican muralist movement, especially David Alfaro Siqueiros, who had worked in Chicago and trained some of the area muralists active in the late 1970s.[41] Mural defense movements, like that which mobilized to save *Breaking the Chains*, were followed by decades of preservation (often with support from elected officials) and continued expansion of the urban public mural movement of the 1970s.

The Chicago public art movement was well organized. Members hosted artists from other countries and cities, published manuals on how to prepare exterior walls for painting, and held workshops to train community members in the selection of paints well suited to the often harsh winters of Chicago. In many ways, the institutionalization of this movement, often with the support of nonprofit organizations, led to a professionalization of the practice of public art and public art instruction, even as the actual execution of the art projects themselves required community support and as time progressed became a part of the political and social fabric of many of Chicago's communities.[42] In fact, by the late twentieth century, as many of the original murals of the movement such as *Metaphysics (Peace)* were demolished along with the buildings they were painted on or were sandblasted by new owners, murals became a point of pride in the *barrios* of Humboldt Park and Pilsen and reflected a growing concern with immigration, nationalism, and Puerto Rican independence. By the twenty-first century the protection of murals was still weak, but cooperative arrangements in Pilsen have made it one of the most mural-rich neighborhoods in the United States during a period of rapid gentrification. New owners in redeveloped sections of Humboldt Park have often preserved and maintained the murals out of respect and the desire of new residents to see these artworks maintained as part of the visual environment of the modern city.[43] The Chicano mural movement in Chicago was diverse and often pan-Latino and pan-ethnic, a fact reflected in the participation of Puerto Ricans in Chicano groups such as the Brown Berets and Chicano participation in Puerto Rican groups such as the Young Lords, as well as the establishment of pan-Latino organizations such as LADO, which incorporated all Latino people.

Chicano Art in Los Angeles, San Francisco, and Texas

The Estrada Housing Courts were built by the federal government during World War II in response to the housing shortage in Southern California resulting from the boom in wartime work in the cities. The Courts were later converted into federally subsidized low-income housing whose large walls became the object of community demands for control of the visual environment. The Ramona Gardens public housing project had experienced a similar history of decline. Efforts to claim visual space in this low-income section of Los Angeles led to the planning and execution of a series of murals throughout the 1970s. Muralists in fact painted over a thousand murals across the city of Los Angeles and environs during the 1970s, many of which challenged the official history of the city and the history of the nation, by inserting Mexican Americans, Native Americans, and other Third World people into the historical narrative, including them in the visual efforts to claim space in a city that by 1990 would surpass Chicago as the second-largest city in the United States. As the city grew and transformed the landscape for poor people, African Americans and Chicanos sought to claim space through political activism. Artists saw their work as part of the Chicano and Black Power movements and an effort to mark out and claim visual territory in the modern city.[44]

For Los Angeles artists, the mural movement was, as was the case in Chicago, an expression of a desire to convert ugly spaces into places of beauty. As artist Charles 'Cat' Felix, the driving force behind the Estrada Housing Court murals, put it while giving a tour of the murals: 'the buildings are always the same drab color . . . everything starts looking the same color as the smog' in a neighborhood ringed by factories, warehouses, and dull brick buildings.[45] At the Estrada Courts, local residents from the neighborhood, young children, working artists, volunteers, and activists came together to alter the dreary façades of these public housing projects and in the process created 23 of the most colorful and iconic images in Chicano mural art by the end of December 1973. Estrada Housing Courts were clearly becoming an open air art museum that featured paintings done by collective action. At the same time there were several other murals in progress and plans for more, led by artists yet completed by families, children, and young people.[46] The murals inspired residents to paint the exterior walls and other sections of the housing project in bright colors—on their own initiative—because, as Felix put it, they 'want them to look as nice as the murals being done on the buildings.'[47] Artists supported the idea that mural art was part of a beautification effort meant to 'paint up the ugliness of the city' while also providing an avenue for professional artists to work with *barrio* youth and not lose touch with their 'roots in the *barrio*.'[48] The Estrada housing murals and others across the city were changing the visual environment in meaningful ways as *barrio* residents and the wider community of Los Angeles took note of the transformation of public space in one of the poorest neighborhoods in the city.[49]

In other sections of the city, change and improvement came not through the revitalization and improvement of existing neighborhoods and structures but with the creation of new spaces after community uprisings. This was the case at the Maravilla housing projects in East Los Angeles, where young Chicanos rebelled and engaged in 'street warfare' with sheriffs' deputies following the police riot at the Chicano Moratorium at Laguna Park in East Los Angeles in which reporter Rubén Salazar was killed. The Nueva Maravilla homes replaced the formerly decrepit and graffiti-scarred brick buildings of the housing project. Despite the improvement in the built environment, residents and activists alike noted that deep structural issues, poverty, and a weak educational system fueled the poverty and gang problems so long faced in East Los Angeles. Murals were part of a bigger long-term effort to make the *barrio* a safe place for all Chicanos young and old.[50] Artists likewise struggled with issues of poverty and the dislocation faced by even educated Chicanos, as artists Joe and John Gonzalez struggled to pay rent and Judy Baca painted while suffering unemployment despite her training as a teacher.[51]

By the late 1970s the Chicano mural movement had grown to make much of East Los Angeles and some other parts of the city a living outdoor museum that featured the lives and history of Chicanos. The murals at Estrada Courts surpassed 80, and Ramona Gardens were home to a large number of completed and planned murals. Murals were painted on storefronts and even commissioned by banks, schools, parks, and businesses. Whittier Boulevard, the main drag of East Los Angeles, had become a museum of the streets as murals graced the walls of many buildings new and old. Even as the murals became part of the visual landscape, the message was still one deeply immersed in the Chicano Movement—these murals celebrated the heroic Mexican and indigenous past of the Chicano people as they also critiqued police brutality, injustice, and the exploitation of the poor in the United States. They continued to give visual form to the hard arguments of Chicano nationalism's critique of American society, as they also made East Los Angeles a beautiful place despite its many social and political problems and enabled Chicano Movement-era artists to work and teach others as the iconography and history of Chicanos became an important part of East and Greater Los Angeles culture. While gangs continued to be a problem in areas such as Ramona Gardens (and American cities generally) the murals were part of a long-term effort on the part of artists and activists to improve the quality of life for residents.[52]

In San Francisco opposition to urban renewal in the historically Chicano Mission District led to the development of a series of mural programs throughout the 1970s. By the 1980s the Chicano mural movement had made the Mission, the historic center of San Francisco, into a dense neighborhood of public art centered at Balmy Alley—telling the story of Chicano nationalism, mestizo culture, and civil rights much as in Los Angeles and Chicago. A driving force behind the movement was Chicago native and Casa Aztlán artist Ray Patlan, a resident of Balmy Alley, who, together with Susan Cervantes, a San Francisco native, and others, became a proponent of mural painting as a way to engage youth in artistic production and learning in this longtime immigrant and working-class neighborhood in San Francisco.[53] By the time the city was becoming less and less affordable for low-income people in the 1990s, the murals had spread to the entire city, encompassing its diversity and highlighting the history of working-class Mexican Americans, Filipinos, Chinese Americans, and others, as the murals increasingly told the story of a people who were finally being effectively displaced decades after urban renewal had attempted to move them out.[54]

In Texas the mural movement took root in San Antonio and El Paso as well as other cities in the state. In San Antonio, much as was done in California, public housing became the canvas upon which much of that city's mural art was painted. San Antonio's West Side, the historic heart of the Mexican American community, was also a section of the city plagued by gang activity, poverty, and violence, where Chicano activists organized community action and politics to bring about positive change through the development of the Brown Berets and La Raza Unida Party. In the 1970s and for decades afterward, artists also came together with youth programs and citywide arts initiatives to paint murals to beautify the *barrio*. The Cassiano Homes Murals became the central tapestry upon which murals were painted. The idea was much the same as that in California and Illinois—the murals would transform the drab visual landscape of public housing in a low-income neighborhood and make it beautiful by celebrating the history, culture, and struggles of its residents.[55] El Paso, where the mural movement began earlier than in other cities—though the subject matter was focused on veterans initially—grew to become one of the most mural-rich in the nation, with over 100 murals by the 1970s, and for a time rivaled Los Angeles in the sheer number of murals. Over time the Anglo elite and business community accepted the murals, even though they continued to depict scenes of employment discrimination, immigration issues, and the symbols and rhetoric of the Chicano Movement.[56]

Chicano Park and Preservation in San Diego

San Diego in the early 1970s was home to over 250,000 Mexican Americans yet lived in the shadow of Los Angeles to the north. The Logan Heights *barrio*, known to residents as 'Barrio Logan,' had become a center of Mexican American life in the city of San Diego and by 1970 suffered a similar form of spatial demolition via the construction of Interstate 5 and the Coronado Bay Bridge. Urban renewal and the construction of the Coronado Bay Bridge had leveled a wide section of this historic Mexican American *barrio*. Residents of Barrio Logan were upset to find out that the state planned to use the land under the bridge at the heart of their community for a California Highway Patrol station. Residents complained that they were not consulted regarding any of the proposed highway plans nor the plan to establish a police station in a neighborhood many felt was already over-policed. One resident complained that 'we have lost so much with the freeway cutting right through.'[57] By the early 1970s the Mexican American community had organized all the various Chicano-serving groups and agencies into the Chicano Federation and was prepared to mount well-organized protest efforts on behalf of the people. Adding insult to injury, the city zoned much of the neighborhood as commercial and industrial, bringing heavy industry and junk-yards into a once mainly residential neighborhood.[58]

Prior to the protests, residents had sought to work with the city and state to establish the area under the Coronado Bay Bridge as a recreational park and a space for art. They felt that an agreement had been reached after three years of community meetings and discussions, yet they soon found out that the state had different plans for some of the land near the proposed park. On April 22, 1970, heavy machinery moved into the area near the park and began construction work—not for a park but for a California Highway Patrol station on land owned by the state. Barrio Logan residents, nearby college students from the area, and artists reacted quickly and organized to halt construction through an occupation and human chain circles to block the tractors. During the occupation, the activists prepared the land as a park and planted vegetation, and artists made plans for murals at the site and flew the 'Chicano' flag (similar to the UFW red flag with a black eagle), as resident families brought food each day to support the occupation.[59] As activist and *barrio* resident Laura Rodriguez put it: 'that's the way we got it, we wouldn't let the tractors work, we just stood right there and let them roll over us.'[60] Another activist remarked that 'it was the first time that we had all come together in a sense of unity' and the occupation inspired others to join the cause and support it.[61] The movement relied on local residents and activists who not only did the work of building the park as a grassroots effort but also, through the Chicano Federation, began the process of negotiations with the city and state for the creation of a park. Occupation continued, as local leaders and activists from outside San Diego volunteered to help create a Chicano Park on the land being occupied by protesters and negotiations continued with the city. This dual strategy method bore fruit in May of 1971 when the park—via a separate bill for its creation—was signed into law by California Governor Ronald Reagan (who interestingly had been a vocal opponent of the United Farm Workers), after which community members and artists began the process of creating the murals of Chicano Park.[62]

Following the establishment of the park, the mural movement at Chicano Park grew rapidly in the first few years after the occupation yielded victory. In 1973 the mural movement took off after a breakdown in negotiations with the city. Artists and hundreds of community members painted on the walls, and while the first effort included layers of graffiti amidst the original plan as a result of hundreds of participants in the unsanctioned artistic 'attack' on the walls (the artists and community members began painting without permission), the artists continued to work on the murals for much of 1973 and formalized, revised, and finished these spontaneous artistic actions. Several important murals were completed by collective artists' organizations and community volunteers led by Los Toltecas en Aztlán and El Congreso de Artistas Chicanos en Aztlán. This first mural effort claimed the visual space of the park on behalf of the residents of Barrio Logan with landmark murals *Quetzalcóatl* and *Historical Mural* completed in 1973. Both explored pre-Columbian and indigenous themes as well as the key elements of Chicano nationalism—pride in diverse ancestry, Mexican and Chicano heroes, and the iconography of Aztec and other indigenous groups. In the mid 1970s the range of artists expanded to include many from Sacramento's Royal Chicano Air Force (RCAF) collective and Los Angeles who memorialized the Chicano Park effort through the creation of the *Chicano Park Logo* mural in 1974 as well as several others painted by RCAF women that included families and women as central to the making of Chicano history, for instance, *La Mujer Cósmica* and *Female Inteligencia* in 1975. By the late 1970s the park had become an important cultural center for Chicano arts, artists, and Barrio Logan residents who used the park as a recreation center surrounded by an ever growing number of murals.[63]

The 'take-over' succeeded and the park became the artistic and cultural center of Barrio Logan, healing an open wound in the landscape created by the interstate highway and the Coronado Bay Bridge. On the 7.4-acre site 40 murals were painted within the first 10 years, as residents transformed the space under the bridge into an important landmark of Chicano Movement art and activism. The park was also a usable space for picnics, parties, and celebrations and featured an Aztec pyramid bandstand by the late 1970s. To residents Chicano Park became 'sacred ground' for the telling of the history of the Chicano people from indigenous origins to the present, dedicated to the preservation of the history of Barrio Logan and the protests that led to the take-over of the space and the creation of the park. The leaders of the movement to establish the park and scenes depicting the occupation are documented in several of the oldest of the murals. The park itself became a center for protest meetings, community discussions, and an effort to press the City of San Diego for changes—the heart of the Chicano Movement's political effort.[64]

In the late 1970s the park and the mural movement entered a new phase as the murals now reflected the history of the effort to establish Chicano Park during a period of increased community activism to fight negative zoning changes passed by the City of San Diego. Barrio Logan may have been victorious in the creation of the park, but the City of San Diego too often neglected the community when it came to including them in decisions of vital importance. Much as had been true in the case of Chicano Park, area residents were left out of the process of determining what impact zoning should have on the quality of life in their neighborhood. By the middle 1970s zoning had led to further loss of housing stock for *barrio* residents and the establishment of large-scale junkyards and compressing facilities—the environmental and noise pollution was seen as yet another assault on the besieged residents of Barrio Logan and an example of what scholars refer to as 'environmental racism.'[65]

Nearly every mural in Chicano Park has its own history of design, implementation, and struggle, and the evolution of the park since its founding has been marked by protest. One classic mural, *Varrio Sí, Yonkes No* (neighborhood yes, junkyards no), completed in 1977, reveals typical trends facing minority communities in the 1970s. The mural was a specific response to events shaping Logan Heights. The rezoning of the neighborhood by the city brought in several junkyards which led to noise and air pollution, traffic congestion, and created an unsafe environment for area residents. Injuries that resulted from some cars falling on a resident led the community to protest the demarcation of their neighborhood as a haven for junkyards. In meetings to organize resistance, the rallying cry 'Varrio Sí, Yonkes No' was used by those who marched to protest the ring of junkyards in Barrio Logan. The mural shows a march moving toward the viewer with the Coronado Bridge and an industrial site in the background. The protesters hold placards that read 'Más Casas, Menos Yonkes' (more houses, fewer junkyards) and, borrowing from the United Farm Workers, 'La Unidad Es La Fuerza' (unity is strength). The protests led to a successful rezoning of Barrio Logan and an end to junkyards in the neighborhood. The mural is a documentary representation in social realist style of the successful activism of everyday people. Yet, despite the battle for public space and the passage of a state law to create the park, Chicano Park has always been in jeopardy and the murals have always been on the precipice of destruction for a variety of reasons.

Following the earthquakes of 1989 and 1994, the California Department of Transportation was charged with inspecting and making all bridges and highways safe for drivers. This 'seismic strengthening program' endangered the murals of Chicano Park, but the relationship between the state and the residents of Barrio Logan had changed. At the center of the seismic modernization program was the replacement of columns such as those upon which all of the murals were painted. However, California had (and continues to have) one of the toughest Environmental Quality laws in the nation, which provided for the protection of historical properties and extensive review before any work can be done that might have an impact on culturally and historically important sites. The state found that the park was historically significant and initiated the process of placing it on the National Register of Historic Places and the California Register of Historical Resources. The consultants hired to do the work spoke of making up for 'past sins' by undertaking the effort to both complete the seismic strengthening and protect the park.

In order to protect the structures, the state had to apply for an exemption since the murals were less than 50 years old. The threshold for such protections can be difficult to attain, but the California Transportation Department pressed forward, making a case that Chicano Park's murals were of 'exceptional significance' under the law. For example, such exemptions are generally granted to the homes of artists and writers. California's environmental laws offer significant protections and provide in many ways a model for the preservation of community art of the recent past. The exemption at both the federal and state levels and the willingness of California government and local officials to work to protect culturally significant spaces in low-income communities are significantly different from the Chicago case where there are no protections and the murals survive at the whim of property owners who maintain private property rights. The lack of historical protection for public art and an unwillingness to extend environmental protection law to cover culturally significant work, as is the case in California, means that once the trend shifts toward gentrification, mural art of significance to minority and low-income communities is often destroyed. Nearly every city in the United States has, in recent years, witnessed the destruction or 'hiding' (as vacant lots are built up through gentrification) of important public art in Chicano, Puerto Rican, and African American neighborhoods undergoing gentrification, yet the mural movement continues to expand as artists replicate the Chicano mural style nationwide.[66]

Conclusion

Chicano and Latino urban murals in Chicago, Los Angeles, Texas, San Diego, and elsewhere represented the Chicano Movement and related civil rights struggle as a visual narrative and became the subject of territorially grounded community social movements, as the buildings on which they are often painted became (and continue to be) the targets of urban renewal and gentrification. Through mural art, Chicanos claimed specific space as their own through the making of visual homelands in *barrios* nationwide. Both urban renewal in the decades of the 1960s and 1970s and gentrification in the late twentieth and early twenty-first centuries work on the physical landscape in similar ways and often do so as direct attacks on the territorial claims of Chicanos and other low-income minority people. Old buildings are torn down, and the community often undergoes a passive form of ethnic and racial cleansing, as working-class minorities and ethnics are pushed out of neighborhoods due to a lack of income to maintain homes, pay inflated rents, and—as new buildings are erected—purchase housing in these newly upscale districts.

In much the same way that the interstate highway system and urban renewal tore through historically African American, Mexican American, and white ethnic neighborhoods nationwide in the 1960s, gentrification in the twenty-first century is also leading to massive displacement. This process has happened nationwide as empty lots are sold, new housing and businesses are constructed, and murals are lost to the march of progress.[67] Some Chicano and Latino murals have outlived the communities they once represented, surrounded by the new businesses and residents of the gentrified city. Yet, some of the murals painted by artists in the 1970s remain, even as neighborhoods become increasingly economically and ethnically diverse. Moreover, many new residents actually desire the preservation of diversity in their recently adopted neighborhoods and work to preserve historic murals rather than have them destroyed.[68]

In California a rigorous environmental protection law that has a mandate to preserve culturally significant space provides a model for communities that seek to preserve these important expressions of late twentieth-century urban life. Yet, even as the murals of Chicano Park have protection and it is apparent that the state of California will protect this space, gentrification has now moved right up to the boundary of Chicano Park itself, much as has happened in Chicago. The murals on the walls of public housing projects have faced attack from those who disagreed with their message and from young graffiti artists, yet they have been part of an ongoing process of preservation and restoration. The issue gets more complicated for those murals painted on the sides of private property such as groceries and taverns and in the spaces between empty lots. In these cases the issues of property rights, advertising rules, and even graffiti prohibition ordinances come into play and weaken the position of public art as an environmentally protected part of the urban scene. In some cities, murals painted to show the linkages of local history to larger themes of Mexican American history and the Chicano movement have been destroyed by new owners not obliged to maintain the murals.

Even with the many preservation issues facing Chicano Movement murals and the public mural movement generally, mural activity expanded throughout the 1970s and continues in the twenty-first century. In places such as Kansas City, Missouri, South Toledo, Ohio, and Woodburn, Oregon, artists inspired by *Los tres grandes* and the legacy of Chicano Park, Pilsen, and Los Angeles now are commissioned to create murals nationwide for Chicano and Mexican immigrant communities. With the changing demographics of Mexican-ancestry neighborhoods, themes of immigration, transnationalism, and immigrant rights are increasingly part of the long narrative of Chicano, Mexican, and immigrant history within the increasingly diverse modern Latino *barrio*. The Chicano Movement lives on in an important way in the continued efforts to represent Chicano history and claim the visual and territorial space of the *barrio* as Aztlán—a homeland for Mexican-ancestry people in places as far away as the Great Lakes and the Pacific Northwest—as Mexican immigrants and Mexican Americans become part of community life nationwide.[69] The murals and the Chicano activist artists who painted and continue to paint them are signal markers of the fact that these neighborhoods are communities and important to the Chicanos and Latinos who live there, as they give concrete form to the territorial claims of residents for space and territory.

Notes

1 The strategic use of essentialism and ethnicity have a long (and some might say problematic) history in the study of ethnic groups. Gayatri Chakravorty Spivak's notion of 'strategic essentialism' here deployed as 'strategic ethnicity' also falls squarely in the tradition of Stanford Lymann, Herbert Gans, and Felix Padilla. Some scholars of Latino social and political life, such as Padilla, show how the public display of ethnicity may be strategically used to mobilize around certain pan-ethnic issues. The term 'strategic ethnicity' here combines social movement principals with the utilization of symbols in art that represent ethnicity in a collective way as part of activist movements for spatial, visual, and cultural representation. See Stanford Lyman, *Color, Culture, Civilization: Race and Minority Issues in American Society* (Urbana: University of Illinois Press, 1995); Herbert J. Gans, *People, Plans, and Policies: Essays on Poverty, Racism, and Other National Urban Problems* (New York: Columbia University Press, 1991); Herbert J. Gans, 'Symbolic Ethnicity: The Future of Ethnic Groups and Cultures in America,' *Ethnic and Racial Studies* 2, no. 1 (January 1979): 1–20; Felix M. Padilla, *Latino Ethnic Consciousness: The Case of Mexican Americans and Puerto Ricans in Chicago* (Notre Dame: University of Notre Dame Press, 1985); Gayatri Chakravorty Spivak and Sarah Harasym, *The Post-Colonial Critic: Interviews, Strategies, Dialogues* (New York: Routledge, 1990).

2 See Desmond Rochfort, *Mexican Muralists: Orozco, Rivera, Siqueiros* (San Francisco: Chronicle Books, 1993).

3 See David Craven, *Art and Revolution in Latin America, 1910–1990* (New Haven: Yale University Press, 2006), 30–3.

4 For the New York City example of urban renewal see Samuel Zipp, *Manhattan Projects: The Rise and Fall of Urban Renewal in Cold War New York* (Oxford: Oxford University Press, 2010). For an international perspective see Christopher Klemek, *The Transatlantic Collapse of Urban Renewal: Postwar Urbanism from New York to Berlin* (Chicago: University of Chicago Press, 2011): for a devastating local example see James R. Saunders and Renae N. Shackelford, *Urban Renewal and the End of Black Culture in Charlottesville, Virginia: An Oral History of Vinegar Hill* (Jefferson: McFarland, 2005); Susan Hanson and Genevieve Giuliano, *The Geography of Urban Transportation* (New York: The Guilford Press, 2004), 347–53.

5 For thought-provoking considerations of *barrio* space and place, see Raúl Homero Villa, *Barrio-Logos: Space and Place in Urban Chicano Literature and Culture* (Austin: University of Texas Press, 2000); David R. Diaz, *Barrio Urbanism: Chicanos, Planning, and American Cities* (New York: Routledge, 2005).

6 See an example in Jane M. Jacobs, *Edge of Empire: Postcolonialism and the City* (London: Routledge, 1996), 147–9.

7 See Daniel D. Arreola, *Hispanic Spaces, Latino Places: Community and Cultural Diversity in Contemporary America* (Austin: University of Texas Press, 2004), 110–14.

8 For examples of this work conceptualized in poetry, see Miguel R. López and Francisco Lomelí, *Chicano Timespace: The Poetry and Politics of Ricardo Sánchez* (College Station: Texas A&M University Press, 2001), 85–92.

9 For a recent example of this decades long struggle see Rachel Rinaldo, 'Space of Resistance: The Puerto Rican Cultural Center and Humboldt Park,' *Cultural Critique*, no. 50 (Winter, 2002), 135–74.

10 See Juan Gómez-Quiñones and Irene Vásquez, *Making Aztlán: Ideology and Culture of the Chicana and Chicano Movement, 1966–1977* (Albuquerque: University of New Mexico Press, 2014), 278–9.

11 Peter Howard Selz, *Art of Engagement: Visual Politics in California and Beyond* (Berkeley: University of California Press, 2006), 168–9.

12 Carlos F. Jackson, *Chicana and Chicano Art: Protestarte* (Tucson: University of Arizona Press, 2009), 81–3.

13 See Amelia Jones, 'Traitor Prophets: Asco's Art as a Politics of the In-Between,' in *Asco: Elite of the Obscure, a Retrospective, 1972–1987*, ed. C. Ondine Chavoya, Rita Gonzalez, David E. James, Amelia Jones, Chon A. Noriega, Jesse Lerner, Deborah Cullen, Maris Bustamante, and Colin Gunckel (Ostfildern: Hatje Cantz Verlag, 2011); Harry Gamboa and Chon A. Noriega, eds., *Urban Exile: Collected Writings of Harry Gamboa, Jr.* (Minneapolis: University of Minnesota Press, 1998); Victor Valle, 'Chicano Art: An Emerging Generation,' *Los Angeles Times*, August 7, 1983, 4.

14 See *MARCH: Movimiento Artístico Chicano*. Chicago: MARCH, 1975/1976, retrieved from: http://icaadocs.mfah.org/icaadocs/en-us/home.aspx.

15 José G. González and Marc Zimmerman, *Bringing Aztlán to Mexican Chicago: My Life, My Work, My Art* (Urbana: University of Illinois Press, 2010), 60–83.

16 See Margaret LaWare, 'Encountering Visions of Aztlán: Arguments for Ethnic Pride, Community Activism, and Cultural Revitalization in Chicano Murals,' *Argumentation and Advocacy* 34, no. 3 (Winter, 1998): 140–53; Jerry Romotsky and Sally Robertson, 'Barrio School Murals,' *Children Today* (September–October 1974): 16–19; David Kahn, 'Chicano Street Murals: People's Art in the East Los Angeles Barrio,' *Aztlán* 6, no. 1 (Spring, 1975): 117–21.

17 See, generally, Michael Innis-Jiménez, *Steel Barrio: The Great Mexican Migration to South Chicago, 1915–1940* (New York: New York University Press, 2013).

18 David K. Fremon, *Chicago Politics, Ward by Ward* (Bloomington: Indiana University Press, 1988), 58–9, 162–4; James R. Green, *Death in the Haymarket: A Story of Chicago, the First Labor Movement, and the Bombing That Divided Gilded Age America* (New York: Pantheon Books, 2006).

19 John J. Betancur, 'The Politics of Gentrification: The Case of West Town in Chicago,' *Urban Affairs Review* 37, no. 6 (July 2002): 780–814; Isidro Lucas, 'Puerto Rican Politics in Chicago,' in *Puerto Rican Politics in Urban America*, ed. James Jennings and Monte Rivera (Westport: Greenwood Press, 1984), 99–114; Mérida M. Rúa, *A Grounded Identidad: Making New Lives in Chicago's Puerto Rican Neighborhoods* (Oxford: Oxford University Press, 2012).

20 Lilia Fernandez, *Brown in the Windy City: Mexicans and Puerto Ricans in Postwar Chicago* (Chicago: University of Chicago Press, 2012), 99–129.

21 See discussion of deindustrialization and the Rust Belt in Lisa M. Fine, 'The "Fall" of Reo in Lansing, Michigan, 1955–1975,' in *Beyond the Ruins: The Meanings of Deindustrialization*, ed. Jefferson Cowie and Joseph Heathcott (Ithaca: Cornell University Press, 2003), 44–63.

22 Jeff Huebner, 'The Outlaw Artist of 18th Street: Marcos Raya: His Life, His Work, His Demon,' *Chicago Reader*, February 1, 1996.

23 Olga U. Herrera, V.A. Sorell, and Gilberto Cárdenas, *Toward the Preservation of a Heritage: Latin American and Latino Art in the Midwestern United States* (Notre Dame: Institute for Latino Studies, 2008), 46–8; Jay Pridmore, 'Inside The "Pilsen/Little Village" Exhibit,' *Chicago Tribune*, December 13, 1996.

24 Huebner, 'The Outlaw Artist of 18th Street'; Victor A. Sorrell, 'Barrio Murals in Chicago: Painting the Hispanic American Experience on "Our Community" Walls,' *Revista Chicano-Riqueña* 4, no. 4 (1976): 50–72.

25 David Carrasco and Scott Sessions, *Daily Life of the Aztecs* (Santa Barbara: Greenwood, 2011), 258–60.

26 See LaWare, 'Encountering Visions of Aztlán.'

27 Quoted in Huebner, 'The Outlaw Artist of 18th Street.'

28 Quoted in Huebner, 'The Outlaw Artist of 18th Street.'

29 Dan Viens, interview with Ray Patlan, 'Murals and Their Power to Change: Video from a Real Earl Production Documentary' (2010) video at: http://vimeo. com/4236498.

30 On urban renewal, see generally Martin Anderson, *The Federal Bulldozer: A Critical Analysis of Urban Renewal, 1949–1962* (Cambridge: Massachusetts Institute of Technology Press, 1965); A. Scott Henderson, *Housing & the Democratic Ideal: The Life and Thought of Charles Abrams* (New York: Columbia University Press, 2000); David R. Diaz and Rodolfo D. Torres, *Latino Urbanism: The Politics of Planning, Policy, and Redevelopment* (New York: New York University Press, 2012).

31 See Natalie Voorhees Center for Neighborhood and Community Improvement, *Gentrification in West Town: Contested Ground* (Chicago: University of Illinois, 2001); Judson Jeffries, 'From Gang-Bangers to Urban Revolutionaries: The Young Lords of Chicago,' *Journal of the Illinois State Historical Society* 96, no. 3 (2003): 288–304; Gina M. Pérez, *The Near Northwest Side Story: Migration, Displacement, and Puerto Rican Families* (Berkeley: University of California Press, 2004), 127–61.

32 'Rioters in Chicago Burn Police Cars in a 5-Hour Melee,' *New York Times*, June 13, 1966; 'Police Leaders Huddle to Cool Riot Zone,' *Chicago Defender*, June 14, 1966.

33 'King Calls for Puerto Rican Meet,' *Chicago Defender*, June 15, 1966.

34 Roberto Suro, 'Humboldt Park: Community without Dreams,' *Chicago Tribune*, June 4, 1978; Frederick Lowe and Derrick Blakley, 'Humboldt Park Riot,' *Chicago Tribune*, June 5, 1977; '2 Killed, 49 Injured in Chicago as Riot Starts after Puerto Rican Demonstration,' *Los Angeles Times*, June 5, 1977.

35 Frederick Lowe, 'Citizens Keep Round-the-Clock Vigil on Threatened Mural Site,' *Chicago Tribune*, April 13, 1978.

36 'Dedication of Wall Mural Set for Sunday,' *Chicago Defender*, October 2, 1971; 'Latin Youths Paint Murals,' *Chicago Tribune*, October 7, 1971.

37 'OK Demolition at "Cultural" Site on N.W. Side,' *Chicago Sun-Times*, April 8, 1978.

38 Charles Leroux and Rogers Worthington, 'It's a Crime against Property, but Arson Hurts People the Most,' *Chicago Tribune*, June 7, 1978.

39 Leroux and Worthington, 'It's a Crime.'

40 Lowe, 'Citizens Keep Round-the-Clock Vigil.'

41 'The Walls of the City Blossom into a Museum of the Streets,' *Chicago Tribune*, May 5, 1978.

42 See Mark Rogovin, *Mural Manual: How to Paint Murals for the Classroom, Community Center, and Street Corner* (Boston: Beacon Press, 1975).

43 John Betancur, 'Gentrification before Gentrification?' White Paper, Voorhees Center for Neighborhood and Community Improvement, University of Illinois, Chicago (Summer, 2005), retrieved from: www.uic.edu/cuppa/voorheesctr/Publications/Gen trification%20before%20Gentrification.pdf.

44 See Sarah Schrank, *Art and the City: Civic Imagination and Cultural Authority in Los Angeles* (Philadelphia: University of Pennsylvania Press, 2008), 166–8.

45 Frank Del Olmo, 'Murals Changing Face of East L.A.,' *Los Angeles Times*, December 3, 1973, 3; 'Charles W. Felix Jr., 46, Created Murals in Los Angeles,' *Los Angeles Times*, January 7, 1990.

46 John Pastier, 'Architecture: Painting the Town Red, Blue, Green, Etc.,' *Los Angeles Times*, June 2, 1975, 2.

47 Del Olmo, 'Murals Changing Face of East L.A.'

48 Del Olmo, 'Murals Changing Face of East L.A.'

49 Mike Castro, 'Murals Replacing Graffiti on Walls of Apartment Complex,' *Los Angeles Times*, August 10, 1973, 1.

50 Frank Del Olmo, 'Riot-Torn Barrio: 5 Years After,' *Los Angeles Times*, September 1, 1975, 2.

51 George Beronius, 'The Murals of East Los Angeles,' *Los Angeles Times*, April 11, 1976, 6.

52 Beronius, 'The Murals of East Los Angeles,' 6; see generally Eva S. Cockcroft and Holly Barnet-Sánchez, eds., *Signs from the Heart: California Chicano Murals* (Venice: Social and Public Art Resource Center, 1993).

53 Nancy Scott, 'Murals Beautify San Francisco's Mission Area,' *Chicago Tribune*, March 13, 1988; Horace Sutton, 'Traveler's Diary,' *Los Angeles Times*, October 30, 1988.

54 Nan Chase, 'The Mural Majority,' *Washington Post*, May 7, 1995, 3; Anne Meredith Nyborg, 'Gentrified Barrio: Gentrification and the Latino Community in San Francisco's Mission District,' MA thesis, University of California, San Diego, 2008.

55 Pat Jasper and Kay Turner, 'Art among Us/Arte entre Nosotros: Mexican-American Folk Art in San Antonio,' in *Hecho en Tejas: Texas-Mexican Folk Arts and Crafts*, ed. Joe S. Graham (Denton: University of North Texas Press, 1991), 48–76; Diaz, *Barrio Urbanism*, 133–4; Richard West, 'An American Family,' *Texas Monthly* (March 1980), 109–81.

56 Virginia Price with Maria Natividad, *Mural Manual: A Resource Guide* (El Paso: Museum and Cultural Affairs Department, City of El Paso, Texas, 2008); Miguel Juárez, *Colors on Desert Walls: The Murals of El Paso* (El Paso: Texas Western Press, 1997).

57 Patricia Murphy, 'Building Chicano Clout in San Diego,' *Los Angeles Times*, April 2, 1972.

58 Murphy, 'Building Chicano Clout in San Diego.'

59 Cindy Lyle, 'Chicano Mural Art a Mixture of the Barrio's Rage and Pride,' *New York Times*, August 17, 1975; Lynne Muller, 'Mexico's History and Legend Come Alive in the Murals of San Diego's Chicano Park,' *Chicago Tribune*, January 24, 1982; Mario Barrera, Marilyn Mulford, Juan Felipe Herrera, and Gary Weimberg, *Chicano Park* (New York: Cinema Guild, 1991).

60 Quoted in Barrera et al., *Chicano Park*.

61 Quoted in Barrera et al., *Chicano Park*.

62 Elise Miller, 'Artists' Vision Fuses Political Spirit, Heritage in Chicano Park Murals,' *Los Angeles Times*, September 10, 1978.

63 California Office of Historic Preservation, 'National Register of Historic Places Registration Form, Chicano Park' (2012), Part 8, 8–10.

64 Josie S. Talamantez, 'Chicano Park and the Chicano Park Murals: A National Register Nomination,' MA thesis, History Department, California State University, Sacramento, 2011, 5–6.

65 On the struggle to expand and maintain the park and the neighborhood, see Barrera et al., *Chicano Park*. On environmental racism and social movements, see Luke W. Cole and Sheila R. Foster, *From the Ground Up: Environmental Racism and the Rise of the Environmental Justice Movement* (New York: New York University Press, 2001).

66 On the ongoing tensions between preservation and attacks on murals, see Karen M. Davalos, *Exhibiting Mestizaje: Mexican American Museums in the Diaspora* (Albuquerque: University of New Mexico Press, 2001), 67–72; Martin D. Rosen and James Fisher,

'Chicano Park and the Chicano Park Murals: Barrio Logan, City of San Diego, California,' *Public Historian* 23, no. 4 (Fall 2001): 91–111.

67 On displacement and gentrification generally, see Japonica Brown-Saracino, *A Neighborhood That Never Changes: Gentrification, Social Preservation, and the Search for Authenticity* (Chicago: University of Chicago Press, 2009); Linda Lutton, 'Racial Change in Pilsen: Mi casa? Tu casa?' (August 30, 2012), retrieved from: www.wbez.org/series/race-out-loud/racial-change-pilsen-mi-casa-tu-casa-102030.

68 This is not a statement of acceptance on my part of the low culture/high culture divide in art. For more on this debate, see Brenda J. Bright and Elizabeth Bakewell, *Looking High and Low: Art and Cultural Identity* (Tucson: University of Arizona Press, 1995).

69 Phil Hawkins, 'CAPACES Unveils Woodburn's First Mural,' *Woodburn Independent*, September 25, 2013 (Woodburn); Tahree Lane, 'Dazzling Murals Light Up Old South End,' *The Blade*, September 2, 2012 (Toledo); 'Avenida Cesar E. Chavez–Kansas City,' July 23, 2010, retrieved from: http://sevigraffiti.blogspot.com/2010/07/avenida-cesar-e-chavez-kansas-city.html (Kansas City).

CONCLUSION

Rethinking to Move Forward

Rethinking and Reformulating Chicano History

The Chicano movement of the 1960s and 1970s changed the nature of American citizenship, defined the topography of a distinct Chicano cultural expression, and expanded the nature of what it meant to be an ethnic minority in the United States. As the African American civil rights and Black Power movements likewise altered the meaning and representation of race in the United States and other movements expanded the terrain for equality and inclusion, the Chicano Movement in important ways—by pushing for alternate understandings of race and ethnicity that embraced hybridity via a mestizo (mixed race) understanding of self—created a framework for the expansion of rights and the expression of personhood in an increasingly multiracial, mixed-race North America.

Rethinking the Chicano Movement, rather than merely re-presenting it, locates the radical reformist project of imagining a Chicano nation and culture at the center of the story of the movement. Whether in the form of poetry, essays, journalism, labor and political activism, student organizing, or spatially grounded artistic expression, the movement had as its primary goal the establishment of a national outlook among Mexican Americans. It also sought recognition from the governmental, educational, economic, cultural, and political institutions, at both the local and national level, that often negatively affected people's lives. By creating a space and a voice for the expression of a Chicano worldview within both the mainstream and the *barrio*, the Chicano Movement sought to place a historically marginalized people at the center of national debates.

Chicano nationalism, from the perspective of the twenty-first century, may appear naïve in retrospect, yet it had a real impact on the individuals and communities who embraced its various formulations. Chicanos and Chicanas took their political and cultural work seriously. For Mexican Americans, a people long surviving between the Mexican nation and the United States, their very in-between status placed them in cultural limbo. The Chicano Movement in its various national, regional, and local manifestations sought to stake out the territory of memory, history, and culture for a group that lived between and across the territories and cultures of Mexico and the United States in ways that those from Mexico and those who saw themselves as Americans (Anglo-Americans) did not. This accomplishment—staking out this truly transnational and transcultural space—is perhaps one of the most lasting impacts of the Chicano Movement.

The Chicano freedom movement was part of the long history of Mexican American civil rights activism in the United States. Earlier citizenship-driven movements, despite their limitations, made the case for greater freedom and opportunity for Mexican Americans. These efforts, while hampered by a tactical embrace of whiteness politics and limited understandings of equal protection jurisprudence, provided both the stimulus for further and more militant activism and a point of departure for radical reformulations of Mexican American identity politics. While criticism of the Mexican Americanist political ideology is valid, the basic tenets of this worldview lived on in the Chicano Movement in the form of demands for educational and economic opportunity within the various institutions of daily life for Mexican Americans and by extension other Latinos. Thus the farm workers' struggle in California, Texas, and the Midwest, as well as the fight for political rights in South Texas and elsewhere, expanded upon older movements within the community. These movements (such as the United Farm Workers, the Los Cinco effort), may not have been part of the Chicano Movement per se, yet they ran parallel to it and provided training and grassroots experience to the young people who made up the vanguard of the Chicano Movement.

A mix of radical and reformist tendencies developed in reaction to the War on Poverty in Chicano neighborhoods. Activist leaders such as Rodolfo Gonzales and many others worked for War on Poverty programs in the various cities and states where they also led key components of the Chicano Movement. Some eventually rejected government assistance, yet many more sought to make the War on Poverty and other programs work for the benefit of *barrio* residents and migratory farm workers in need. Other groups such as MAYO in Texas used War on Poverty funding to provide employment and training opportunities to activists who either used these programs to accomplish the militant goals of the organization or to support other work outside their employment. The strategic use of governmental support was a central—and often understudied—aspect of the Chicano Movement presented in this reconsideration.

One of the central demands of the student walkouts in California, Texas, and elsewhere was for acceptance and assistance for Latino students as well as bilingual and bicultural education. Their efforts led to the development of bilingual and bicultural curricular changes as well as an expansion of bilingual and bicultural staffing and guidance at schools nationwide. While many of the initial programs did not prove durable, the concept of bilingual education has found significant acceptance among educators and has led to an expansion of language programs to include a variety of heritage languages, immigrant languages, and immersion programs. In the schoolyards of Texas and elsewhere, where Spanish was once a forbidden language, the protests of the Chicano youth movement, the walkouts, and subsequent educational reforms at the federal and state level brought about real change—not only for Spanish speakers and those Chicanos seeking to reclaim a heritage language but for other language minorities and those seeking more language options in schools nationwide. The issue of Spanish-language use in the public sphere remains controversial, yet the Chicano Movement efforts have helped to make Spanish an acceptable language of public discourse and instruction in places where it was once forbidden.[1]

The Chicano Movement gave Mexican Americans and other Latinos increasing access to higher education and the private sector. One of the lasting impacts of the movement was the expansion of affirmative action and diversity policies to include Mexican Americans (and all Latinos and Hispanics) as targeted groups. The activism of Mexican Americans over the course of the twentieth century, culminating in the militancy of the Chicano Movement, yielded benefits for many other Latino groups and several generations of Latin American immigrants. Thus, the Chicano Movement created pathways of upward mobility for Mexican Americans and for the new Latin American and Mexican immigrants who flowed into the United States in ever-larger numbers after the 1980s. The movement also contributed to the growing presence of a Mexican American middle class in Texas, California, and elsewhere. Most scholars of the Chicano experience to date have neglected the post-movement expansion of the middle class (and Chicano professional class). The rise of second- and third-generation Chicano college enrollments, graduate and professional school attendance, political participation, and suburbanization in Texas, California, and Illinois seem to indicate that the movement facilitated the growth of the once small Mexican American middle class in important ways, yet this development awaits its historian.

Thus, the legacy of the Chicano Movement is multifaceted and continues in the twenty-first century. The movement succeeded in ways that perhaps the activists themselves never expected. By pressing for a place in politics, labor unions, education, arts, and the media, the movement opened up real opportunities for subsequent generations, and the institutions created at colleges and universities and in *barrio* communities have served to support the continuous discovery and rediscovery of selfhood among Chicanos and Chicanas within an increasingly diverse Latino population. Through numerous neighborhood art galleries, youth programs, and educational institutions, the Chicano Movement lives on in the increasingly complex social world of *barrios* in East Los Angeles, San Antonio, and Chicago as well as smaller settlements across the country. In student outreach and educational programs at community colleges, universities, and state colleges, Chicano Studies reaches those Mexican American and other students who wish to learn about the history of one of the largest and longest-settled US minority groups. In the face of a demographic revolution that tends to foster the image of Latinos as 'new' immigrants, Chicano Studies presents the long-term history of Mexican Americans as a people with roots spanning centuries. The Chicano place in the United States pre-dates in many cases the mass immigration of European ethnics to the United States and continues to evolve within the context of an increasingly translocal and transnational understanding of history, culture, and life.[2]

Latinos All: Chicanos, Mexicans, Puerto Ricans, and Latin Americans

The demographic revolution that followed the Chicano Movement has altered not only the ethnic and linguistic makeup of the *barrio* but also that of the nation at large. This transformation has been significant and rapid and has changed the culture of Chicano neighborhoods, remaking them in a more highly Mexican and Latin American mold, a process that has revitalized the traditional ties to Mexican culture and sparked new relationships (and also divisions) among Latinos, as long-term Latinos (US-born and mainly of Mexican American and Puerto Rican descent) live and work with more recent immigrants from Latin America, the Caribbean, and Mexico, who are all nominally Latino or Hispanic yet may know little about the history of the struggles of Mexican Americans (and Puerto Ricans) in the United States. The Latino presence is growing not only in traditional population centers but also in the Southern states and small towns of the Great Plains where settlement had previously been limited. The greater acceptance of Latino cultural citizenship enjoyed by new immigrants today is a direct result of the activism of those Latinos who participated in the Chicano and Puerto Rican civil rights efforts in the 1960s and 1970s.[3]

The Chicano Movement allowed Mexican Americans to break with the accommodationist past of whiteness politics. By making claims to whiteness, Mexican American lawyers and activists had long been forced to embrace the language of racial superiority and distinction when fighting for civil rights. In the evolutionary process that was the Chicano Movement, Mexican Americans in phases gave up the false guise of whiteness in favor of a racial status as brown people. There were limits to this change: many Mexican Americans and other Latinos continued to claim a white racial status. For some, this was a reflection of Latin American racial understandings and prejudice rather than those of the United States. Meanwhile, others increasingly embraced their mixed racial, ethnic, and linguistic heritage in a process that made Latino ethnic culture acceptable and that grew in tandem with the expansion of bilingual and Spanish-language print and media. By shedding the baggage of whiteness, Chicanos and other Latinos could embrace with pride their mixed ethno-racial ancestry and confront the long history of racial discrimination in the United States.

Many Americans and new immigrants today misunderstand the Chicano Movement and the important role it played in creating the infrastructure to accommodate the Latino demographic revolution of the late twentieth century.

As new immigrants find a US media environment that caters to Spanish-language shoppers via several Spanish-language broadcast networks (often owned by large mainstream media conglomerates), offers Spanish-language options in many retail and institutional environments, and has a vast network of businesses that cater to their specific needs, it may seem that there is little wrong with the host society. However, this view fails to recognize the long-term efforts of Chicanos (and other Latinos) to create these spaces and make them acceptable to all Americans. These and other changes are the result of a vast opening of American society that grew from the efforts of Chicanos, Puerto Ricans, and other Latinos in the 1960s and 1970s, that benefit new Latino immigrants from the Caribbean and Latin America.

While Chicanos continue to represent a significant percentage of the broader Latino community, they have some social and cultural practices that set them apart. Many do not speak Spanish as a first language, although many are nominally bilingual. Many US-born Chicanos have long spoken mainly English in the second and third generation (especially in California and areas outside of Texas and New Mexico) and have yet maintained ties to their ethnic community institutions including churches, social service and educational agencies, artistic venues, and local politics. Chicanos have long lived in a bilingual and bicultural milieu where a significant number may no longer speak Spanish fluently but strongly support efforts to provide Spanish-language options in public life and the media. One must remember that until comparatively recently schools did not offer Spanish instruction in many Mexican American-serving districts, and the language was forbidden in schoolyards, and discouraged in the public sphere. Thus, the language Chicanos and Mexican Americans spoke or knew was mainly an oral-tradition Spanish that had evolved within an English dominant society that did not support language maintenance.

Newly arrived immigrants may also lack the identity crisis experienced by some Chicanos in the 1960s, as they have generally arrived in the United States with clear national allegiances to Mexico or other Latin American nations and a well-developed sense of their place within the world as Mexicans, Cubans, El Salvadorians, Dominicans, and other Latin Americans. These new Latino transnational identities challenge Chicano claims to historical position while also enlivening and strengthening ties to a broader Mexican and pan-Latino identity. The Chicano Movement created the infrastructure for these Latino groups to advance through efforts to expand the meaning of affirmative action, minority electoral representation legislation, and educational outreach to all Latinos (or Hispanics).[4]

Even with the changing nature of intragroup dynamics, there are moments where unity drives a new pan-Latino politics. The example of community-wide participation in the immigration rights efforts of the late twentieth and early twenty-first century have provided opportunities for both cross-Latino community organizing and greater understanding between Chicanos and more recent

Mexican immigrants and their children. The mass media covered the immigrant rights marches in 2006 in large population centers such as Los Angeles and Chicago, but the immigration rights movement mobilized protest movements in the many small towns and medium-sized cities nationwide with long-term Chicano residents as well as in the new growth regions of the United States. The American South, the Pacific Northwest, and the Midwest as well as New York City and many cities of the eastern seaboard witnessed large-scale protests in favor of immigration reform—and in some cases the protesters were joined by European immigrants (and ethnics) and the many other immigrant peoples from the rest of the world. The tactics and practices of the Chicano Movement, as well as Chicano Movement-era organizations such as the Mexican American Legal Defense and Educational Fund (MALDEF), have supported the call for immigration rights and defended the rights of new immigrants.[5]

Current Debates and Persistent Problems

Immigration rights—and the status of the more than 11 million unauthorized immigrants, many of whom entered the country as undocumented workers—have become the dominant issue for many Latinos and their families. This is especially true for those in the numerous mixed-status families within the larger Latino community, where parents and some children may be citizens of Mexico (or other nations of Latin America) but lack legal documentation in the United States, and others may be US citizens by birth. While some families may be unaware of the role of the Chicano Movement in developing the organizational infrastructure and networks to support immigrant rights efforts, Chicano Movement groups and activists have long led the fight for immigrant rights in the United States.[6] The immigration reform issue has inspired young people to take up the activist mantle of the Chicano Movement in real ways, and this effort to support the rights of their families has led many in colleges, universities, and community organizations nationwide to seek out a greater understanding of the Chicano Movement and Latino civil rights history. Moreover, many Chicano Movement activists of the 1960s and 1970s supported the development of new immigrant rights groups and the expansion of their civil rights orientation to include rights for the undocumented, and 'dreamers' (undocumented children seeking educational opportunity in the United States).[7]

The Chicano Movement's impact on education cannot be overstated. Within the past 50 years, the number of Mexican American students at colleges and universities has expanded significantly. Likewise, the number of teachers, professors, and administrators of Mexican American ancestry has grown from California to New York and has helped to support the development of a Chicano middle class in many communities. These changes have also meant that Chicanos hold many administrative positions in Mexican American–serving school systems nationally.

Yet, even with these reforms and the positive results of change, educational out-comes for low-income Chicanos and Latinos are still a problem. While the demo-graphics of these communities have shifted, educational outcomes, dropout rates, and retention rates for at-risk Latino students continue to be abysmal. Whereas a Chicano middle class now can send its children to top tier and Ivy League colleges and universities, many of the high schools in Texas and East Los Ange-les as well as *barrios* nationwide that were the sites of protest in the 1960s and 1970s continue to suffer from an unconscionably high dropout rate. This issue has led some observers to question the continued utility of policies that neglect the impact of persistent poverty and income stratification on low-income minority student outcomes in favor of a focus on diversity or multiculturalism. Educa-tional reform was one of the central demands of the Chicano Movement, and while much progress has been made when it comes to expanding opportunity for middle-class and some low-income Latinos, there remain persistent problems when it comes to educational advancement for poor and disadvantaged students from elementary school to college.[8]

One issue of concern to many within the Chicano Movement was the issue of incarceration rates among Mexican Americans in the United States. Much like their African American counterparts, Chicano activists considered the criminal justice system deeply flawed and in need of serious reform. Now, as in the 1960s and 1970s, Chicano and Latino youth who enter the juvenile justice system tend to come from urban neighborhoods scarred by poverty and are less likely to be high school graduates. Incarceration rates tend to hover at the 3 percent mark for US-born Latinos (classified generally as Hispanics by the criminal justice system), but many consider this an undercount due to many Hispanics being recorded as white. Urban young women and men are often the target of policing poli-cies that mark them out as gang members because they are Latinos and live in urban neighborhoods where gang activity is common. While the problem of gang violence is a serious one, Chicano and Latino youth face a constant threat of arrest for minor violations that middle-class suburban youth do not often face, leading to high rates of incarceration among the former. The issue of police bru-tality and harassment was one of the targets of the Chicano Movement (which led many actual and potential gang members to become community activists), and there have been some improvements—increased numbers of Chicano and Latino officers on many police forces, community outreach police programs—but entrenched policing habits still result in a high rate of incarceration among urban Chicano youth.[9]

Political representation has expanded significantly following the Chicano Movement and continues today. California, Texas, New Mexico, Colorado, Illi-nois, and many cities nationwide have witnessed increased numbers of Chicanos and Mexican Americans as elected officials alongside other Latinos. While the vast majority of Latino elected officials tend to be Democrats, several high profile

Republicans have joined the ranks. Latino issues run the gamut from the traditional concerns of the Chicano Movement to the increasingly important issue of immigration reform and immigration-related policies in Mexican American and Latino majority districts. While it may seem that immigration is the dominant issue, many of the issues Latino elected officials confront are those common to minority-majority and low-income districts as they often represent urban, minority, and disadvantaged areas. Most Chicano and Latino elected officials are at the local level yet are making inroads into state government and the federal level.[10]

In many important ways, the Chicano Movement created the foundation for the development of the immigration rights movement and educational, criminal justice, and political reform movements nationwide. Reforms often took place as more moderate Latinos responded to the radicalism of groups such as La Raza Unida Party (RUP) in Texas—and made the case for representation and cooperation. These efforts however grew as a direct result of the hard-fought battle for representation within Chicano/Mexican-ancestry-majority neighborhoods nationwide. The movement and its legacy have redefined the essence of what it means to be an American and tested the mainstream's understanding of what defines Americanism and liberty within the context of a changing society. The process has taken place within contested space, as many who consider themselves 'Americans' have struggled to understand and come to terms with the demographic and cultural changes brought by the rapid rise of the Latino population in the past 50 years.[11] The Chicano Movement was no mere flash in the activist pan of post-World War II America; rather, along with the African American civil rights movement, it has created one of the most enduring social movement legacies of the late twentieth century.

Notes

1 See Fredric W. Field, *Bilingualism in the USA: The Case of the Chicano-Latino Community* (Amsterdam: John Benjamins Pub. Company, 2011); Charles M. Tatum, *Chicano Popular Culture: Que Hable El Pueblo* (Tucson: University of Arizona Press, 2001); Armando L. Trujillo, *Chicano Empowerment and Bilingual Education: Movimiento Politics in Crystal City, Texas* (New York: Garland Publishing, 1998).

2 See José Á. Gutiérrez, *The Texas Association of Chicanos in Higher Education* (Charleston: Arcadia Publishing, 2013); Adalberto Aguirre and Ruben O. Martinez, *Chicanos in Higher Education: Issues and Dilemmas for the 21st Century* (Washington, DC: School of Education and Human Development, George Washington University, 1993).

3 See William A.V. Clark, *Immigrants and the American Dream: Remaking the Middle Class* (New York: Guilford Press, 2003); Ronald L. Mize and Grace Delgado, *Latino Immigrants in the United States* (Cambridge: Polity, 2012); Mary E. Odem and Elaine C. Lacy, *Latino Immigrants and the Transformation of the U.S. South* (Athens: University of Georgia Press, 2009).

4 Pew Hispanic Center, *When Labels Don't Fit: Hispanics and Their Views of Identity* (Washington, DC: Pew Research Center, April 4, 2012); Mark Hugo Lopez and Ana

Gonzalez-Barrera, 'What Is the Future of Spanish in the United States?' Retrieved from: www.pewresearch.org/fact-tank/2013/09/05/what-is-the-future-of-spanish-in-the-united-states/.

5 See Amalia Pallares and Nilda Flores-González, *¡Marcha! Latino Chicago and the Immigrant Rights Movement* (Urbana: University of Illinois Press, 2010); Leo R. Chavez, *The Latino Threat: Constructing Immigrants, Citizens, and the Nation* (Stanford: Stanford University Press, 2008).

6 Jeffrey Passel, D'Vera Cohn, and Ana Gonzalez, 'Population Decline of Unauthorized Immigrants Stalls, May Have Reversed,' Pew Research Hispanic Trends Project (September 23, 2013), retrieved from: www.pewhispanic.org/2013/09/23/population-decline-of-unauthorized-immigrants-stalls-may-have-reversed/.

7 Walter Nicholls, *The Dreamers: How the Undocumented Youth Movement Transformed the Immigrant Rights Debate* (Palo Alto: Stanford University Press, 2013).

8 See Richard R. Valencia, *Chicano School Failure and Success: Past, Present, and Future* (London: Routledge/Falmer, 2002).

9 See Ruth E. Zambrana, *Latinos in American Society: Families and Communities in Transition* (Ithaca: Cornell University Press, 2011), 163–97; Suzanne Oboler, *Behind Bars: Latino/as and Prison in the United States* (Basingstoke: Palgrave Macmillan, 2009).

10 See Lisa Magaña, *Mexican Americans and the Politics of Diversity: ¡Querer Es Poder!* (Tucson: University of Arizona Press, 2005); Kevin Davis, 'California Leads in Percentage Growth of Latino Officials,' *Los Angeles Times*, September 15, 1989, 3; Seema Mehta, 'Texas Latinos Hope to be Reflected in New District Lines; Their Growth Is Evident Everywhere but among the State's Elected Officials,' *Los Angeles Times*, April 24, 2011.

11 There is nothing new about this process. During past periods of massive immigration to the United States, nativism was an important political and social issue. See John Higham, *Strangers in the Land: Patterns of American Nativism, 1860–1925* (New York: Atheneum Press, 1963); Ray A. Billington, *The Protestant Crusade, 1800–1860* (New York: Macmillan, 1938). See also Editorial, 'The New Nativism,' *Nation*, August 10, 2006, retrieved from: www.thenation.com/article/new-nativism.

BIBLIOGRAPHY

Abeyta, Elena. 'I am María.' *Bronce* (Berkeley), June 1969.

Acuña, Rodolfo. *The Making of Chicana/o Studies: In the Trenches of Academe.* New Brunswick: Rutgers University Press, 2011.

————. *Occupied America: The Chicano's Struggle toward Liberation.* San Francisco: Canfield Press, 1972.

Adelante (Riverside, California). 'Chicanos 20% of Viet Dead.' October 14, 1969.

Aguirre, Adalberto, and Ruben O. Martinez. *Chicanos in Higher Education: Issues and Dilemmas for the 21st Century.* Washington, DC: School of Education and Human Development, George Washington University, 1993.

Alamo Messenger (San Antonio). 'Dissenting Paso Group Scores Crystal City Coup.' April 19, 1963.

Albro, Ward S. *Always a Rebel: Ricardo Flores Magón and the Mexican Revolution.* Fort Worth: Texas Christian University Press, 1992.

Allswang, John M. *A House for All Peoples: Ethnic Politics in Chicago, 1890–1936.* Lexington: University Press of Kentucky, 1971.

Almaguer, Tomás. *Racial Fault Lines: The Historical Origins of White Supremacy in California.* Berkeley: University of California Press, 1994.

Alonzo, Armando C. *Tejano Legacy: Rancheros and Settlers in South Texas, 1734–1900.* Albuquerque: University of New Mexico Press, 1998.

Anaya, Rudolfo, and Francisco Lomelí, eds. *Aztlán: Essays on the Chicano Homeland.* Albuquerque: University of New Mexico Press, 1991.

Anderson, Benedict. *Imagined Communities: Reflections on the Origin and Spread of Nationalism.* London: Verso Books, 1991.

Anderson, Martin. *The Federal Bulldozer: A Critical Analysis of Urban Renewal, 1949–1962.* Cambridge: Massachusetts Institute of Technology Press, 1965.

Andrade, Francisco Manuel. 'The History of *La Raza* Newspaper and Magazine, and Its Role in the Chicano Community from 1967 to 1977.' MA thesis, California State University, Fullerton, 1978.

Anft, Michael. 'Giving a Voice to Hispanics.' *Chronicle of Philanthropy*, January 20, 2005.

Arreola, Daniel D. *Hispanic Spaces, Latino Places: Community and Cultural Diversity in Contemporary America.* Austin: University of Texas Press, 2004.

Atlanta Daily World. 'Mexican-Americans Stage Demonstration in Calif.' January 14, 1971, 5.

Auerbach, Stuart, and Paul Valentine. 'Marchers Blocked at Justice Department.' *Washington Post,* June 4, 1968, A1.

Avena, Richard. 'One Last Vote for Willie Velasquez.' *Los Angeles Times,* June 18, 1988, A8.

Bardacke, Frank. *Trampling Out the Vintage: Cesar Chavez and the Two Souls of the United Farm Workers.* New York: Verso Books, 2012.

Barrera, Mario. *Race and Class in the Southwest: A Theory of Racial Inequality.* Notre Dame: University of Notre Dame Press, 1979.

Barrera, Mario, Marilyn Mulford, Juan Felipe Herrera, and Gary Weimberg. *Chicano Park.* New York: Cinema Guild, 1991.

Barrett, James R., and David Roediger. 'Inbetween Peoples: Race, Nationality and the "New Immigrant" Working Class.' *Journal Of American Ethnic History* 16, no. 3 (Spring 1997): 3–45.

Bass, Jack, and Walter DeVries. *The Transformation of Southern Politics: Social Change and Political Consequences since 1945.* Athens: University of Georgia Press, 1995.

Bauman, Robert. 'The Neighborhood Adult Participation Project: Black-Brown Strife in the War on Poverty in Los Angeles.' In *The Struggle in Black and Brown: African American and Mexican American Relations during the Civil Rights Era,* edited by Brian D. Behnken, 104–24. Lincoln: University of Nebraska Press, 2012.

———. *Race and the War on Poverty: From Watts to East L.A.* Norman: University of Oklahoma Press, 2008.

Beaudrie, Sara M., and Marta Ana Fairclough. *Spanish as a Heritage Language in the United States: The State of the Field.* Washington, DC: Georgetown University Press, 2012.

Bebout, Lee. *Mythohistorical Interventions: The Chicano Movement and Its Legacies.* Minneapolis: University of Minnesota Press, 2011.

Behnken, Brian. *Fighting Their Own Battles: Mexican Americans, African Americans, and the Struggle for Civil Rights in Texas.* Chapel Hill: University of North Carolina Press, 2011.

Beltrán, Christina. *The Trouble with Unity: Latino Politics and the Creation of Identity.* Oxford: Oxford University Press, 2010.

Berman, Art. 'Chavez a Modern Zapata to Grape Strikers.' *Los Angeles Times,* May 6, 1966.

———. 'Latin-American Quits Antipoverty Job in Row.' *Los Angeles Times,* September 16, 1966, 32.

Bernal, Dolores D. 'Grassroots Leadership Reconceptualized: Chicana Oral Histories and the 1968 East Los Angeles School Blowouts.' *Frontiers* 19, no. 2 (1998): 113–42.

Bernstein, Harry. 'Benefits in End of Bracero Plan Told by Brown.' *Los Angeles Times,* March 15, 1966.

———. 'Catholic Bishops Help Union, Grape Growers OK Pact.' *Los Angeles Times,* April 2, 1970.

———. 'Chavez Revolt Catching Fire across State.' *Los Angeles Times,* June 14, 1970.

———. 'Chavez Scores Major Victory, Signs Pact with Huge Farm.' *Los Angeles Times,* June 11, 1970.

———. 'Grape Growers in Delano Sign Union Contracts.' *Los Angeles Times,* May 21, 1970.

———. 'Grape Growers Sue Unions for $25 Million over Boycott.' *Los Angeles Times,* July 12, 1968.

———. 'Grape Growers Sue 6 Unions for $25 Million in Damages.' *Los Angeles Times,* July 12, 1968.

————. 'Massive Boycott Mounted against State's Grapes.' *Los Angeles Times*, August 12, 1968.

————. 'Talks between Teamsters and Chavez's Farm Union Collapse.' *Los Angeles Times*, December 25, 1970.

————. 'Yule Gifts for Grape Strikers Called Stunt.' *Los Angeles Times*, December 24, 1965.

Bernstein, Shana. *Bridges of Reform: Interracial Civil Rights Activism in Twentieth-Century Los Angeles*. New York: Oxford University Press, 2011.

Beronius, George. 'The Murals of East Los Angeles.' *Los Angeles Times*, April 11, 1976, 6.

Berry, Faith. 'The Anger and Problems and Sickness of the Poor of the Whole Nation.' *New York Times*, July 7, 1968, SM5.

Berta-Ávila, Margarita, Anita Tijerina Revilla, and Julie López Figueroa. *Marching Students: Chicana and Chicano Activism in Education, 1968 to the Present*. Reno: University of Nevada Press, 2011.

Betancur, John. 'Gentrification before Gentrification?' White Paper, Voorhees Center for Neighborhood and Community Improvement, University of Illinois, Chicago (Summer 2005). Retrieved from: www.uic.edu/cuppa/voorheesctr/Publications/Gentrifi cation%20before%20Gentrification.pdf.

————. 'The Politics of Gentrification: The Case of West Town in Chicago.' *Urban Affairs Review* 37, no. 6 (July 2002): 780–814.

Bigarts, Homer. 'A New Mexican-American Militancy.' *New York Times*, April 20, 1969, 1.

Billington, Ray A. *The Protestant Crusade, 1800–1860: A Study of the Origins of American Nativism*. New York: Macmillan, 1938.

Blackwell, Maylei. *¡Chicana Power! Contested Histories of Feminism in the Chicano Movement*. Austin: University of Texas Press, 2011.

Blake, J. Herman. 'Guest Editor's Comments: The Full Circle: TRIO Programs, Higher Education, and the American Future—Toward a New Vision of Democracy.' *Journal of Negro Education* 67, no. 4 (Autumn, 1998): 329–32.

Braun, Mark Edward. *Social Change and the Empowerment of the Poor: Poverty Representation in Milwaukee's Community Action Programs, 1964–1972*. Lanham: Lexington Books, 2001.

Bright, Brenda J., and Elizabeth Bakewell. *Looking High and Low: Art and Cultural Identity*. Tucson: University of Arizona Press, 1995.

Brilliant, Mark. *The Color of America Has Changed: How Racial Diversity Shaped Civil Rights Reform in California, 1941–1978*. New York: Oxford University Press, 2010.

Brown-Saracino, Japonica. *A Neighborhood That Never Changes: Gentrification, Social Preservation, and the Search for Authenticity*. Chicago: University of Chicago Press, 2009.

Bruce-Novoa, Juan. *RetroSpace: Collected Essays on Chicano Literature*. Houston: Arte Público Press, 1990.

Burciaga, José Antonio. *Drink Cultura: Chicanismo*. Santa Barbara: Joshua Odell Editions, Capra Press, 1993.

Bustamante, Jorge. 'Julian Samora: Mentor.' In *Moving beyond Borders: Julian Samora and the Establishment of Latino Studies*, edited by Alberto L. Pulido, A.B. Driscoll, and Carmen Samora, 174–9. Urbana: University of Illinois Press, 2009.

Busto, Rudy V. *King Tiger: The Religious Vision of Reies López Tijerina*. Albuquerque: University of New Mexico Press, 2005.

Calderón, José. '"Hispanic" and "Latino": The Viability of Categories for Panethnic Unity.' *Latin American Perspectives* 19, no. 4 (Autumn, 1992): 37–44.

California Office of Historic Preservation. 'National Register of Historic Places Registration Form, Chicano Park.' Part 8, 8–10, 2012.

Camarillo, Albert. *Chicanos in a Changing Society: From Mexican Pueblos to American Barrios in Santa Barbara and Southern California, 1848–1930*. Cambridge: Harvard University Press, 1979.

Carrasco, David, and Scott Sessions. *Daily Life of the Aztecs*. Santa Barbara: Greenwood, 2011.

Carrigan, William D. *The Making of a Lynching Culture: Violence and Vigilantism in Central Texas, 1836–1916*. Urbana: University of Illinois Press, 2004.

Carroll, Patrick James. *Felix Longoria's Wake: Bereavement, Racism, and the Rise of Mexican American Activism*. Austin: University of Texas Press, 2003.

Castañeda, Antonia. Telephone conversation, September 10, 2012.

Castillo, Ana. *Massacre of the Dreamers: Essays on Xicanisma*. Albuquerque: University of New Mexico Press, 1994.

Castro, Mike. 'Murals Replacing Graffiti on Walls of Apartment Complex.' *Los Angeles Times*, August 10, 1973, 1.

———. '2 Women of Mexican Origin Conquer Machismo.' *Los Angeles Times*, September 12, 1974, SF1.

Castro, Sal. Remarks. 'A Discussion of Mario T. García and Sal Castro *Blowout!*' Western History Association annual meeting, Oakland, October 15, 2011.

———. Remarks. 'Hispanic Experience Panel.' *Los Angeles Times* Festival of Books, University of Southern California, April 30, 2011. Retrieved from: www.c-spanvideo.org/program/HispanicEx.

Chabrán, Richard, and Rafael Chabrán. 'The Spanish-Language and Latino Press of the United States: Newspapers and Periodicals.' In *Handbook of Hispanic Cultures in the United States: Literature and Art*, edited by Alfredo Jiménez, Nicolás Kanellos, and Fabregat C. Esteva, 360–83. Houston: Arte Público Press, 1994.

Chase, Nan. 'The Mural Majority.' *Washington Post*, May 7, 1995, 3.

Chávez, Ernesto. *'¡Mi Raza Primero!' (My People First!): Nationalism, Identity, and Insurgency in the Chicano Movement in Los Angeles, 1966–1978*. Berkeley: University of California Press, 2002.

Chávez, John R. *Eastside Landmark: A History of the East Los Angeles Community Union, 1968–1993*. Stanford: Stanford University Press, 1998.

———. *The Lost Land: The Chicano Image of the Southwest*. Albuquerque: University of New Mexico Press, 1984.

Chavez, Leo R. *The Latino Threat: Constructing Immigrants, Citizens, and the Nation*. Stanford: Stanford University Press, 2008.

Cherney, Robert W., and William Issel, eds. *American Labor and the Cold War*. New Brunswick: Rutgers University Press, 2004.

Chicago Daily Defender. 'Bishop Pike Backs Farm Workers Strike.' March 24, 1966.

———. 'Dedication of Wall Mural Set for Sunday.' October 2, 1971.

———. 'Grape Pickers Call off Strike against Schenley.' April 7, 1966.

———. 'Hatcher Backs Grape Boycott.' October 31, 1968.

———. 'King Calls for Puerto Rican Meet.' June 15, 1966.

———. 'Police Leaders Huddle to Cool Riot Zone.' June 14, 1966.

Chicago Sun-Times. 'OK Demolition at "Cultural" Site on N.W. Side.' April 8, 1978.

Chicago Tribune. 'Clash in Denver.' March 21, 1969, 6.

———. 'Latin Youths Paint Murals.' October 7, 1971.

———. 'The Walls of the City Blossom into a Museum of the Streets.' May 5, 1978.

———. 'Workers Reach Destination.' April 11, 1966.

Chicano Coordinating Council on Higher Education. *El Plan De Santa Bárbara: A Chicano Plan for Higher Education*. Santa Barbara: La Causa Publications, 1970.

Chicano Student News (Los Angeles). 'Outside Agitators.' March 15, 1968, 3.

————. 'Student Demands.' N.d., 1968.

————. 'Walkout.' February 1969, 1–2.

————. 'Who Are the Brown Berets.' March 15, 1968, 6.

Chicano Times (San Antonio). 'Awake Freedom.' August 21, 1970. '

————. 'OLL Faculty Members Blare Racism.' May–June, 1973.

————. 'OLL Labeled Racist and Discriminatory.' March–April, 1973.

Chispas (Berkeley). 'On Mecha/UC Berkeley.' 2, no. 3, August, 1974.

Chriss, Nicholas. 'Texas Farm Laborers March to Protest Pay.' *Los Angeles Times*, July 12, 1966.

Cimons, Marlene. 'From Follower to Leader.' *Los Angeles Times*, February 10, 1972.

Clark, William A.V. *Immigrants and the American Dream: Remaking the Middle Class*. New York: Guilford Press, 2003.

Clayson, William S. *Freedom Is Not Enough: The War on Poverty and the Civil Rights Movement in Texas*. Austin: University of Texas Press, 2010.

Cockcroft, Eva S., and Holly Barnet-Sánchez, eds. *Signs from the Heart: California Chicano Murals*. Venice: Social and Public Art Resource Center, 1993.

Cole, Luke W., and Sheila R. Foster. *From the Ground Up: Environmental Racism and the Rise of the Environmental Justice Movement*. New York: New York University Press, 2001.

Connally Papers, Zavala County Folder. O.W. Nolen to John Connally. May 1, 1963.

————. 'Pena, Ploch Trade Oral Jabs over Crystal City.' Newspaper clipping dated May 10, 1963.

Con Safos (Los Angeles). No. 6, Summer, 1970.

————. 2, no. 5, 1970.

————. 'Answers to the Barriology Examination #4.' No. 7, Winter, 1971.

————. 'The Autobiography of a Brown Buffalo.' No. 7, Winter, 1971.

————. 'Editorial.' 1, no. 2, Fall 1968.

————. Editorial section. No. 7, Winter, 1971.

————. 'Glossary.' 1, no. 3, March 1969.

Correa, Jennifer G. 'The Targeting of the East Los Angeles Brown Berets by a Racial Patriarchal Capitalist State: Merging Intersectionality and Social Movement Research.' *Critical Sociology* 37, no. 1 (2001): 83–101.

Craven, David. *Art and Revolution in Latin America, 1910–1990*. New Haven: Yale University Press, 2006.

Crossen, Cynthia. 'Against All Odds: 1960s Grape Pickers Won Right to Bargain.' *Wall Street Journal*, May 1, 2006.

Cypess, Sandra M. *La Malinche in Mexican Literature from History to Myth*. Austin: University of Texas Press, 1991.

Dallas Morning News. 'Crystal City Expected to Affect More Elections.' May 9, 1963.

Davalos, Karen M. *Exhibiting Mestizaje: Mexican American Museums in the Diaspora*. Albuquerque: University of New Mexico Press, 2001.

Davies, Lawrence. 'Farm Union Vote Set on the Coast.' *New York Times*, August 28, 1966.

————. 'Religion Inspires Grape Marchers.' *New York Times*, March 25, 1966.

————. '2d Grape Grower Agrees to a Union.' *New York Times*, April 8, 1966.

Davis, Kevin. 'California Leads in Percentage Growth of Latino Officials.' *Los Angeles Times*, September 15, 1989, 3.

de la Garza, Beatriz. *A Law for the Lion: A Tale of Crime and Injustice in the Borderlands*. Austin: University of Texas Press, 2003.

De Leon, Arnoldo. '*In Re Ricardo Rodríguez*: An Attempt at Chicano Disenfranchisement in San Antonio, 1896–1897.' In *En Aquel Entonces: Readings in Mexican-American History*, edited by Manuel G. Gonzalez and Cynthia G. Gonzales, 57–63. Bloomington: Indiana University Press, 2000.

Del Olmo, Frank. 'Cesar Chavez—Out of Sight but Still in Fight.' *Los Angeles Times*, February 14, 1972.

———. 'Murals Changing Face of East L.A.' *Los Angeles Times*, December 3, 1973, 3.

———. 'Riot-Torn Barrio: 5 Years After.' *Los Angeles Times*, September 1, 1975, 2.

———. 'Special Preparations to Police Chicano Marches Being Made.' *Los Angeles Times*, January 27, 1971, A3.

Denersesian, Angie Chabram. 'And, Yes . . . the Earth Did Part: On the Splitting of Chicano/a Subjectivity.' In *Building with Our Hands: New Directions in Chicana Studies*, edited by Adela de la Torre and Beatriz M. Pesquera, 34–56. Berkeley: University of California Press, 1993.

DeSipio, Luis. 'The Pressures of Perpetual Promise: Latinos and Politics, 1960–2003.' In *The Columbia History of Latinos in the United States since 1960*, edited by David G. Gutiérrez, 422–5. New York: Columbia University Press, 2004.

Deverell, William. *Whitewashed Adobe: The Rise of Los Angeles and the Remaking of Its Mexican Past*. Berkeley: University of California Press, 2004.

Diaz, David R. *Barrio Urbanism: Chicanos, Planning, and American Cities*. New York: Routledge, 2005.

Diaz, David R., and Rodolfo D. Torres. *Latino Urbanism: The Politics of Planning, Policy, and Redevelopment*. New York: New York University Press, 2012.

Dougherty, Jack. *More Than One Struggle: The Evolution of Black School Reform in Milwaukee*. Chapel Hill: University of North Carolina Press, 2004.

D-Q University National Park Service, November 17, 2004. Retrieved from: www.cr.nps. gov/history/online_books/5views/5views1h18.htm.

Dubon, Armando. 'The Inside Word.' *Vida* (Los Angeles), December 1974.

Einstoss, Ron. 'DA's Office Hits Back at Criticism in Sal Castro Case.' *Los Angeles Times*, October 2, 1968, 3.

El Chicano (Colton). 'Mexican-American or Chicano?' April 26, 1972.

———. 'Parents Unite to Oppose Closing of Westside Schools.' May 21, 1971.

———. 'Vilma Martinez Speaks on Court Decisions and Chicanos.' March 20, 1975.

El Chicano (San Bernardino). 'Chicano Country.' April 5, 1970.

El Clarin Chicano (Chicago). 'Chicanas Caucus, Wichita, Kansas.' July 17, 1974.

El Clarin Mexico-Americano (Chicago). 'Las Mujeres LULAC Seminar Smashing Success.' March 29, 1975.

El Grito del Norte (Espanola). 'La Raza en Las Americas.' May 19, 1969.

El Griton (Porterville). 'Education and Culturally Different Children.' June, 1972.

———. 'I am an Angry Chicano.' 1973.

Elizondo, Sergio. 'La Voz Del Barrio: Chicano Liberation.' *El Chicano* (Colton, California), May 28, 1971, 3.

El Malcriado (Delano). 'The Fast.' March 15, 1968.

———. 'Kennedy Chooses Chavez.' April 1, 1968.

———. 'Paid Political Advertisement.' June 1, 1968.

———. 'Triumph and Tragedy' and 'Our Friend, May He Rest in Peace.' June 15, 1968.

'El Plan Espiritual de Aztlán.' In *Chicano Resource Journal & Service Handbook*. Berkeley: MEChA, University of California, Fall 1972.

El Travieso (Los Angeles). 'El Travieso Believes.' July, 1969.

Encuentro Femenil (San Fernando). 'The Realities of Being a Woman/Chicana.' 1, no. 1, Spring 1973.

Escobar, Edward J. 'The Dialectics of Repression: The Los Angeles Police Department and the Chicano Movement, 1968–1971.' *Journal of American History* 79, no. 4 (March 1993): 1483–514.

Espinoza, John L. 'Corky Speaks on Spectrum of Movement.' *El Diario De La Gente*. Boulder: United Mexican American Students, Chicano Studies, 1972.

Espinoza, Richard. 'Machismo.' *¡Es Tiempo!* (Los Altos Hills) 2, no. 2, August, 1972.

Es Tiempo! (Los Altos Hills). 'Biculturalism: Its Effect on the Personality of the Mexican-American.' June 1972.

Fanucchi, Kenneth. 'Latins Demand Poverty Probe.' *Los Angeles Times*, October 3, 1966, sf8.

———. 'Lettuce Boycott Ends with Pro-Chavez Vote.' *Los Angeles Times*, January 8, 1971.

Fernandez, Lilia. *Brown in the Windy City: Mexicans and Puerto Ricans in Postwar Chicago*. Chicago: University of Chicago Press, 2012.

Ferriss, Susan, Ricardo Sandoval, and Diana Hembree. *The Fight in the Fields: Cesar Chavez and the Farmworkers Movement*. New York: Harcourt Brace, 1997.

Field, Fredric W. *Bilingualism in the USA: The Case of the Chicano-Latino Community*. Amsterdam: John Benjamins Pub. Company, 2011.

Fields, Rona M. 'Interviews with Brown Berets, Part 1.' June 17, 2013. Retrieved from: www.youtube.com/watch?v=Q3wupE4eatU.

Fine, Lisa M. 'The "Fall" of Reo in Lansing, Michigan, 1955–1975.' In *Beyond the Ruins: The Meanings of Deindustrialization*, edited by Jefferson Cowie and Joseph Heathcott, 44–63. Ithaca: Cornell University Press, 2003.

Fixico, Donald. *The American Indian Mind in a Linear World: American Indian Studies and Traditional Knowledge*. New York: Routledge, 2003.

Foley, Neil. *Quest for Equality: The Failed Promise of Black-Brown Solidarity*. Cambridge: Harvard University Press, 2010.

Fox, Jack. 'Grape Boycott: Small, Soft-Spoken Cesar Chavez Leads Quietly Determined Drive to Unionize Agricultural Workers.' *Washington Post*, November 14, 1968.

Fremon, David K. *Chicago Politics, Ward by Ward*. Bloomington: Indiana University Press, 1988.

Gamboa, Harry, and Chon A. Noriega, eds. *Urban Exile: Collected Writings of Harry Gamboa, Jr.* Minneapolis: University of Minnesota Press, 1998.

Gans, Herbert J. *People, Plans, and Policies: Essays on Poverty, Racism, and Other National Urban Problems*. New York: Columbia University Press, 1991.

———. 'Symbolic Ethnicity: The Future of Ethnic Groups and Cultures in America.' *Ethnic and Racial Studies* 2, no. 1 (January 1979): 1–20.

Ganz, Marshall. *Why David Sometimes Wins: Leadership, Organization, and Strategy in the California Farm Worker Movement*. New York: Oxford University Press, 2009.

García, Alma M., ed. *Chicana Feminist Thought: The Basic Historical Writings*. New York: Routledge, 1997.

Garcia, E. 'Flower of Aztlan: The Chicana.' *Es Tiempo!* (Los Altos Hills) 2, no. 2, August, 1972.

García, Ignacio M. *Chicanismo: The Forging of a Militant Ethos among Mexican Americans*. Tucson: University of Arizona Press, 1997.

———. *Hector P. Garcia: In Relentless Pursuit of Justice*. Houston: Arte Público Press, 2002.

———. *United We Win: The Rise and Fall of La Raza Unida Party*. Tucson: University of Arizona Press, 1989.

————. *Viva Kennedy: Mexican Americans in Search of Camelot.* College Station: Texas A&M University Press, 2000.

————. *White But Not Equal: Mexican Americans, Jury Discrimination, and the Supreme Court.* Tucson: University of Arizona Press, 2008.

García, Juan R. *Mexicans in the Midwest: 1900–1932.* Tucson: University of Arizona Press, 1996.

García, María-Cristina. 'Juarez-Lincoln University.' *Handbook of Texas Online,* June 15, 2010. Retrieved from: www.tshaonline.org/handbook/online/articles/kcj03.

García, Mario T. *Mexican Americans: Leadership, Ideology, and Identity, 1930–1960.* New Haven: Yale University Press, 1991.

García, Mario T., and Sal Castro. *Blowout! Sal Castro and the Chicano Struggle for Educational Justice.* Chapel Hill: University of North Carolina Press, 2011.

Garcia, Matt. *From the Jaws of Victory: The Triumph and Tragedy of Cesar Chavez and the Farm Worker Movement.* Berkeley: University of California Press, 2012.

Gaskie, Jack. 'Gonzales Views His Poverty Role.' *Rocky Mountain News,* September 25, 1965.

Gillon, Steven M. *That's Not What We Meant to Do: Reform and Its Unintended Consequences in Twentieth-Century America.* New York: W.W. Norton, 2000.

Gómez-Quiñones, Juan. *Chicano Politics: Reality and Promise 1940–1990.* Albuquerque: University of New Mexico Press, 1990.

Gómez-Quiñones, Juan, and Irene Vásquez. *Making Aztlán: Ideology and Culture of the Chicana and Chicano Movement, 1966–1977.* Albuquerque: University of New Mexico Press, 2014.

Gonzales, Rodolfo. *I Am Joaquín/Yo Soy Joaquín; an Epic Poem. With a Chronology of People and Events in Mexican and Mexican American History.* Toronto: Bantam Books, 1972.

————. *Message to Aztlán: Selected Writings of Rodolfo 'Corky' Gonzales.* Houston: Arte Público Press, 2001.

Gonzalez, Eloy L. 'Where Are You, My America?' *El Renacimiento* (Lansing), June 25, 1973.

Gonzalez, Gilbert G., and Raul A. Fernandez. *A Century of Chicano History: Empire, Nations, and Migration.* New York: Routledge, 2003.

González, José G., and Marc Zimmerman. *Bringing Aztlán to Mexican Chicago: My Life, My Work, My Art.* Urbana: University of Illinois Press, 2010.

Gosse, Van. *Rethinking the New Left: An Interpretative History.* New York: Palgrave Macmillan, 2005.

Graham, Hugh Davis. *Collision Course: The Strange Convergence of Affirmative Action and Immigration Policy in America.* Oxford: Oxford University Press, 2002.

Grebler, Leo, Joan W. Moore, and Ralph C. Guzman. *The Mexican American People: The Nation's Second Largest Minority.* New York: Free Press, 1970.

Green, James R. *Death in the Haymarket: A Story of Chicago, the First Labor Movement, and the Bombing That Divided Gilded Age America.* New York: Pantheon Books, 2006.

Greene, Victor. *American Immigrant Leaders, 1800–1910: Marginality and Identity.* Baltimore: Johns Hopkins University Press, 1987.

Greenstone, J.D., and Paul E. Peterson. *Race and Authority in Urban Politics: Community Participation and the War on Poverty.* Chicago: University of Chicago Press, 1976.

Gregory, James N. *The Southern Diaspora: How the Great Migrations of Black and White Southerners Transformed America.* Chapel Hill: University of North Carolina Press, 2005.

Greider, William. 'A Family Fight Embitters Chicanos.' *Washington Post,* May 25, 1969, B1.

Griswold del Castillo, Richard. *The Treaty of Guadalupe Hidalgo: A Legacy of Conflict*. Norman: University of Oklahoma Press, 1990.

———, ed. *World War II and Mexican American Civil Rights*. Austin: University of Texas Press, 2008.

Guajardo, Cesilia. 'De origen . . .' *El Sueño*, Supplement to *El Hispano* (Sacramento), December 14, 1971.

Guerrero, Carlos. 'Silent No More: The Voice of a Farm Worker Press, 1964–1975.' PhD thesis, Claremont Graduate University, 2004.

Gurda, John. 'The Latin Community on Milwaukee's Near South Side.' Milwaukee: Milwaukee Urban Observatory, University of Wisconsin-Milwaukee, 1976.

Gutiérrez, David G. *Walls and Mirrors: Mexican Americans, Mexican Immigrants, and the Politics of Ethnicity*. Berkeley: University of California Press, 1995.

Gutiérrez, José Á. *The Making of a Chicano Militant: Lessons from Cristal* [sic]. Madison: University of Wisconsin Press, 1998.

———. *The Texas Association of Chicanos in Higher Education*. Charleston: Arcadia Publishing, 2013.

———. *We Won't Back Down: Severita Lara's Rise from Student Leader to Mayor*. Houston: Piñata Books, 2005.

Gutiérrez, Ramón. 'Community, Patriarchy and Individualism: The Politics of Chicano History.' *American Quarterly* 45 (March 1993): 44–72.

Halcon, John. 'A New Direction for MECHA.' *Vida* (Los Angeles), October 1973.

Hancock, Velia. 'Viva La Chicana.' *El Mestizo* (Irvine) 1, no. 3, 1971.

Handbook of Texas Online. 'Allee, Alfred Young.' Retrieved from: www.tsha.utexas.edu/handbook/online/articles/AA/fal97.html (accessed July 19, 2006).

Haney-López, Ian F. 'Protest, Repression, and Race: Legal Violence and the Chicano Movement.' *University of Pennsylvania Law Review* 150 (2001): 205–44.

———. *Racism on Trial: The Chicano Fight for Justice*. Cambridge: Belknap Press of Harvard University Press, 2003.

Hanson, Susan, and Genevieve Giuliano. *The Geography of Urban Transportation*. New York: The Guilford Press, 2004.

Harris, Dean A., ed. *Multiculturalism from the Margins: Non-dominant Voices on Difference and Diversity*. Westport: Bergin & Garvey, 1995.

Hawkins, Phil. 'CAPACES Unveils Woodburn's First Mural.' *Woodburn Independent*, September 25, 2013.

Henderson, A. Scott. *Housing & the Democratic Ideal: The Life and Thought of Charles Abrams*. New York: Columbia University Press, 2000.

Henderson, Timothy J. *A Glorious Defeat: Mexico and Its War with the United States*. New York: Hill and Wang, 2007.

Herber-Valdez, Christiane R. 'Understanding a Hispanic-Serving Institution beyond the Federal Definition: A Qualitative Analysis of Mexican American Student Perceptions and Experiences.' PhD thesis, University of Texas at El Paso, 2008.

Hernández, Fernando. *The Cubans: Our Legacy in the United States: A Collective Biography*. Berkeley: Berkeley Press, 2012.

Herrera, Olga U., V.A. Sorell, and Gilberto Cárdenas. *Toward the Preservation of a Heritage: Latin American and Latino Art in the Midwestern United States*. Notre Dame: Institute for Latino Studies, 2008.

Hietala, Thomas R. *Manifest Design: American Exceptionalism and Empire*. Ithaca: Cornell University Press, 2003.

Higham, John. *Strangers in the Land: Patterns of American Nativism, 1860–1925*. New York: Atheneum Press, 1963.

Hijas de Cuauhtémoc (Long Beach). 'Interview with La Señora Minerva Castillo.' April/ May 1971.

Hill, Gladwin. 'Big Farms Blamed for Migrant Woes.' *New York Times*, August 13, 1950.

———. 'Los Angeles Rioting Is Checked.' *New York Times*, August 16, 1965, 1.

———. 'Penalty for Hiring "Wetbacks" Hailed.' *New York Times*, May 6, 1951.

Horsman, Reginald. *Race and Manifest Destiny: The Origins of American Racial Anglo-Saxonism*. Cambridge: Harvard University Press, 1981.

Horton, John. *The Politics of Diversity Immigration, Resistance, and Change in Monterey Park, California*. Philadelphia: Temple University Press, 1995.

Houston, Paul, and Ted Thackrey Jr. '1 Slain, 24 Hurt in Violence after Chicanos' Rally.' *Los Angeles Times*, February 1, 1971, 1.

Huebner, Jeff. 'The Outlaw Artist of 18th Street: Marcos Raya: His Life, His Work, His Demon.' *Chicago Reader*, February 1, 1996.

Huerta, Dolores. 'Dolores Huerta Talks.' *La Voz del Pueblo* (Berkeley), November–December, 1972.

Innis-Jiménez, Michael. *Steel Barrio: The Great Mexican Migration to South Chicago, 1915–1940*. New York: New York University Press, 2013.

Jackson, Carlos F. *Chicana and Chicano Art: Protestarte*. Tucson: University of Arizona Press, 2009.

Jackson, H. Joaquín, with David Marion Wilkinson. *One Ranger: A Memoir*. Austin: University of Texas Press, 2005.

Jacobs, Jane M. *Edge of Empire: Postcolonialism and the City*. London: Routledge, 1996.

Jasper, Pat, and Kay Turner. 'Art among Us/Arte entre Nosotros: Mexican-American Folk Art in San Antonio.' In *Hecho en Tejas: Texas-Mexican Folk Arts and Crafts*, edited by Joe S. Graham, 48–76. Denton: University of North Texas Press, 1991.

Jeffries, Judson. 'From Gang-Bangers to Urban Revolutionaries: The Young Lords of Chicago.' *Journal of the Illinois State Historical Society* 96, no. 3 (2003): 288–304.

Johannsen, Robert Walter. *To the Halls of the Montezumas: The Mexican War in the American Imagination*. New York: Oxford University Press, 1985.

Johnson, Benjamin Heber. *Revolution in Texas: How a Forgotten Rebellion and Its Bloody Suppression Turned Mexicans into Americans*. New Haven: Yale University Press, 2003.

Johnson, David K. *The Lavender Scare: The Cold War Persecution of Gays and Lesbians in the Federal Government*. Chicago: University of Chicago Press, 2006.

Jones, Amelia. 'Traitor Prophets: Asco's Art as a Politics of the In-Between.' In *Asco: Elite of the Obscure, a Retrospective, 1972–1987*, edited by C. Ondine Chavoya, Rita Gonzalez, David E. James, Amelia Jones, Chon A. Noriega, Jesse Lerner, Deborah Cullen, Maris Bustamante, and Colin Gunckel Ostfildern: Hatje Cantz Verlag, 2011.

Jones, Jack. 'Chicanos 3-Month March to Capital Reaches Salton Sea.' *Los Angeles Times*, May 13, 1971, B1.

———. 'Education of Latin-Americans in L.A. Area Called Inadequate.' *Los Angeles Times*, May 1, 1968, SG1.

———. 'Efforts to Divide and Control Poverty Project Stir Dispute.' *Los Angeles Times*, November 8, 1966, A1.

———. 'Watts Riot Shows Need for Responsible Adults.' *Los Angeles Times*, March 20, 1966, B.

Journal of Negro Education. 'The Full Circle: TRIO Programs, Higher Education, and the American Future.' 67, no. 4 (Autumn, 1998).

Juárez, Miguel. *Colors on Desert Walls: The Murals of El Paso.* El Paso: Texas Western Press, 1997.

Julian Samora Legacy Project. 'Timeline.' Retrieved from: http://samoralegacymedia. org/?page_id=1052.

Kahn, David. 'Chicano Street Murals: People's Art in the East Los Angeles Barrio.' *Aztlán* 6, no. 1 (Spring 1975): 117–21.

Kaplan, Geoff. *Power to the People: The Graphic Design of the Radical Press and the Rise of the Counter-Culture, 1964–1974.* Chicago: University of Chicago Press, 2013.

Kaplowitz, Craig A. *LULAC, Mexican Americans, and National Policy.* College Station: Texas A&M University Press, 2005.

Kazin, Michael, and Joseph Anthony McCartin. *Americanism: New Perspectives on the History of an Ideal.* Chapel Hill: University of North Carolina Press, 2006.

Kennedy, Howard. 'Lettuce Farm Strike Part of Deliberate Union Plan.' *Los Angeles Times,* January 23, 1961.

Kistler, Robert. 'Police Reports over Militant's Arrest Differ.' *Los Angeles Times,* August 31, 1970, 3.

Klemek, Christopher. *The Transatlantic Collapse of Urban Renewal: Postwar Urbanism from New York to Berlin.* Chicago: University of Chicago Press, 2011.

Klunder, Jan. 'Chicana Council Promises to Resist Male Domination.' *Los Angeles Times,* November 18, 1979, SEA3.

Kornbluth, Jesse. 'This Place of Entertainment Has No Fire Exit: The Underground Press and How It Went.' *The Antioch Review* 29, no. 1 (Spring, 1969): 91–9.

La Hormiga (Oakland, California). 'Freemont Demands' and 'Chicano Students Blow Out!' October 7, 1968, 2.

Lammers, Dave. 'Chicanos Blast Hesburgh Policy.' *The Observer* (Notre Dame), April 23, 1970, 1.

Lane, Tahree. 'Dazzling Murals Light Up Old South End.' *The Blade* (Toledo), September 2, 2012.

La Raza. 'Chicano Moratorium.' December 10, 1969.

———. 'Chicano Vietnam.' November 1969.

———. 'Time of Studies & Statistics Over!' December 25, 1967, 3.

La Raza Habla (Las Cruces). 'La Década de la Mujer.' February 1978.

La Raza, Yearbook (Los Angeles). 'Blow Out.' September 1968, 16.

———. '*La Raza* Interviews Mrs. Cardenas.' September 1968, 10–11.

———. 'Sheriffs Harass Brown Berets.' September 1968, 29.

———. 'Teachers and Parents.' September 1968, 14.

Latin Times (East Chicago). 'Form Midwest Council of "La Raza".' April 24, 1970.

———. 'Was It Discrimination at Notre Dame?' May 28, 1971.

LaWare, Margaret. 'Encountering Visions of Aztlán: Arguments for Ethnic Pride, Community Activism, and Cultural Revitalization in Chicano Murals.' *Argumentation and Advocacy* 34, no. 3 (Winter, 1998): 140–53.

Leal, Luis. 'Octavio Paz and the Chicano.' *Latin American Literary Review* 5, no. 10 (Spring, 1977): 115–23.

Leroux, Charles, and Rogers Worthington. 'It's a Crime against Property, but Arson Hurts People the Most.' *Chicago Tribune,* June 7, 1978.

Levy, Peter B. *The New Left and Labor in the 1960s.* Urbana: University of Illinois Press, 1994.

Lewin, Kurt. 'Action Research and Minority Problems.' *Journal of Social Issues* 2, no. 4 (November, 1946).

Limón, José E. *Américo Paredes: Culture and Critique.* Austin: University of Texas Press, 2012.

Lipski, John M. *Varieties of Spanish in the United States.* Washington, DC: Georgetown University Press, 2008.

Lomnitz, Claudio. *The Return of Comrade Ricardo Flores Magón.* New York: Zone Books, 2014.

López, Dennis. 'Good-Bye Revolution—Hello Cultural Mystique: Quinto Sol Publications and Chicano Literary Nationalism.' *MELUS* 35, no. 3 (Fall 2010): 183–210.

Lopez, Joe. 'La Raza.' *Chicago Defender,* February 2, 1974.

Lopez, Mark Hugo, and Ana Gonzalez-Barrera. 'What Is the Future of Spanish in the United States?' Retrieved from: www.pewresearch.org/fact-tank/2013/09/05/what-is-the-future-of-spanish-in-the-united-states/.

López, Miguel R., and Francisco Lomelí. *Chicano Timespace: The Poetry and Politics of Ricardo Sánchez.* College Station: Texas A&M University Press, 2001.

Lopez Saenz, Lionila. 'Machismo, No! Igualdad, Si!' *La Luz* (Denver), May 1972, 19–21.

Los Angeles Times. 'Charles W. Felix Jr., 46, Created Murals in Los Angeles.' January 7, 1990.

———. 'Chavez Declares Senate Report "Lot of Garbage".' September 8, 1967.

———. 'Chicano Group Plans Walk to Sacramento.' May 5, 1971, C7A.

———. 'Chicanos Hit Sheriff Searches in East L.A.' September 5, 1970, A10.

———. 'Chicanos Plan Rally, Service for War Dead.' June 17, 1971.

———. 'Chicanos' Plans for Big Antiwar Rally Here Told.' March 29, 1970, B.

———. 'The Grape Boycott.' September 23, 1968.

———. 'Grape Strikers, Nearing End of Walk to Capitol, Rap Brown.' April 10, 1966.

———. 'Humphrey Backs Farm Union's Grape Boycott.' August 8, 1968.

———. 'Kennedy Wins Race.' June 5, 1968.

———. 'Pickets Urge Teachers to Remain at Lincoln.' October 23, 1968, 1.

———. 'Red Influence in 1966 Grape Strike Seen by Burns.' June 9, 1967.

———. 'Teamsters Quitting Drive to Organize DiGiorgio Workers.' June 8, 1966.

———. 'Won't Change Plan for Jan. 31 March, Chicano Leader Says.' January 12, 1971, 3.

———. '2 Killed, 49 Injured in Chicago as Riot Starts after Puerto Rican Demonstration.' June 5, 1977.

Lowe, Frederick. 'Citizens Keep Round-the-Clock Vigil on Threatened Mural Site.' *Chicago Tribune,* April 13, 1978.

Lowe, Frederick, and Derrick Blakley. 'Humboldt Park Riot.' *Chicago Tribune,* June 5, 1977.

Lozada, Forben, and Mariana Hernandez. 'The Chicano Moratorium—How It Developed.' *The Militant,* September 4, 1970.

Lucas, Isidro. 'Puerto Rican Politics in Chicago.' In *Puerto Rican Politics in Urban America,* edited by James Jennings and Monte Rivera, 99–114. Westport: Greenwood Press, 1984.

Lutton, Linda. 'Racial Change in Pilsen: Mi casa? Tu casa?' August 30, 2012. Retrieved from: www.wbez.org/series/race-out-loud/racial-change-pilsen-mi-casa-tu-casa-102030.

Lyle, Cindy. 'Chicano Mural Art a Mixture of the Barrio's Rage and Pride.' *New York Times,* August 17, 1975.

Lyman, Stanford. *Color, Culture, Civilization: Race and Minority Issues in American Society.* Urbana: University of Illinois Press, 1995.

Maciel, David, and Erlinda Gonzales-Berry. *The Contested Homeland: A Chicano History of New Mexico.* Albuquerque: University of New Mexico Press, 2000.

Magaña, Lisa. *Mexican Americans and the Politics of Diversity: Querer Es ¡Poder!* Tucson: University of Arizona Press, 2005.

Mann, Bert. 'Wiggins Confers with Militant Mexican Americans in Washington.' *Los Angeles Times,* June 17, 1968, C8.

Mantler, Gordon. *Power to the Poor: Black-Brown Coalition and the Fight for Economic Justice, 1960–1974.* Chapel Hill: University of North Carolina Press, 2013.

MARCH: Movimiento Artístico Chicano. Chicago: MARCH, 1975/1976. Retrieved from: http://icaadocs.mfah.org/icaadocs/en-us/home.aspx.

Marin, Christine. 'Rodolfo "Corky" Gonzales: The Mexican American Movement Spokesman, 1966–1972.' *Journal of the West* 14, no. 4 (1975): 107–20.

Mariscal, George. *Brown-Eyed Children of the Sun: Lessons from the Chicano Movement, 1965–1975.* Albuquerque: University of New Mexico Press, 2005.

———. 'Left Turns in the Chicano Movement, 1965–1975.' *Monthly Review* 54, no. 3 (July 2002): 59.

Márquez, Benjamin. *LULAC: The Evolution of a Mexican American Political Organization.* Austin: University of Texas Press, 1993.

Martínez, George A. 'The Legal Construction of Race: Mexican-Americans and Whiteness.' *Harvard Latino Law Review* 321, 328 (1997).

Martínez Caraza, Leopoldo. *La Intervención Norteamericana en México, 1846–1848: Historia Político-Militar de la Pérdida de Gran Parte del Territorio Mexicano.* Mexico: Panorama Editorial, 1981.

Matovina, Timothy M. *The Alamo Remembered: Tejano Accounts and Perspectives.* Austin: University of Texas Press, 1995.

May, Glenn A. *Sonny Montes and Mexican American Activism in Oregon.* Corvallis: Oregon State University Press, 2011.

May, Lawrence. 'Emergence of Militancy Seen for Chicanos.' *Los Angeles Times,* August 25, 1969, A24.

MAYO Newsletter (San Antonio). 'El Colegio Holds Seminar.' January 29, 1971.

McCurdy, Jack. 'Castro Restored to Teaching Job.' *Los Angeles Times,* October 4, 1968, 1.

———. 'East Side Still Plagued with Hangover from School Boycott.' *Los Angeles Times,* September 15, 1968, eb.

———. 'Latins Urge Reinstatement of Teacher Who Led Walkout.' *Los Angeles Times,* August 30, 1968, B.

———. 'Lincoln High Pickets Protest Absence of Indicted Teacher.' *Los Angeles Times,* September 17, 1968, 3.

———. 'Student Disorders Erupt at 4 High Schools.' *Los Angeles Times,* March 7, 1968, 3.

———. 'Student-Parent Sit-in Continuing on Weekend.' *Los Angeles Times,* September 28, 1968, 2.

———. '40 Teachers Ask for Transfers after Reinstatement of Castro.' *Los Angeles Times,* October 8, 1968, 1.

McDermott, Jim. 'MECHA Seeks Aid, Chicano Counselor.' *The Observer* (Notre Dame), February 22, 1971.

McMillian, John. *Smoking Typewriters: The Sixties Underground Press and the Rise of Alternative Media in America.* New York: Oxford University Press, 2011.

MECHA Newsletter (Stanford). 'MECHA Meeting.' 1, no. 1, 1972.

Meeks, Erik. *Border Citizens: The Making of Indians, Mexicans, and Anglos in Arizona.* Austin: University of Texas Press, 2007.

Mehta, Seema. 'Texas Latinos Hope to be Reflected in New District Lines; Their Growth Is Evident Everywhere but among the State's Elected Official.' *Los Angeles Times*, April 24, 2011.

Meister, Dick. '"La Huelga" Becomes "La Causa".' *New York Times*, November 17, 1968.

Mellard, Jason. *Progressive Country: How the 1970s Transformed the Texan in Popular Culture.* Austin: University of Texas Press, 2013.

Merrifield, Fr. Donald P. 'Chicanos and the Rest of Us at Loyola Marymount.' *Vida* (Los Angeles), February, 1974.

Merry, Robert W. *A Country of Vast Designs: James K. Polk, the Mexican War, and the Conquest of the American Continent.* New York: Simon & Schuster, 2009.

Michaels, Walter Benn. *The Trouble with Diversity: How We Learned to Love Identity and Ignore Inequality.* New York: Metropolitan Books, 2006.

Miller, Elise. 'Artists' Vision Fuses Political Spirit, Heritage in Chicano Park Murals.' *Los Angeles Times*, September 10, 1978.

Mize, Ronald L., and Grace Delgado. *Latino Immigrants in the United States.* Cambridge: Polity, 2012.

Montejano, David M. *Anglos and Mexicans in the Making of Texas, 1836–1986.* Austin: University of Texas Press, 1987.

———. *Sancho's Journal: Exploring the Political Edge with the Brown Berets.* Austin: University of Texas Press, 2012.

———. *Quixote's Soldiers: A Local History of the Chicano Movement, 1966–1981.* Austin: University of Texas Press, 2010.

Montoya, María. *Translating Property: The Maxwell Land Grant and the Conflict over Land in the American West, 1840–1900.* Lawrence: University Press of Kansas, 2005.

Moore, Joan W., and Robert Garcia. *Homeboys: Gangs, Drugs, and Prison in the Barrios of Los Angeles.* Philadelphia: Temple University Press, 1978.

Morales, Ed. *Living in Spanglish: The Search for Latino Identity in America.* New York: St. Martin's Press, 2013.

Movimiento Estudiantil Chicano de Aztlán (MEChA). 'About Us.' Retrieved from: www.nationalmecha.org/about.html.

Muller, Lynne. 'Mexico's History and Legend Come Alive in the Murals of San Diego's Chicano Park.' *Chicago Tribune*, January 24, 1982.

Muñoz, Carlos. 'The Politics of Protest and Chicano Liberation: A Case Study of Repression and Cooptation.' *Aztlán* 5, no. 1–2 (Spring–Fall, 1974): 119–41.

———. 'UC Irvine Philosophy.' *El Mestizo* (Irvine) 1, no. 1, May, 1971.

———. *Youth, Identity, Power: The Chicano Movement, Revised and Expanded Edition.* New York: Verso Press, 2007.

Murguía, Edward. *Chicano Intermarriage: A Theoretical and Empirical Study.* San Antonio: Trinity University Press, 1982.

Murphy, Patricia. 'Building Chicano Clout in San Diego.' *Los Angeles Times*, April 2, 1972.

Natalie Voorhees Center for Neighborhood and Community Improvement. *Gentrification in West Town: Contested Ground.* Chicago: University of Illinois, 2001.

Nation, The. 'The New Nativism.' Editorial, August 10, 2006. Retrieved from: www.thenation.com/article/new-nativism.

National Latino Communications Center and Galan Productions. *Taking Back the Schools.* Los Angeles: distributed by NLCC Educational Media, 1996.

Nava, Julian. *Julian Nava: My Mexican-American Journey.* Houston: Arte Público Press, 2002.

Navarro, Armando. *The Cristal* [sic] *Experiment: A Chicano Struggle for Community Control.* Madison: University of Wisconsin Press, 1998.

———. *La Raza Unida Party: A Chicano Challenge to the U.S. Two-Party Dictatorship.* Philadelphia: Temple University Press, 2000.

———. *Mexican American Youth Organization: Avant-Garde of the Chicano Movement in Texas.* Austin: University of Texas Press, 1995.

———. *Mexicano Political Experience in Occupied Aztlán: Struggles and Change.* Walnut Creek: Altamira Press, 2005.

Navarro, Irma. 'MECHA Students at OLL Plan Active Campaign.' *Chicano Times* (San Antonio), November 1972, 6.

New York Times. 'A Challenge to Build a New Society.' April 20, 1969, 55.

———. 'Denver Man Killed, 6 Wounded in Gunfight at Chicano Building.' March 18, 1973, 46.

———. 'Grape and Lettuce Boycott to Widen.' November 10, 1973.

———. 'Here to Spur Boycott of Lettuce, Farm Workers Urge: Remember the Grape.' October 9, 1970.

———. 'Rioters in Chicago Burn Police Cars in a 5-Hour Melee.' June 13, 1966.

———. 'Union Accuses U.S. on Wetback Pact.' February 14, 1952.

———. 'Vast Di Giorgio Farm Empire Nearing End after Many Woes.' December 25, 1968.

———. 'Wisconsin Migrants March to Capital to Protest Pay.' August 16, 1966.

Nicholls, Walter. *The Dreamers: How the Undocumented Youth Movement Transformed the Immigrant Rights Debate.* Palo Alto: Stanford University Press, 2013.

Nieto, Consuelo. 'The Chicana and the Women's Rights Movement.' *LULAC News,* December 1974.

Nieto, Nancy. 'Macho Attitudes.' *Hijas de Cuauhtémoc* (Long Beach), April/May, 1971.

Nieto-Gomez, Anna. 'Chicana Identify.' *Hijas de Cuauhtémoc* (Long Beach), April/May, 1971.

Noriega, Chon A. *The Chicano Studies Reader: An Anthology of Aztlán, 1970–2000.* Los Angeles: UCLA Chicano Studies Research Center Publications, 2001.

Nyborg, Anne Meredith. 'Gentrified Barrio: Gentrification and the Latino Community in San Francisco's Mission District.' MA thesis, University of California, San Diego, 2008.

Oboler, Suzanne. *Behind Bars: Latino/as and Prison in the United States.* Basingstoke: Palgrave Macmillan, 2009.

———. *Ethnic Labels, Latino Lives: Identity and the Politics of (Re)Presentation in the United States.* Minneapolis: University of Minnesota Press, 1995.

Odem, Mary E., and Elaine C. Lacy. *Latino Immigrants and the Transformation of the U.S. South.* Athens: University of Georgia Press, 2009.

Olivas, Michael A., ed. *'Colored Men' and 'Hombres Aquí': Hernandez v. Texas and the Emergence of Mexican-American Lawyering.* Houston: Arte Público Press, 2006.

———. 'Hernandez v. Texas: A Litigation History.' In *'Colored Men' and 'Hombres Aquí,'* 209–24.

Ontiveros, Randy. *The Spirit of a New People: The Cultural Politics of the Chicano Movement.* New York: New York University Press, 2013.

Orleck, Annelise, and Lisa Gayle Hazirjian, eds. *The War on Poverty: A New Grassroots History, 1964–1980.* Athens: University of Georgia Press, 2011.

Oropeza, Lorena. *¡Raza Sí! ¡Guerra No! Chicano Protest and Patriotism during the Viet Nam War.* Berkeley: University of California Press, 2005.

Orozco, Cynthia E. *No Mexicans, Women, or Dogs Allowed: The Rise of the Mexican American Civil Rights Movement.* Austin: University of Texas Press, 2009.

Orr, Richard. 'Chicago Labor Backs Grape Boycott.' *Chicago Tribune*, November 13, 1969.

———. 'Shuman Raps Jewel's New Policy on Grapes.' *Chicago Tribune*, May 7, 1970.

Pacific Northwest Labor and Civil Rights Projects. 'Chicano/a Movement in Washington State History Project.' University of Washington, Digital Collection. Retrieved from: https://depts.washington.edu/civilr/mecha_intro.htm.

Padilla, Felix M. *Latino Ethnic Consciousness: The Case of Mexican Americans and Puerto Ricans in Chicago.* Notre Dame: University of Notre Dame Press, 1985.

Padilla, Fernando V. 'Early Chicano Legal Recognition: 1846–1897.' *Journal of Popular Culture* 13, no. 3 (Spring, 1980): 564–74.

Pallares, Amalia, and Nilda Flores-González. *¡Marcha! Latino Chicago and the Immigrant Rights Movement.* Urbana: University of Illinois Press, 2010.

Paredes, Américo. '*With His Pistol in His Hand': A Border Ballad and Its Hero.* Austin: University of Texas Press, 1986.

Pastier, John. 'Architecture: Painting the Town Red, Blue, Green, Etc.' *Los Angeles Times*, June 2, 1975, 2.

Pawel, Miriam. *The Union of Their Dreams: Power, Faith, and Struggle in Cesar Chavez's Farm Worker Movement.* New York: Bloomsbury Press, 2009.

Peña, Albert Jr. Interview by José Ángel Gutiérrez. July 2, 1996, CMAS 15, TVOH.

Pendes, Miguel. 'I Am Joaquín/Yo Soy Joaquín.' *El Renacimiento* (Lansing), September 24, 1973.

Perea, Juan F. 'Ethnicity and the Constitution: Beyond the Black and White Binary Constitution.' *William and Mary Law Review* 36, no. 2 (1995): 571–611.

Pérez, Gina M. *The Near Northwest Side Story: Migration, Displacement, and Puerto Rican Families.* Berkeley: University of California Press, 2004.

Pérez-Torres, Rafael. *Mestizaje: Critical Uses of Race in Chicano Culture.* Minneapolis: University of Minnesota Press, 2006.

Pew Hispanic Center. *When Labels Don't Fit: Hispanics and Their Views of Identity.* Washington DC: Pew Research Center, April 4, 2012.

Pitti, Stephen J. *The Devil in Silicon Valley: Northern California, Race, and Mexican Americans.* Princeton: Princeton University Press, 2003.

Pittsburgh Courier. 'Protest March Stirs up New Boycott, Wine Grower to Talk to Union.' April 23, 1966.

Poling-Kempes, Lesley. *Valley of Shining Stone: The Story of Abiquiu.* Tucson: University of Arizona Press, 1997.

Price, Virginia, with Maria Natividad. *Mural Manual: A Resource Guide.* El Paso: Museum and Cultural Affairs Department, City of El Paso, Texas, 2008.

Pridmore, Jay. 'Inside The "Pilsen/Little Village" Exhibit.' *Chicago Tribune*, December 13, 1996.

Pulido, Laura. *Black, Brown, Yellow, and Left: Radical Activism in Los Angeles.* Berkeley: University of California Press, 2006.

Raat, W. Dirk. *Revoltosos: Mexico's Rebels in the United States, 1903–1923.* College Station: Texas A&M University Press, 1981.

Raices (Fresno). 'FSC Kills La Raza Studies.' September 16, 1970.

Ramos, Henry A.J. *The American GI Forum: In Pursuit of the Dream, 1948–1983.* Houston: Arte Público Press, 1998.

Ramos, Raúl A. *Beyond the Alamo: Forging Mexican Ethnicity in San Antonio, 1821–1861.* Chapel Hill: University of North Carolina Press, 2008.

Rangel, Javier. 'The Educational Legacy of El Plan de Santa Barbara: An Interview with Reynaldo Macias.' *Journal Of Latinos & Education* 6, no. 2 (April, 2007): 191-9.

Rangel, Jeffrey J. 'Art and Activism in the Chicano Movement: Judith F. Baca, Youth, and the Politics of Cultural Work.' In *Generations of Youth: Youth Cultures and History in Twentieth-Century America,* edited by Joe Austin and Michael Nevin Willard, 223–39. New York: New York University Press, 1998.

Rendón, Armando B. *Chicano Manifesto.* New York: Macmillan, 1971.

Rentería, Tamis H. *Chicano Professionals: Culture, Conflict, and Identity.* New York: Garland Publishing, 1998.

Reyna, Teresa. 'I Ain't No Women's Libber.' *La Voz del Pueblo* (Berkeley), November–December, 1972.

Rinaldo, Rachel. 'Space of Resistance: The Puerto Rican Cultural Center and Humboldt Park.' *Cultural Critique,* no. 50 (Winter, 2002): 135–74

Ripley, Anthony. 'Chicanos Seeking a National Role.' *New York Times,* November 29, 1971, 33.

Rivas-Rodriguez, Maggie. *35 Years: The Center for Mexican American Studies, the University of Texas at Austin.* Austin: Center for Mexican American Studies, 2005.

Roberts, Steven. 'First Grapes with Union Label Shipped to Market from Coast.' *New York Times,* May 31, 1970.

Rochfort, Desmond. *Mexican Muralists: Orozco, Rivera, Siqueiros.* San Francisco: Chronicle Books, 1993.

Rodriguez, América. *Making Latino News: Race, Language, Class.* Thousand Oaks: Sage Press, 1999.

Rodriguez, Joseph A. 'Latinos at UWM: A History of the Spanish-Speaking Outreach Institute and the Roberto Hernandez Center.' Unpublished Paper, 2005. Retrieved from: https://pantherfile.uwm.edu/joerod/www/ssoi.html.

Rodriguez, Marc S. 'Defining the Space of Participation in a Northern City: Tejanos and the War on Poverty in Milwaukee.' In *The War on Poverty: A New Grassroots History, 1964–1980,* edited by Annelise Orkeck and Lisa Gayle Hazirjian, 110–30. Athens: University of Georgia Press, 2011.

———. *The Tejano Diaspora: Mexican Americanism and Ethnic Politics in Texas and Wisconsin.* Chapel Hill: University of North Carolina Press, 2011.

Rodríguez, Richard T. *Next of Kin: The Family in Chicano/a Cultural Politics.* Durham, NC: Duke University Press, 2009.

Rogers, Ray. 'Unique School Problems Linked to Latins Here.' *Los Angeles Times,* June 9, 1967, 13.

Rogovin, Mark. *Mural Manual: How to Paint Murals for the Classroom, Community Center, and Street Corner.* Boston: Beacon Press, 1975.

Romano-V., Octavio Ignacio. *Voices: Readings from El Grito, a Journal of Contemporary Mexican American Thought, 1967–1971.* Berkeley: Quinto Sol Publications, 1971.

Romero II, Tom I. 'Wearing the Red, White, and Blue Trunks of Aztlán: Rodolfo "Corky" Gonzales and the Convergence of American and Chicano Nationalism.' *Aztlán* 29, no. 1 (2004): 83–117.

Romo, Ricardo. *East Los Angeles: History of a Barrio.* Austin: University of Texas Press, 1983.

Romotsky, Jerry, and Sally Robertson. 'Barrio School Murals.' *Children Today* (September–October 1974): 16–19.

Rosen, Martin D., and James Fisher. 'Chicano Park and the Chicano Park Murals: Barrio Logan, City of San Diego, California.' *Public Historian* 23, no. 4 (Fall 2001): 91–111.

Rossinow, Doug. *The Politics of Authenticity: Liberalism, Christianity, and the New Left in America.* New York: Columbia University Press, 1998.

Rúa, Mérida M. *A Grounded Identidad: Making New Lives in Chicago's Puerto Rican Neighborhoods.* Oxford: Oxford University Press, 2012.

Ruiz, Raul. 'One Year Ago.' *Chicano Student Movement* (Los Angeles), March 1969, 1.

———. 'Sal Castro,' *Chicano Student News* (Los Angeles), April 25, 1968, 2.

Salazar, Rubén. 'Anglo "Integration" Rejected by Chicanos.' *Los Angeles Times*, April 7, 1969, C4.

———. 'Brown Berets Hail "La Raza" and Scorn the Establishment.' *Los Angeles Times*, June 16, 1969, 3.

———. 'Chicano Must Be Nationalist to Last in U.S.' *Los Angeles Times*, April 18, 1969, SF1.

———. 'Chicanos Hold 5-State Event in Colorado.' *Los Angeles Times*, March 30, 1969, 8.

———. 'Mexican-Americans to Hold Youth Conference.' *Los Angeles Times*, March 23, 1969, B3.

———. 'Militants Denounce Traditional Stands at Chicano Parley.' *Los Angeles Times*, March 31, 1969, 3.

———. 'Who Is a Chicano? And What Is It the Chicanos Want?' *Los Angeles Times*, February 6, 1970, B7.

Salazar Mallén, Rubén, and Mario T. García, *Border Correspondent: Selected Writings, 1955–1970.* Berkeley: University of California Press, 1995.

Salazar, Sophie. 'A Reply to "Who Is El Chicano?"' *El Chicano* (Colton), March 1, 1970.

Salgado, Armida (Pee-Wee). 'A Letter from Our Editor.' *Carnalas de MAYO* (California Rehabilitation Center, Santa Barbara), November 1974.

Sal Si Puedes (Santa Barbara). 'Chicano Moratorium.' January 1970.

Samora, Julian, Joe Bernal, and Albert Peña. *Gunpowder Justice: A Reassessment of the Texas Rangers.* Notre Dame: University of Notre Dame Press, 1979.

Sánchez, George. *Becoming Mexican American: Ethnicity, Culture, and Identity in Chicano Los Angeles, 1900–1945.* New York: Oxford University Press, 1995.

Saragossa, Elvira. 'Chicana: Slave? Companion? Co-Partner? La Mujer in the Chicano Movement.' *Bronce* (Berkeley), June 1976.

Saunders, James R., and Renae N. Shackelford. *Urban Renewal and the End of Black Culture in Charlottesville, Virginia: An Oral History of Vinegar Hill.* Jefferson: McFarland, 2005.

Schmidt Camacho, Alicia. *Migrant Imaginaries: Latino Cultural Politics in the U.S.-Mexico Borderlands.* New York: New York University Press, 2008.

Schrank, Sarah. *Art and the City: Civic Imagination and Cultural Authority in Los Angeles.* Philadelphia: University of Pennsylvania Press, 2008.

Schuck, Peter H. *Diversity in America: Keeping Government at a Safe Distance.* Cambridge: Harvard University Press, 2003.

Scott, Nancy. 'Murals Beautify San Francisco's Mission Area.' *Chicago Tribune*, March 13, 1988.

Selz, Peter Howard. *Art of Engagement: Visual Politics in California and Beyond.* Berkeley: University of California Press, 2006.

Sepúlveda, Juan. *The Life and Times of Willie Velásquez: Su Voto Es Su Voz.* Houston: Arte Público Press, 2003.

Serros, Juana. 'A La Mujer.' *Nuestra Cosa* (Riverside), January 1975.

sevigraffiti.blogspot. 'Avenida Cesar E Chavez—Kansas City.' July 23, 2010. Retrieved from: http://sevigraffiti.blogspot.com/2010/07/avenida-cesar-e-chavez-kansas-city.html.

Shaw, Randy. *Beyond the Fields: Cesar Chavez, the UFW, and the Struggle for Justice in the 21st Century.* Berkeley: University of California Press, 2011.

Shockley, John S. *Chicano Revolt in a Texas Town.* Notre Dame: University of Notre Dame Press, 1974.

Shuit, Doug, and John Sheibe. 'Rioting Spreads to Wilmington.' *Los Angeles Times,* August 31, 1970, 1.

Soldatenko, Michael. *Chicano Studies: The Genesis of a Discipline.* Tucson: University of Arizona Press, 2009.

Sorrell, Victor A. 'Barrio Murals in Chicago: Painting the Hispanic American Experience on "Our Community" Walls.' *Revista Chicano-Riqueña* 4, no. 4 (1976): 50–72.

Spivak, Gayatri Chakravorty, and Sarah Harasym. *The Post-Colonial Critic: Interviews, Strategies, Dialogues.* New York: Routledge, 1990.

Stavans, Ilan. *Spanglish: The Making of a New American Language.* New York: Rayo, 2003.

Stein, Jean. *American Journey: The Times of Robert F. Kennedy.* New York: Harcourt, Brace, Jovanovich, 1970.

Stern, Laurence, and Richard Harwood. 'Ford Foundation: Its Works Spark a Backlash.' *Washington Post,* November 2, 1969, A1.

Storrs, Landon R.Y. *The Second Red Scare and the Unmaking of the New Deal Left.* Princeton: Princeton University Press, 2012.

Stromquist, Shelton, ed. *Labor's Cold War: Local Politics in a Global Context.* Urbana: University of Illinois Press, 2008.

Suro, Roberto. 'Humboldt Park: Community without Dreams.' *Chicago Tribune,* June 4, 1978.

Suttles, Gerald. *The Social Order of the Slum: Ethnicity and Territory in the Inner City.* Chicago: University of Chicago Press, 1970.

Sutton, Horace. 'Traveler's Diary.' *Los Angeles Times,* October 30, 1988.

Talamantez, Josie S. 'Chicano Park and the Chicano Park Murals: A National Register Nomination.' MA thesis, History Department, California State University, Sacramento, 2011.

Tatum, Charles M. *Chicano and Chicana Literature: Otra Voz Del Pueblo.* Tucson: University of Arizona Press, 2006.

———. *Chicano Popular Culture: Que Hable El Pueblo.* Tucson: University of Arizona Press, 2001.

Telles, Edward Eric, and Vilma Ortiz. *Generations of Exclusion: Mexican Americans, Assimilation, and Race.* New York: Russell Sage Foundation, 2008.

Tenopia, Tia. 'Latinopia Literature Arte Público Press: Interview with Nicolas Kanellos.' May 1, 2011. Retrieved from: http://latinopia.com/latino-literature/latinopia-literature-arte-publico-press/.

Thomas Jr., Robert. 'Julian Samora, 75, a Pioneering Sociologist.' *New York Times,* February 6, 1996.

Tiersten, Sylvia. 'What's In a Name? The Long Saga of Third College.' *At USCD* 7, no 2 (May 2010). Retrieved from: http://ucsdmag.ucsd.edu/magazine/vol7no2/features/feat4.htm.

Torgerson, Dial. 'Start of a Revolution?' *Los Angeles Times,* March 17, 1968, B1.

Torres, Rudy. 'Bi-Culturalism: Its Effect on the Personality of the Mexican American.' *Es Tiempo!* (Los Altos Hills), June 1972.

———. 'Teacher Expectations in the Chicano Classroom.' *Es Tiempo!* (Los Altos Hills) 2, no. 2, August 1972.

Trevino, Oscar Jr. 'Students.' *Chispas* (Berkeley) 2, no. 3, August 1974.

Truchas y Mujer (San Pedro). 'Aztlán.' November 1972.

———. 'The Program of El Plan Espiritual De Aztlan.' November 1972.

Trujillo, Armando L. *Chicano Empowerment and Bilingual Education: Movimiento Politics in Crystal City, Texas.* New York: Garland Publishing, 1998.

Tushnet, Mark V. *Making Civil Rights Law: Thurgood Marshall and the Supreme Court, 1956–1961.* New York: Oxford University Press, 1996.

US Senate, Committee on Commerce, Federal Trade Commission Oversight. 104–5.

Valadez, Kathy. 'Women in Politics—Where Does the Chicana Fit in?' *El Chicano* (Colton), February 6, 1975.

Valdes, Daniel, and Tom Pino, 'Labels Tell You What You Are.' *La Luz* (Denver), 1, no. 3, 1973.

Valdés, Dennis N. *Barrios Norteños: St. Paul and Midwestern Mexican Communities in the Twentieth Century.* Austin: University of Texas Press, 2000.

Valdez, Andres. 'They Will Know.' *El Chicano* (Colton), August 23, 1969.

Valdez, Avelardo. 'Selective Determinants in Maintaining Social Movement Organizations: Three Case Studies from the Chicano Community.' In *Latinos and the Political System*, edited by F. Chris Garcia, 236–54. Notre Dame: University of Notre Dame Press, 1988.

Valdez, Luis Miguel. 'El Machete.' *El Excéntrico* (San José), January 5, 1964.

Valencia, Richard R. *Chicano School Failure and Success: Past, Present, and Future.* London: Routledge/Falmer, 2002.

Valentine, Paul. 'Civil Rights Leaders Set up "Poor Peoples Embassy".' *Washington Post*, September 7, 1968, B2.

Valle, Victor. 'Chicano Art: An Emerging Generation.' *Los Angeles Times*, August 7, 1983, 4.

Vargas, Zaragosa. *Crucible of Struggle: A History of Mexican Americans from Colonial Times to the Present Era.* Oxford: Oxford University Press, 2011.

———. *Labor Rights Are Civil Rights: Mexican American Workers in Twentieth-Century America.* Princeton: Princeton University Press, 2005.

Vasconcelos, José, and Didier Tisdel Jaén. *The Cosmic Race: A Bilingual Edition.* Baltimore: Johns Hopkins University Press, 1997.

Vasquez, Catherine. 'Dr. Pantoja Urges Women to Trust One Another, Assume Positions of Leadership.' *LULAC News*, December 1979.

Venceremos (Kansas City). 'El Plan Espiritual De Aztlán.' January 1971.

———. 'Puerto Rico.' January 1971.

Vento, Arnoldo C. *Mestizo: The History, Culture, and Politics of the Mexican and the Chicano: The Emerging Mestizo-Americans.* Lanham: University Press of America, 1998.

Vidal, Mirta. 'New Voice of La Raza: Chicanas Speak Out.' In *Chicana Feminist Thought: The Basic Historical Writings*, edited by Alma M. García. New York: Routledge, 1997.

Viens, Dan. 'Murals and Their Power to Change: Video from a Real Earl Production Documentary.' Interview with Ray Patlan, 2010. Video at: http://vimeo.com/4236498.

Vigil, Ernesto B. *The Crusade for Justice: Chicano Militancy and the Government's War on Dissent.* Madison: University of Wisconsin Press, 1999.

———. 'A Poem of Dedication.' *El Chicano* (Colton), August 23, 1969.

Villa, Raúl Homero. *Barrio-Logos: Space and Place in Urban Chicano Literature and Culture.* Austin: University of Texas Press, 2000.

Washington Post. 'L.A. Police Seal off Chicano Riot Area.' August 31, 1970, A4.

Waters, Mary C., Reed Ueda, and Helen B. Marrow, eds. *The New Americans: A Guide to Immigration since 1965.* Cambridge: Harvard University Press, 2007.

White, William S. 'After Los Angeles.' *Washington Post,* August 25, 1965, A19.

Wiebe, Robert H. *Who We Are: A History of Popular Nationalism.* Princeton: Princeton University Press, 2002.

Wise, Bert. 'Mexican-American Militancy Rises.' *Washington Post,* April 1, 1969, A1.

Works Progress Administration. *Chicago Foreign Language Press Survey.* Washington, DC: Works Progress Administration, 1942. This collection has been digitalized by the Newberry Library and is available at: http://flps.newberry.org/.

Wright, Robert A. 'East Los Angeles Calm after Riot.' *New York Times,* August 31, 1970, 30.

———. 'Farm Workers Union Signs First Table-Grape Contract with Two California Growers.' *New York Times,* April 2, 1970.

Yamane, David. *Student Movements for Multiculturalism: Challenging the Curricular Color Line in Higher Education.* Baltimore: Johns Hopkins University Press, 2001.

Yosso, Tara J., Laurence Parker, Daniel G. Solórzano, and Marvin Lynn. 'From Jim Crow to Affirmative Action and Back Again: A Critical Race Discussion of Racialized Rationales and Access to Higher Education.' *Review of Research in Education* 28 (2004): 1–25.

Zambrana, Ruth E. *Latinos in American Society: Families and Communities in Transition.* Ithaca: Cornell University Press, 2011.

Zamora, Emilio. *Claiming Rights and Righting Wrongs in Texas: Mexican Workers and Job Politics during World War II.* College Station: Texas A&M University Press, 2009.

———. *The World of the Mexican Worker in Texas.* College Station: Texas A&M University Press, 2000.

Zavala County Sentinel. 'Latin Ticket Wins Council Race.' April 5, 1963.

———. 'New Council Takes Office Apr. 16.' April 5, 1963.

Zeman, Ray. 'Reds Accused of Role Win in Delano Grape Strike.' *Los Angeles Times,* September 8, 1967.

Zipp, Samuel. *Manhattan Projects: The Rise and Fall of Urban Renewal in Cold War New York.* Oxford: Oxford University Press, 2010.

Zurek, Katharine. 'Publishing Profiles: Dr. Nicolas Kanellos of Arte Público Press, Creating a Thriving Latino Literary Community from the Ground Up.' *Independent Publisher,* n.d. Retrieved from: www.independentpublisher.com/article.php?page=1687.

INDEX

access 6, 9
acculturation 24
Acosta, Oscar Zeta 67, 131
affirmative action 17, 93–4, 96–7, 112, 167
African American civil rights movement 1,
    8, 8–9, 10, 36, 47, 79, 80, 108, 165, 172
African Americans: incarceration rates
    171; murals and mural movements 147;
    poverty 63; tensions with 57–8, 62,
    63–4
Agricultural Workers Organizing
    Committee (AWOC) 13, 40, 41
Alianza Hispano-Americana 25
Alinsky, Saul 73
Allee, Alfred Y. 38
Almaraz, Carlos 144
American Dream, Chicano version 100
American exceptionalism 20n25
American Federation of Labor and
    Congress of Industrial Organizations 40
American GI Forum (AGIF) 8, 9, 13,
    29–30; civil rights argument 69;
    expansion 30; and formation of MAPA
    33; *Hernandez v. Texas* 30–1; role in
    Texas 36; status 31–2; and Viva Kennedy
    Clubs 34; and the War on Poverty 57
American Indian Movement 121
Americanism 53, 55; Cold War 28;
    rejection of 67, 125
Americas Review 132
ancestry 3
Anglo, definition 19n17

Anguiano, Lupe 129
anti-colonialism 10, 11, 58, 73
anti-Communism 28, 28–9, 43
antiwar movement 58, 69–70, 121
Arizona 110–1
armed resistence 54
art collectives 139
Arte Público Press 132, 133
artistic expression 16, 145; encouragement
    of 144; in newspapers 130–3. *see also*
    murals and mural movements
Asco 144
Asian Americans 1
assimilation, rejection of 59
Aztlán 11, 21n28, 53, 54, 61, 94, 96, 98,
    123–5, 126, 139, 143, 145, 159
Aztlán 132

barrios 21n31, 53, 54, 97–8, 143–5
beauty, and space 142
biculturalism 123–4
bilingual education 1, 166–7, 169
Bilingual Review/Press 133
bilingualism 3–4
Black Commandos 80
Black Power Movement 1, 5, 8, 54, 58,
    60–1, 64, 68, 73, 75, 111, 121, 122, 152,
    165
Black Student Union (BSU) 103, 107
Bracero guest worker program 40–1
Braceros 3
Brown, Edmund 33

Brown, H. Rap 64
Brown Berets, the 14, 65, 66, 68, 72, 75–7, 84, 107, 145, 147, 154
Brown Power 66, 82
Brown v. Board of Education 1, 26
Bustamante, Jorge 108

California: Chicano population 62–3; Chicano Studies program development 100–4; *cholos* 12; election campaigns 33; grape boycott 13, 23–4, 39–46, 129; labor rights 5; Mexican Americanism in 32–3; student activism 100–4
California State University, Los Angeles 103
Cárdenas, Gilberto 108
Carmichael, Stokely 64
carnalismo 12, 76, 126
Castillo, Mario 146–7, 149, 151
Castro, Sal 65, 66, 67–8, 87n38, 89n58
Catholic Church 53, 72
Cesar Chavez College 110
Chavarria, Jesus 101
Chavez, Cesar 13, 15, 23–4, 33, 40–1, 41–2, 43, 44–5, 46, 64, 81, 148
Chavez, Dennis 34
Chicago 6, 79, 80, 142; *Breaking the Chains* 150–1; demographics 145–6; Humboldt Park 149–51; Latino politics 146; Lincoln Park 149; *Metaphysics (Peace)* (Castillo) 146–7, 149, 151; murals and mural movements 144, 145–51, 159; the Patlan murals 147–8; Urban Progress Center 146–7
Chicago Mural Group 150
Chicago Tribune 151
Chicanismo 10–12, 126
Chicano Blowouts, the 14
Chicano identity 10, 54, 67, 124–6, 166
Chicano Liberation 68
Chicano Liberation Committee (CLC) 111
Chicano Moratorium movement 69–71
Chicano nationalism 10–12, 54, 58–9, 77, 84, 94, 124, 127, 165–6
Chicano Park, San Diego 140, 154–8, 159
Chicano Power 121
Chicano Press Association (CPA) 15, 117, 131
Chicano Press Movement 120, 122–7, 133
Chicano scholarship, publication 133
Chicano Studies 15, 93, 94, 97, 111–13, 167–8; California program development

100–4; model 98; Texas program development 100–4; Washington State program development 106–8; Wisconsin program development 105–6, 107
Chicano university model 109–10
Chicanos: definition 2–3, 18n10; demographics 3; emergence of 7–8; language 3–4; racial status 7–8, 9–10, 27, 30, 68, 168; rejection of term Mexican American 125; social class 4; terminology 2–3, 17n1
Chicanos por La Causa (CPLC) 110–11
Christianity 25
citizenship 13; activism 7; eligibility 7–8; groups 3; rights 39, 42
civil liberties, Cold War attack on 28–9
civil rights 7–8, 14, 36, 69, 170; activism 4–5, 13, 27, 60, 166, 167; organizations 23–5, 46–7
Cleveland 146
Coahuila y Tejas 7
Cold War, the 10, 23, 24, 28–9, 43, 47, 54, 67
college attendance 4
colonial theory 8, 10–2
colonias 53, 54
Committee for Barrio Betterment (CBB) 73
Community Action Agencies (CAA) 55
community arts movement, and space 142–3
community betterment and uplift 71, 143–5
community control 12–14, 84
community mural movement 16
Community Service Organization (CSO) 32–3, 40–1
community service, students 99–100
community space: the *barrios* 143–5; Chicago 145–51; claiming 139, 142–3; and mural movements 139–59
community uplift and betterment 71, 143–5
Compean, Mario 73, 74, 80–1, 82
Con Safos: Reflections on Life in the Barrio 131
Connally, John 38
Constitution, the 68; Fourteenth Amendment 9, 30
Cornejo, Juan 37, 38–9
Corpus Christi, Texas 26
countercultural press 121
Crusade for Justice 15, 54, 58–60

Crystal City, Texas 9, 12–13, 14, 47, 54;
Anglo backlash 38–9; city council
elections, 1963 23, 38–9; high school
walkouts 81–2; impact 39; revolt 35–9;
youth participation 37–8
Cuba 10
cultural nationalism 58, 68, 72, 83, 96–7

Daley, Richard J. 79
Deganwidah Quetzalcoatl University 110
Delano, California 40–1, 47
demands 6
Democratic Party of California 33
demographic revolution, Latino
community 168–70
Denver, Colorado 54, 56–60, 84
Detroit 145, 146
DiGiorgio Corporation 43
direct action 6
discrimination 13, 23, 26, 31, 66, 68, 70–1,
130
diversity, action for 6
diversity policies 167, 171
dreamers 170
dropout rates 94, 98–9

East LA 13, the 66–8
The East Los Angeles Community Union
(TELACU) 71, 89n71
East Los Angeles Labor Community
Action Committee (ELALCAC) 71
Economic and Youth Opportunities
Agency (EYOA) 63
economic mobility 99
Economic Opportunity Act (EOA) 54,
79, 97
Editorial Quinto Sol 132
education: bilingual 1, 166–7, 169; dropout
rates 94, 98–9; impact on 170–1; level 4;
opportunities 1; outcomes 171; reform
campaigns 65–6, 67–8; strategic use of
96–7. *see also* student activism
Educational Opportunity Program (EOP)
107
*El Grito: A Journal of Contemporary Mexican-
American Thought* 131–2, 132
El Huitlacoche 133
El Malcriado 122
El Paso 154
El Plan de Santa Bárbara (PDSB) 93,
96–100
El Plan Espiritual de Aztlán (El Plan) 61,
95, 123

election campaigns 33
employment 4
employment opportunities 1, 72
employment-training programs 57
Encuentro Femenil 129
English language 169
equality, desire for 5
Espinoza, Joe 30–1
ethnic consciousness 39
ethnic identity 47, 55
ethnic nationalism 86n19
ethnic newspapers 118–9
ethnic pride 10

Farm Workers Movement 64
Felix, Charles 152
Felix Longoria Affair, the 29–30
Filipino agricultural workers 41
Flores-Magón, Jesús 119–20
Flores-Magón, Ricardo 119–20
Ford Foundation 109
Free Speech movements 111
Freeman Ranches, the 46
Fresno State College 103

Galarza, Ernesto 41, 108
Gandhi, Mohandas 45
Garcia, Hector 9, 29–30, 35, 36
gender relations 128–9
gender roles 61
gentrification 158–9
global revolutionary context 118
goals 10
Gómez-Quiñones, Juan 101, 103
Gonzales, Rodolfo 'Corky' 54, 56–62, 64,
70, 73, 83, 95, 124–5, 127–8, 166;
'Yo soy Joaquín' (I am Joaquín) 11,
58–60
Gonzalez, Henry B. 34–5, 36, 37, 39, 74
Gonzalez, Joe and John 153
González, José Gamaliel 144–5
grape boycott, California 13, 23–4, 39–46,
129
Groppi, James 60
Guadalupe Hidalgo, Treaty of 7–8, 27
guest workers 3, 40, 40–1
Guevara, Che 11
Gutiérrez, José Ángel 48n7, 73, 74–5,
80–4, 90n75

Hampton, Fred 79
Hernández, Judithe 144
Hernandez, Pete 30–1

Hernandez v. Texas 1, 9, 26, 30–1
high school 99; Crystal City walkouts
    81–2; graduation 4; Los Angeles
    walkouts 14, 15, 66, 67–8, 89n58, 166
Higher Education Act 97
Higher Education Amendments, 1968 97
Higher Education Amendments, 1972 97
Hispanics 2
Hoffa, James R. 38
homeland. *see* Aztlán
Huerta, Dolores 13, 23–4, 33, 41, 42, 43,
    44, 45, 122, 129
hyphenated Americans 26, 48n6, 95,
    118–9

identity: bicultural 123–4; Chicano 10, 54,
    67, 124–6, 166; construction of 6, 10;
    ethnic 47, 55; Mexican-American 2; and
    mural movements 139; and newspapers
    117–18, 124–6, 133; pan-Latino 169;
    racial 9, 10, 27; rejection of Mexican-
    American 11; women 127–30
imagined communities 117
immigration 168–70
immigration rights movement 170
In re Rodríguez 27
incarceration rates 171
indigenismo 141
Industrial Areas Foundation (IAF) 32
intermarriage 99, 100
internal colonialism 8, 19n19, 20n21
Itliong, Larry 13, 41, 42, 44

Jacinto Treviño College 109
Jim Crow 27, 35, 36
Johnson, Lyndon Baines 30, 34, 54, 72
Jones, Opal 63
journalism movement 15–16
Juárez-Lincoln Center 109
Juárez-Lincoln University 109
juries, bias 30–1
juvenile justice system 171

Kanellos, Nicolás 132–3
Karenga, Ron 64
Keller, Gary 133
Kennedy, John F. 34, 35, 54
Kennedy, Robert F. 45, 59
'Kill the Gringo' rhetoric 74–5
King, Martin Luther, Jr. 42, 45, 59, 86n24,
    108
Klotsche, Martin 106
Korean War 9

La Luz 130
La Sociedad Mutualista Cuauhtémoc 25
La Universidad de los Barrios (LUB) 73, 74
labor newspapers 122–3
labor rights 5
language 3–4, 17, 26, 111, 166–7, 169
Lara, Severita 81–2
Latin American Defense Organization
    (LADO) 150–1
Latin American Education Committee
    (CELA) 105, 106
Latin American Union for Civil Rights
    (LAUCR) 79–80, 105
Latin pride 23
Latinos 2; demographic revolution 168–70
League of United Latin American Citizens
    (LULAC) 8, 9, 13, 48n7, 130; activism
    27; aims 26; establishment 25–6;
    expansion struggle 26–7; *Hernandez v.
    Texas* 30–1; official language 26; and the
    War on Poverty 57; and whiteness 27
legacy 17, 172
Limón, José 104
Longoria, Felix, Jr. 29–30
Lopez, Hank 34
Los Angeles 32, 37, 84; Chicano
    Moratorium movement 69–71;
    Chicano population 62–3; community
    betterment 71; the East LA 13 66–8;
    Great Wall of Los Angeles mural 144; high
    school walkouts 14, 15, 66, 67–8, 89n58,
    166; interracial conflict and cooperation
    63–4; language 3–4; murals and mural
    movements 144, 152–3; Neighborhood
    Adult Participation Project (NAPP) 63;
    Ramona Gardens Housing Projects 144;
    student activism 64, 166; and the War
    on Poverty 62–3, 63–4, 71; Watts Riots
    86n24
Los Angeles Times 129
Los Cinco movement 38–9, 166
Los Four 144
Los Voluntarios 56–7
Lucey, Robert E. 72
Luján, Gilbert 144
LULAC News 119
lynch-law 7

McCarran Internal Security Act 28–9
McCarran-Walter Immigration and
    Nationality Act 29
McCormick, Carlos 34, 35
Manifest Destiny 7

Manning, Timothy 45–6
Marshall, Thurgood 31
masculinity 12, 57, 58–60, 75, 118, 127–8
maximum feasible participation 73, 79, 84
mestizaje 9–10
Mexican American civil rights movement, impact 1–2
Mexican American community 1
Mexican American diaspora 90n87
Mexican-American identity 2
Mexican American Legal Defense and Educational Fund (MALDEF) 170
Mexican American Neighborhood Community Organization (MANCO) 73
Mexican American Political Association (MAPA) 33, 34, 35
Mexican American Student Association (MASA) 110
Mexican American Student Organization (MASO) 110–1
Mexican American Unity Council (MAUC) 73
Mexican American Youth Organization (MAYO) 13, 72, 73–5, 77, 81, 104, 109, 166
Mexican Americanism 47, 84; in California 32–3; confrontational 39; development of 8–10; electoral 33; working class 36–7
Mexican Americanist, definition 47–8n3
Mexican Americans: *see* Chicanos
Mexican consulate-supported groups 24–5
Mexican Muralists 141
Mexican pride 24
Mexican Revolution 7, 42
Mexican-American War 7, 8, 125
Mexicanist, definition 47–8n3
Mexico 7
militancy, emergence of 4–5
military service 9
Milwaukee 77–80, 84, 105, 145, 146
Minority Mobilization Program (MMP) 74
Montoya, Joseph 34
Mount Angel, Oregon 110
Movimiento Artístico Chicano (MARCH) 144–5
Movimiento Estudiantial Chicano de Aztlán (MEChA) 15, 94–6, 97–8, 99, 100, 101, 102, 103, 105, 107, 108–9, 111
Mujeres Por La Raza conference 130
multiculturalism 171
Muniz, Ramsey 83, 105

Munoz, Rosalio 70
murals and mural movements 131; African American 147; artists 16, 139; audience engagement 140; and the *barrios* 143–5; *Breaking the Chains* 150–1; Chicago 144, 145–51, 159; Chicano Park, San Diego 140, 154–8, 159; commonalities 140; community betterment 152–3; community mobilization 143, 147, 149–51, 152, 155, 157; and community space 139–59; environmental reshaping 143–5; goals 148; *Great Wall of Los Angeles* mural 144; iconography 140, 145, 148, 153; and identity 139; legacy 159; Los Angeles 144, 152–3; *Metaphysics (Peace)* (Castillo) 146–7, 149, 151; Mexican 141; Movimiento Artístico Chicano (MARCH) 144–5; preservation 157–8, 158–9; San Francisco 153–4; story 140; territorialized 139; Texas 154; themes 140; youth participation 140
mutual benefit organizations 24–5
mutualistas 24–5

nation-building 68, 123, 143
National Association for the Advancement of Colored People (NAACP) 8–9, 27; Legal Defense Fund (LDF) 31
National Association of Chicana and Chicano Studies (NACCS) 103, 112
National Association of Chicano Social Scientists 103
National Council of La Raza (NCLR) 108
National Farm Labor Union (NFLU) 41
National Farm Workers Association (NFWA) 41–2
national pride 25
nationalism: Chicano 54, 58–9, 77, 84, 94, 124, 127, 165–6; cultural 58, 68, 72, 83, 96–7; ethnic 86n19
nationhood, sense of 124
Native Americans 1, 59–60, 110, 134n15, 152
naturalization 7–8, 24, 49n9
Neighborhood Adult Participation Project (NAPP) 63
Neighborhood Youth Corps (NYC), Denver 57
New Left, the 111
New Mexico 12, 60

newspapers 117–27, 130–4; and
artistic expression 130–3, 145; and
Chicano nationalism 124; Chicano
Press Movement 120, 122, 122–7;
countercultural 121; ethnic 118–9;
global revolutionary context 118;
and identity 117–8, 124–6, 133;
influence 133; labor 122–3; and
masculinity 118; Mexican American
press 119–20; national aspects of 133;
neglect of women 126; poetry 126–7;
underground 120–2
Nixon, Richard M. 34
nonviolence 45, 70–1

Obreros Unidos (OU) 77, 79, 122
Office of Economic Opportunity (OEO)
62, 72, 75, 78, 91n92; creation of 54–5;
demise of 71; funding 53; MAYO and
73–4; reform model 55
oppression 7
Orozco, José 141
Our Lady of the Lake College (OLL) 105

pan-Latino activism 77–80
pan-Latino identity 169
pan-Latino politics 169–70
Paredes, Américo 104
participatory democracy 32
paternalism 12
Patlán, Juan 73
Patlan, Ray 147–8, 150, 153–4
patriarchy 128
patriotism 13, 29
Paz, Octavio 128
Peña, Albert, Jr. 34–5, 36, 37, 39
Perez, Ignacio 73
poetry 11, 58–60, 126–7, 128, 130
police brutality 56–7, 65, 66, 69, 70–1
Political Association of Spanish-Speaking
Organizations (PASSO): collapse 39;
Crystal City revolt 35–9; establishment
34, 34–5; leadership 35; strategy debate
39; unification failure 35–6
political mobilization 14
political participation 12–13
political representation 171–2
Poor People's Campaign, the 59–60
Poor People's Movement 69
population, Chicano 3
poverty 15, 22n36, 171. see also War on
Poverty

Premio Quinto Sol 132
print media. see newspapers; women's
periodicals
Puerto Ricans 2, 6, 77–80, 142, 145–6,
149

race consciousness 36
racial discrimination 10
racial identity 9, 10, 27
racial profiling 71
racial status 7–8, 9–10, 27, 30, 68, 168
racism 27, 46–7, 109
radical movements: interpretations of 5–6;
student 100
Raya, Marcos 148
La Raza Unida Party (RUP) 13, 15, 39, 54,
62, 75, 80–4, 104, 108, 109, 144, 145,
154, 172
Reagan, Ronald 155
reform 6
Regeneración 119–20, 144
religious expression 42
reverse racism 13
Revista Chicano-Requeña 131–2
Rio Grande, the 7
Rivera, Diego 141
Rivera, Tomás 132
Rocha, Roberto de la 144
Rodriguez, Laura 155
Romero, Frank 144
Ross, Fred 33
Royal Chicano Air Force (RCAF) 155
Roybal, Edward 32, 33, 35, 37

Sacramento 33, 70; pilgrimage to 42–3
Salazar, Rubén 69, 86n19, 125
Salón Obreros y Obreras, the 26
Salt of the Earth (film) 128
Samora, Julian 108–9, 133
San Antonio 23, 37, 39, 71–2, 84; Brown
Berets in 72, 75–7; MAYO in 72, 73–5;
murals and mural movements 154;
Neighborhood Councils 72–3, 75; and
the War on Poverty 72–3
San Antonio Neighborhood Youth
Organization (SANYO) 72–3, 75
San Diego 142; Chicano Park 140, 154–8,
159
San Diego State University 103
San Fernando Valley State 101
San Francisco 33, 101–2, 153–4
San Francisco State College (SFSC) 101–2

San José 33
Santa Barbara 93, 94, 96, 101, 103
Saragoza, Elvira 128
Schenley Industries 43
schools, desegregation 36
segregation 5, 8, 12–13, 14, 27, 36
Serros, Juana 129
Service Employment Redevelopment
    (SER)-Jobs for Progress 57
Servicemen's Readjustment Act 29–30
sexism 12, 95
Shafer, Ray 37
Siqueiros, David 141, 151
Smith Act 29
social class 4, 26, 167
Social Development Commission (SDC)
    78, 79
social justice 10
Southern Christian Leadership Conference
    (SCLC) 42, 59–60
Southwest Council of La Raza (SCLR)
    108
Southwest Voter Registration Education
    Project (SVREP) 75, 91n96
space, and community arts 142–3
Spanish language proficiency 3–4, 17, 111,
    166–7, 169
special class status 31
Stanford University 102
strategic essentialism 142, 160n1
strategic ethnicity 160n1
street art, ethnic 140
student activism 64–8, 93–113;
    achievements 111–13; affirmative
    action 93–4, 96–7, 112; Arizona 110–1;
    and the *barrio* 97–8; California 100–4;
    Chicano nationalism 94; Chicano
    Studies model 98; community service
    99–100; cultural nationalism 96–7;
    demands 96–7; and *El Plan Espiritual*
    95; goals 98; Indiana 108–9; Los Angeles
    166; MEChA 94–6; Native Americans
    110; the PDSB 96–9; radical 100;
    strategic use of education 96–7; Texas
    104–5, 166; underground press 121;
    Washington State 106–8; Wisconsin
    105–6
supporters 16
Supreme Court 8, 31

Taft-Hartley Act 28–9
Teamsters 37, 38–9, 43, 46

Tejanos (Texas-Mexicans) 3, 7, 72
terminology 2–3, 17n1
Texas 54; AGIF role 36; Chicano
    population 62; Chicano Studies program
    development 104–5; elections, 1972 83;
    the Felix Longoria Affair 29–30; gringo
    worldview 74–5; *Hernandez v. Texas*
    30–1; murals and mural movements 154;
    pachucos 12; poll tax 37, 38; race relations
    35, 36–7; racial oppression 26; RUP
    activities 80–4; segregation 5, 12–13, 14,
    27; student activism 166. *see also* Crystal
    City, Texas
Texas, Republic of 7
Texas Institute for Educational
    Development (TIED) 73
Texas Rangers 26, 27, 30, 38
Third World Liberation Front (TWLF)
    101–2
Tijerina, Reies López 54, 60, 64, 73, 83,
    84n1
Tucson, Arizona 25, 111
two-class theory 31

underground press 120–2
Underground Press Syndicate (UPS) 120, 121
undocumented, the 170
United Farm Workers (UFW) 13, 23–4,
    81, 144, 166; grape boycott 23–4,
    39–46, 129
United Farm Workers Organizing
    Committee (UFWOC) 13, 14–5, 33,
    42–6, 107, 110, 122
United Mexican American Students
    (UMAS) 65, 94, 95
United Migrant Opportunity Services, Inc.
    (UMOS) 78–9
United Packinghouse Workers of America
    (UPWA) 40
United States Students Press Association
    (USSPA) 121
universities: Chicano enrollments 101,
    109, 112, 167; Chicano model 109–10;
    Chicano recruitment 94, 96, 97, 106;
    dropout rates 94, 98–9; hierarchy. 97;
    minority student admissions 102
University of Arizona 111
University of California, Berkeley
    102
University of Illinois 146
University of Notre Dame, Indiana 108–9,
    144

University of Notre Dame Press 133
University of Texas, Austin (UT) 104
University of Texas, El Paso 104–5
University of Washington 107
University of Wisconsin, Madison (UW)
    105–6
urban renewal 16

Valdez, Luis 42, 135n26
Vasconcelos, José 125, 141
Velásquez, Willie 73, 74, 81, 82, 84, 91n96
Victoria, Texas 34
Vietnam War 4–5, 69, 121
violence, threats of 74–5
Viva Kennedy Clubs 34, 35, 56
Volunteers in Service to America (VISTA)
    74, 75
voter registration 32, 37–9, 91n96

Walker, William 147
War on Poverty 15, 22n36, 53–5, 77,
    84, 166; Los Angeles 62–3, 63–4, 71;
    Milwaukee 77–80; San Antonio 72–3;
    struggles within 57–8
Warren, Earl 31
Washington, Poor People's March on
    59–60
Washington State 106–8
Watts Riots 86n24

Weber, John 150
whiteness 9, 27, 35, 36, 47, 68, 168
'Winter Garden' project, the 80–4
Wisconsin 105–6, 107, 122
women: activism 129, 130; Brown Beret
    membership 76; discrimination 130;
    and El Plan Espiritual 95; employment
    4; identity 127–30; newspapers neglect
    of 126; rights 128; status 11, 12, 59,
    100, 127, 129–30; Youth Liberation
    Conferences 61
women's liberation movement 111
women's periodicals 127–30, 133
working class Mexican Americanism 36–7
World War II 9

Yanez, Gabriel 63
Yanta, John 72–3, 75
Young Chicanos for Community Action
    (YCCA) 64
Young Citizens for Community Action 64
Young Lords Organization [YLO] 80, 151
young people: activism 6, 14, 15; and the
    grape boycott 44; mural movement
    participation 140; participation 37–8;
    Youth Liberation Conferences 60–2
Youth Conferences 15
youth crime 171
Youth Liberation Conferences 60–2